River, Reaper, Rail

SERIES ON OHIO HISTORY AND CULTURE

Series on Ohio History and Culture
    Kevin Kern, Editor

Joyce Dyer, *Gum-Dipped: A Daughter Remembers Rubber Town*

Melanie Payne, *Champions, Cheaters, and Childhood Dreams: Memories of the Soap Box Derby*

John Flower, *Downstairs, Upstairs: The Changed Spirit and Face of College Life in America*

Wayne Embry and Mary Schmitt Boyer, *The Inside Game: Race, Power, and Politics in the NBA*

Robin Yocum, *Dead Before Deadline: . . . And Other Tales from the Police Beat*

A. Martin Byers, *The Ohio Hopewell Episode: Paradigm Lost and Paradigm Gained*

Edward C. Arn, edited by Jerome Mushkat, *Arn's War: Memoirs of a World War II Infantryman, 1940–1946*

Brian Bruce, *Thomas Boyd: Lost Author of the "Lost Generation"*

Kathleen Endres, *Akron's "Better Half": Women's Clubs and the Humanization of a City, 1825–1925*

Russ Musarra and Chuck Ayers, *Walks Around Akron: Rediscovering a City in Transition*

Heinz Poll, edited by Barbara Schubert, *A Time to Dance: The Life of Heinz Poll*

Mark D. Bowles, *Chains of Opportunity: The University of Akron and the Emergence of the Polymer Age, 1909–2007*

Russ Vernon, *West Point Market Cookbook*

Stan Purdum, *Pedaling to Lunch: Bike Rides and Bites in Northeastern Ohio*

Joyce Dyer, *Goosetown: Reconstructing an Akron Neighborhood*

Robert J. Roman, *Ohio State Football: The Forgotten Dawn*

Timothy H. H. Thoresen, *River, Reaper, Rail: Agriculture and Identity in Ohio's Mad River Valley, 1795–1885*

Titles published since 2003.
    For a complete listing of titles published in the series,
    go to www.uakron.edu/uapress.

River, Reaper, Rail

AGRICULTURE AND IDENTITY IN
OHIO'S MAD RIVER VALLEY, 1795–1885

Timothy H. H. Thoresen

The University of Akron Press
Akron, Ohio

ISBN: 978-1-629220-76-5 (paper)
ISBN: 978-1-629220-77-2 (ePDF)
ISBN: 978-1-629220-78-9 (ePub)

A catalog record for this title is available from the Library of Congress.

∞The paper used in this publication meets the minimum requirements of ANSI/NISO Z39.48–1992 (Permanence of Paper).

Cover: (Top) "The Harvesters Discussing the Temperance Lecture," reprinted from A Son of Temperance, *Thrilling Scenes in Cottage Life* (Hartford: Case, Tiffany, and Co., 1855), p 379; (middle) "Mad River, Near Springfield, O.," reprinted from Rev. B. F. Tefft, ed., *The Ladies' Repository* (Cincinnati, 1851), facing p. 321; (bottom) 1851 advertising broadside for Hussey's Reaping Machines, courtesy of the Ohio History Connection. Cover design by Amy Freels.

River, Reaper, Rail was designed and typeset in Adobe Caslon by Amy Freels and printed on sixty-pound natural and bound by Bookmasters of Ashland, Ohio.

For my daughters—SaraLynne, Ahna, Karis

Contents

Introduction   ix

1. The Land   1

2. The People and Their Culture   6

3. Claiming the Land, and Settling In   12

4. Traditions and Revisions   23

5. The Transportation Problem   30

6. Making Do, With Roads and Without   35

7. New Connections, New Directions   41

8. Urbana   51

9. The Prospect of a Railroad   56

10. Changing Prospects   62

11. Reapers   74

12. Improving the Land   95

13. Organizing for Improvement: An Agricultural Society   102

14. Geography, Generation, Gender: Union Township, 1860   114

15. Adaptive Diversity   130

16. The Relevance of Horses   143

17. Making Sense of Civil War   153

18. Distant Fields   170

19. Common Ground   186

Notes 192

Bibliography 239

Index 273

Introduction

This study has its origin in an invitation to participate in the 2005 Champaign County Bi-Centennial lecture series sponsored jointly by the County's Bi-Centennial Commission and Urbana University. While the original lecture gave focus to a personal interest in farm machines and agricultural technology, it was also the stimulus to look at a field of scholarship I had previously barely known. A decade-long project evolved. Loosely an exploration of systemic change in agriculture, the work was from its inception distracted by the personal elements—the lives and stories of the people who experienced the change. I found myself looking for the narratives, the representative and illustrative stories that made sense of the patterns I was seeing. My principal models come from ethnography, my language often draws on economics, and my perspective is always historical.

The initial sources for this project were the commonly available publications in the history of agriculture, selected manuscript schedules and summary statistics of the Census Bureau for the period under review, and the *Annual Report of the Ohio State Board of Agriculture* from its beginning in 1846. Champaign County residents of the 1800s may have kept account books, and a few kept diaries. None of those documents has survived unless they are still hidden away in attic boxes or bottom drawers. A few private letters survived in published form when they were included in pioneer reminiscences following the Civil War. Otherwise, my principal and quite rich primary source has been the weekly Urbana newspapers. The earliest, *The Farmer's Watch Tower*, first appeared in 1812, and only a few issues survive. From 1821 and the appearance of *Ways of the World*, a weekly newspaper in Urbana was fitfully regular. Names changed, as did the "proprietors" (their word for the owner/publisher/

editor). Long-term stability was achieved in 1849 with the *Urbana Citizen and Gazette* which ran continuously for forty years until displaced by the *Urbana Daily Citizen*. The *Citizen* was proudly Whig, then Republican, and was challenged for readership by much less successful Democratic papers. Offsetting its political bias was its self-conscious role as the principal newspaper in the county. Beyond matters of public notice and legal record, the *Citizen* generously provided space for reader comment, letters from the war front or from the "West," and reminiscences of ye olde days. Mixed in on the same unnumbered folio pages were paid advertisements for professional services, retail dry goods, and agricultural implements, allowing the historian a complementary insight into local events and public transactions. Less consistently I also consulted the much more limited surviving files of the other newspapers attempted in the county's several smaller towns. These source materials were encouragingly made available to me by the staffs of the Champaign County Public Library, the Champaign County Historical Society, the Urbana University Library, the Wright State University Library, and the archives of the Ohio History Connection.

The story of Champaign County and its Mad River Valley is a story of the Ohio country and, with reference to agriculture, it is a story of America and its rural heartland. It is the story of land-hungry migrants carrying a market-oriented farm ethos across the Appalachians into the Ohio Valley and displacing the native inhabitants. As the migrants adapted their traditional farming practices to the local conditions, practice was also affected by changes in farming technology, changes in modes of transport and communication, changes in market orientation, and perhaps most obviously into our own day, changes in a dynamic and global industrial economy. For a few brief decades in the middle of the nineteenth century, Champaign County was very near the center of the nation demographically, agriculturally, and industrially. Its people looked optimistically in all directions, stirred especially by big changes in the transportation infrastructure, the mechanization of the harvesting process, and the character of state-sponsored farmer organizations. Driven by dynamics from outside the county, the effect of those developments on life inside the county was intense because of the timing. And yet, through all those changes we should see that the individual farmer, like the evolutionary process itself, has been fundamentally conservative. Change is endured to preserve what otherwise would be at risk. Everything is interrelated. Better yields, higher prices, less work, lower costs are all values within a complex, a network, a system, a culture which understands that change in one place will certainly have unanticipated implications and change in other places. For the farmer, improvement is therefore tested against multiple annual cycles of planting and harvest before it is judged a success, and outsiders, experts, and city folk just don't know. But change did happen, and therein is our story. It begins with the land itself.

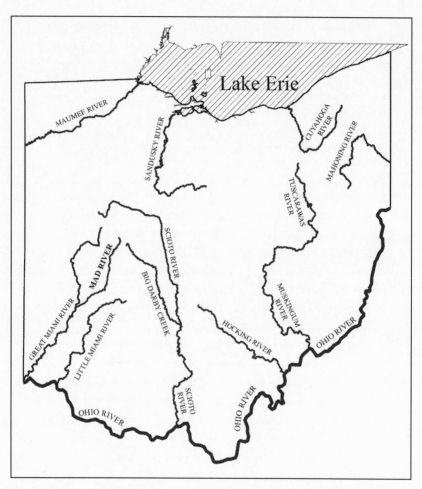

Selected Ohio Waterforms. *Courtesy Champaign County Engineer.*

I.

The Land

Land was the reason. Land gave identity. Land also gave purpose, and for prospective white settlers, that meant working the land in accord with their cultural heritage. Anticipating removal of what those settlers called "the Indian menace," therefore, and with the prospect of obtaining title to as much good land as any hard-working farmer could manage, independent farming was the attraction of the Old Northwest Territory. Officially opened for settlement by terms specified in the Land Ordinance of 1785 and the Northwest Ordinance of 1787, the future Ohio beckoned. Along the Ohio River and gradually upstream its tributaries, forests gave way to farms. By the middle of the 1790s, the leading edge of settlement up the Great Miami River had reached about half the distance from the Ohio River to Lake Erie. From there a lesser edge was spreading eastward to encompass a land nearly perfect for farming.

Through this land runs a river with its sources on the eastern slopes of Campbell Hill, Ohio's high point of elevation. Named Mad, the river flows southward and westward as though wrapping itself around the base of the ancient rock formation of which Campbell Hill is composed. Thousands of years earlier, massive ice flows similarly wrapped and bent around that obstruction of Devonian bedrock, neither thick enough to ride over it nor strong enough to wear it away. On the east, a wall of ice—the Scioto Sub-lobe—seemed to pivot on its rock anchor and move clockwise, just as on the west another wall of ice—the Miami Sub-lobe—mirrored the motion by moving counterclockwise until the two walls of ice lined up facing each other on an almost perfect north/south axis. Whatever had been carried or pushed by those walls of ice now had nowhere to go as the larger glaciers resumed their inexorable southward grind around the stalled portions. When warming temperatures eventually forced the ice to release its hold, the detritus remained as two uneven ridges. End moraines they are, still facing each other across a shared plain, a valley, a natural conduit for collecting and directing water. So it is that the Mad River gathers its waters from the named creeks and nameless rivulets flowing from the rolling hills forming its channel sides. For about two dozen miles, the course of the river is meanderingly southward.[1]

This is the Mad River Valley, and it properly ends where the valley's parallel moraines lose definition. That is where Buck Creek, erratically draining the southern portion of the eastern moraine, descends rapidly and powerfully just before joining with the Mad, and the now larger Mad River turns decidedly westward toward the Great Miami. The fall of Buck Creek and its confluence with the Mad mark the attractions that became the site of Springfield, just as farther downstream the confluence of the Mad with the Great Miami became the site of Dayton. The entire length of the river measures somewhat fewer than seventy miles. Along its upper half, intentionally as near the center of the Mad River Valley as seemed reasonable at the time, a town named Urbana was located. A government far removed from the site delineated administrative boundaries inclusive of much more than the Valley and named it Champaign County. Pending increased settlement by the many additional persons who would be attracted to the land, boundary adjustments were expected. In all the considerations, the fact of the river was always present. So it must also be in the historian's imaginatively and necessarily bifocal perspective, seeing always the changing contemporary in view of the very distant past.

The long view of the land is stated simply as the legacy of the successive North American glaciers. The geologic "floor" is limestone, overlain by a mantle of glacial drift that has weathered into silt and clay loams, in some places very sandy but especially in the lower portions resulting in a richly layered alluvial soil. Located within the very eastern portion of the North American Till Plains stretching from Ohio's Appalachian Plateau westward to the Mississippi River, Champaign County's relatively level land surface is interrupted by a handful of eskers and kames. The larger and more continuous formations are the moraines that guide the Mad River. The highest elevation in the county is 1385 feet at the crest of the Cable Moraine just west of Middleton in Wayne Township. The lowest elevation of 950 feet is at the point where the Mad River crosses from Champaign into Clark County. Overall, the surface formations of bands and ridges are oriented north-south. When white settlement defined the significance of the Mad River in terms of commerce and communication, the flow direction of water set the county's cultural geography in a fundamentally but not uniformly southern orientation. Because the eastern flank of the Cable Moraine drains eastward and not into the Mad River, the county in its eastern third also shares in central Ohio's Scioto Valley drainage by way of Darby Creek. Physically and culturally, therefore, the county lies at the very edge of, and not wholly within, southwestern Ohio's Miami Valley.[2]

At the time of white incursion, much of the county's land area was wooded, mostly deciduous. Jervis Cutler noted in 1812 that on the land south from Urbana to Springfield "the growth varies from oak to beach, ash, sugar-maple, black and white walnut, and cherry." The mesothermal range of temperatures and cycle of seasons, and a predictable rainfall averaging just over forty inches per year, were familiar enough. The soils compared favorably with any of the agricultural lands east of the Alleghenies, and by that same standard were exploitable by the same cultural inventory of agricultural technologies practiced along the Middle Atlantic seaboard at the time. Again in Jervis Cutler's phrasing, the land north from Urbana to the Indian boundary line was "mostly level, the growth large, inclining to beach, the water good, and will admit of many excellent mill seats."[3]

Almost completely unappreciated by the early observers of record was the extent to which the land they were entering had been actively managed by Native Americans for centuries. The horticultural implements may have been simple and few, but they were not significantly different in function from their European counterparts. In the absence of draft animals and plows, the most useful tool was fire. Burning the land cover to control

vegetation was later misunderstood, perhaps inevitably so. Certainly it
was derided by white farmers as the legacy of the uncivilized hunter and
savage warrior, unconformed to proper agricultural principles.[4]

Contributing to misunderstanding, the continuity of Native American land management had been violently disrupted when European
contact on the Atlantic coast aligned with the expansionist ambitions of
the Iroquois Confederacy in the mid-1600s. Ohio's native inhabitants
fled or were killed, and for about half a century, the land between Lake
Erie and the Ohio River was nearly empty. Waning of the Beaver Wars
allowed diverse peoples, red and white, opportunistically to renew life
in Ohio. By 1730 or so, Shawnee were living in the Miami Valley, eventually spreading out their loosely organized villages also along the Mad
River. A modified traditional horticulture resumed. Tranquility did not.
Native Americans were an obstacle to the intentions of the newer white
immigrants. Warrior violence by all partisans seared the land.[5]

Two examples are instructive of the late eighteenth-century situation.
A few miles below the confluence of the Mad River with Buck Creek at
Springfield, residents of a moderately sized Shawnee village worked their
corn fields in the rich bottom land. In 1780 as an action against presumed
British allies in the American Revolutionary War, George Rogers Clark
led a mix of regulars and militia in a raid on that village site where today
a park bears his name. Loss of lives could be counted; loss of livelihood
could not as the raiders burned the fields. Upstream closer to its sources
in what became Logan County, a smaller unconjoined Mad River flows
within a visibly contained floodplain. From the road that today curves
beside the river between West Liberty and Zanesfield, even a casual trav-
eler can see bottomland perfect for minimum-tillage horticulture of corn,
beans, and squash. Just as in the past, the low-rising moraines today make
secure river-safe siting for dwellings, and every autumn the highly visible
color of hunting gear is a reminder of how readily the near-distant woods
have provided access to deer and other wildlife. Nevertheless, safety in
peaceful horticulture did not prevent Wapatomica and other nearby small
villages from being attacked and burned in 1786 by Kentucky militia
under the command of Benjamin Logan.[6]

With only a hint of irony in their lived experience, therefore, and
only as the white settlers' own Atlantic coast agricultural technology was

selectively adapted, did the carriers of the technology appreciate that the upper drainage systems of the Mad and Scioto Rivers could be worked to accommodate a diversity of agricultural values. Even then, common patterns of farming practice confirmed the strength of shared perceptions. The aging memories of the pioneer generation evoked the land of their youth as "primeval," as not yet affected by human ingenuity. That was cultural artifice, a rationale, a moral judgment, a scheme for action. Significantly phrased in very everyday language, always it was the land itself that invited or restricted human opportunities. It was the land that was rich, mixed, transitional, and in some places marginal. In an 1876 agricultural interrogatory, the question was asked whether the soil of Champaign County was "clayey, loamy, gravelly, sandy, or mucky?" The answer was "clayey, loamy, mucky," with "loam" predominating. Or, as Henry Howe explained in his *Historical Collections*, Champaign County "derived its name from the character of its surface. About half of it is level or slightly undulating, one quarter rolling, one fifth rather hilly, and five per cent wet prairie, and best adapted for grazing."[7]

2.

The People and Their Culture

Officially open for white settlement in 1788, the Northwest Territory did not see more than a handful of determined squatters north of the Ohio River until after the 1795 Treaty of Greeneville. The Mad River Valley's first white settler of record, William Owens, arrived in 1797, making his home in what became Mad River Township. As others ventured into the area, a pattern was soon evident. The settlers—initially a mix of squatters and small farmers—tended to come from the south or southeast, up the Miami and Scioto river valleys, having come down the Ohio River from western Pennsylvania, northern Virginia, and northern Kentucky.[1]

Typically the migrants were family units comprised of a married couple and usually several children, often accompanied or soon followed by the unmarried siblings of either marriage partner and sometimes also by a widowed parent. The first settler of record in Jackson Township, Charles Dorsey, was a middle-aged adult when he came to the area alone, entered a claim, built a shelter, cleared a small amount of land, and approximately a year later returned to Virginia to bring his family to the new home site. Similarly, Silas Johnson and his two sons established their claim in 1802 in what became Johnson Township, returning to Kentucky before the worst of winter and then bringing the entire family to the new home in the spring of 1803. With decision-making centered in a pair or trio of adult male siblings, sometimes an entire extended family relocated. In 1796, brothers Mathias and Ichabod Corwin crossed the Ohio River from Kentucky to settle in Warren County, where Mathias' son Tom would make the political base that eventually placed him in the Governor's office. First-cousin Moses, son of Ichabod, also took up the study of law and politics, and just before the outbreak of the War of 1812, arrived in the frontier town of Urbana to begin the practice of law.[2]

For probably most of the migrants, the relocation into Champaign County was not their first major move. Many had come as children from the Virginia/Maryland Piedmont into Kentucky, just as many of their parents or grandparents had followed the trails of the Great Appalachian Valley into Virginia from New Jersey or southeastern Pennsylvania. For many of the younger ones, it would not be their last major move. George Fithian, in 1805 one of the first to settle in the newly platted village of Urbana, and in 1816 the village's first elected mayor, eventually made a final move to Champaign County, Illinois. Young Gershom Flagg, about to make his own next move to Illinois after less than a year in Champaign County, wrote to his brother in 1817 that "There is plenty of Land for sale here. There is as many wishing to sell here and go further West as in Vermont but land is very high."[3]

The reasons for those migrations were embedded in the economic and political culture of the day, and were hardly new. Some of the earliest migrants may have been hoping to establish or recover stations in life disrupted by the War of Revolution and the subsequent economic depression. For others, Revolutionary ferment had precipitated a new possessive attitude toward the land itself. Some saw prospects, if not fortunes, in the land policies of the new Federal government, and a handful of individuals had sufficient money, political connections, or land surveying skill to make substantial investment in future real estate development. William Ward, Joseph Vance, and Duncan McArthur had such traits in combination. Others felt only a vague optimism. Cincinnati's Daniel Drake, in 1815, saw the reasons in "The cheapness of land and the high price of labor," plus "the general fertility of our soil, the security of land titles, and the prohibition of slavery." In 1925, two pioneers in American agricultural history evoked the heritage of "craving for the excitement and romance of a new life in a new country" with a "desire to exchange exhausted farms for cheap, fertile land." For a few persons, the attraction of the Ohio country—the pull—was blurred with an aversive need to make a change—the push. For others, the need arose in an unwillingness or even inability to accommodate to a changing economic environment in the East. As they sought to create familiarity in the Old Northwest, they found themselves moving westward along a constant meridian of latitude in order to maintain an accustomed scheme of agricultural technology.[4]

Some migrants may simply have followed friends and family and, without serious consideration of alternative sites, settled on the nearest available claims. Tax records, such as the 1810 Ohio Tax Duplicate, show multiple instances of extended families on adjacent or near-adjacent farms. In the earliest days of Champaign County, consequently, distinctive minor regional cultural patterns were evident in localities such as the village of Woodstock, where an active Universalist community was decidedly atypical among the county's Methodists and Presbyterians. Overall, the county's dominant cultural pattern was more Middle than Northern, at least on the farms, and as it became increasingly diffuse and generically "American," it still displayed traces of its Piedmont and Upland South heritage in the twentieth century. Common to the entire generation were certain attitudes: "a yearning to own land in abundance, a love of freedom and a contempt for restrictive measures that denied them the rights they claimed, a pragmatic outlook on life, a distrust of urban politicians, and a tendency to become more conservative as their property increased in value." Equally common was a lack of any felt need to record in writing the thoughts and experiences of making life happen in the interior of the Ohio country.[5]

Those who settled in the western two-thirds of the county, the "Congress" lands west of the Ludlow Line, tended to claim tracts of approximately 320 or 160 acres, depending on the date of the entry, with the terrain itself often determining the practicality of the claim's size. In the later-settled northwestern quadrant of the county, farms were likely to be smaller, many comprising fewer than eighty acres. Claims in the Virginia Military District, that is, east of the Ludlow Line, included some very much larger tracts, some consisting of 1,600, 1,800, and 2,000 acres. There, an initial "average" size seems to have been close to 1,000 acres, although almost immediately the larger holdings began a long-term process of break-up and piecemeal sale, whether for speculative profit, for cash to pay tax obligations, for more efficient management, or for legal obligations resulting from re-survey.[6]

Except in the eastern third of the county, the bulk area of most tracts was timbered and required clearing before any crops could be planted. The clearing process was slow, whether by girdling or by chopping, and for the sheer physical labor involved, the pioneer farmer claiming a wooded tract could not expect to become self-sustaining in fewer than three to five years. Roots and burned tree stumps remained to interfere with any use of implements, sometimes for twenty years before rotting completely. Even the relatively open prairie-like portions of the county called "barrens" resisted easy exploitation. "Grubs" were any number of small shrubs whose roots intertwined with the root mass of the prairie grasses, making tough sod even tougher. When James Rawlings bought a farm on the near-level heart of Pretty Prairie southeast of Urbana in 1830, his acquisition included only twenty-five acres of land cleared of "grubs" by the previous owners during fifteen years.[7]

In the still-unimproved portions, unfenced cattle and pigs foraged throughout most of the year. In very much smaller portions, and with minimal hoeing, Indian corn and squash and perhaps potatoes were planted directly into newly "cleared" land. Small grain cultivation came later, usually not sooner than the second season, and usually in the form of buckwheat as a first planting. Plowing was exhausting both to humans and to draft animals, and proceeded at a pace of about one acre per day. The pace also favored use of oxen rather than horses as the initial draft animals because clearing forest cover to create meadow for horses was far less efficient than planting additional acreage to corn to feed both cattle and humans.[8]

All of the initial settlements were along rivers and creeks—Mad River, Buck Creek, King's Creek, Storms Creek, and others. The main reasons were directly related to the farming and industrial technology of the day. Water for all human domestic and animal needs was readily available. Second, by extension of the customs in the areas from where the settlers had come, land immediately along the waterways was perceived as more fertile and generally easier to work than the land away from the water. The favored lands were the gentle slopes just above flood plain, especially those covered by open hardwood stands. The settlers of the Old Northwest were adept at reading the trees as a way of finding the kinds of soil they were familiar with working. A third reason, true only along the larger rivers, was that water was transportation. Fourth, flowing water was power.[9]

Water power was what drove the sawmills and the gristmills. Not every farm had its own mill, but probably many farmers toyed with trying to make one since none of the alternatives—crude spring-pole mortars, small hand-cranked grinders, or time-consuming if not dangerous distances to the nearest "merchant" mill—was ever satisfactory. The fall of the Mad River is minimally adequate for water power, with an overall average drop of just over eight feet per mile along its course. Several of its tributaries have a much higher fall, although seasonal variation in flow usually required compensation through the construction of dams and mill ponds. The earliest mills of record were started on King's Creek between 1803 and 1808. At about the same time, mills were also located on Mad River and Nettle Creek.[10]

Those initial mills were not commercial establishments as much as they were specializations within a local economy—country mills engaged in custom grinding for domestic consumption. Simple in construction, whether "tub" mills or "overshot" mills, they cracked corn enough to allow use of the rough meal in cooking and baking. Regardless of their technical efficiency, they were essential, and the local populace was seriously inconvenienced when the mills were inoperative. In 1883, Mary Guthridge recalled the winter of 1811–1812 along Kings Creek when the severe cold froze the normally flowing water, and the people had to grind their corn in mortars by hand. Whatever the devices, dry milling of corn in small quantities was necessary because of the tendency of the oil in stored meal to become rancid. Frequent trips to a mill tended to make it a natural focus for community interests. Nascent hamlets sometimes developed into villages, even towns. Such happened on the eastern side of the county where the fall of Little Darby Creek was sufficient to power a mill, and where in approximately 1814 the town of Mechanicsburg had its start.[11]

Cheap to raise, Indian corn had little market value in any unprocessed form. By contrast with corn, wheat had cash value, whether as bulk grain or processed as flour, even in relatively small quantities. When the earliest white settlers entered the Ohio country, wheat had already been a commercial cash crop for over a hundred years near the milling and exporting centers in Philadelphia, Wilmington, and Baltimore, and after about 1750, in the Virginia Piedmont as well. Despite some ambivalence about interacting with the world of commerce, wheat was what the new Ohio farmers wanted to grow and to sell.[12]

More than entrepreneurial vision was needed. Wheat grown in Ohio's interior, even when it could be harvested in quantity—which on most farms it could not—had to be transported to mills, packed in barrels, and shipped to relevant markets. Wheat was not a conceptual problem; it was a practical problem. The record of solutions and attempted solutions to that problem is essentially the history of Champaign County.

Therefore, we return to the profile of the initial settlers. They came as families with strong but fluid age and gender expectations, and they came to be farmers. They came with experience in growing corn and wheat and some other grains such as oats and barley. Many had had experience with the growing and marketing of tobacco. They came with an appreciation of the many virtues of swine. They knew how to raise beef cattle but had little knowledge and less interest in dairy. They recognized the value of sheep for wool but they had a strong distaste for mutton. They loved horses but not horseflesh; horses were for transport, traction, and the track. Cattle, in the form of oxen, were slow but strong and could be recycled as beef stew. In the carts or wagons pulled by those oxen was a short inventory of essential farm implements, chiefly the ax, the single-point plow, the hoe in various shapes, a sickle and perhaps a scythe, and some building tools.

Ohio Counties since 1888, showing Champaign County Final Boundaries as of 1818. *Courtesy Champaign County Engineer.*

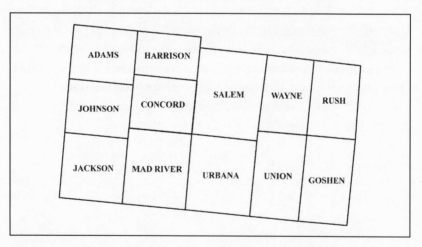

Champaign County Township Boundaries as of 1828. *Courtesy Champaign County Engineer.*

3.

Claiming the Land, and Settling In

They came to the Mad River country in four small and uneven waves, timed to the great political movements and economic forces of the day. Wars and international financial crises were relevant. So also were the less obvious changes in outlook and expectation marking the agricultural and industrial revolutions under way in Great Britain and in the fledgling United States. On the American side of the Atlantic, the opening of the Ohio country for farm settlement was a factor of monumental proportion. Champaign County farmers may not have individually sensed that significance. Merely to survive in the newer settings required at least minimal adaptive innovations in their familiar agricultural practices. They were positioned to ask, perhaps even without reflection, Is there a better way to do what we know how to do? Certainly some asked that question. Nevertheless, through the first two waves of immigration, new technologies were not particularly sought; they simply happened. Intentionality in making farming "better" was more evident with a third wave that took shape somewhere in the 1820s. It was a common but not pervasive attitude. Before that account, the waves need to be seen in sequence, as does a representative township.[1]

A decade-long first wave of settlement began in 1795 with demarcation of the Greeneville Treaty Line and its promise of land legitimacy. The handful of settlers venturing up the Miami Valley to locate in what became Champaign County scattered themselves within and along the interior edges of the Mad River Valley "trough." Prior to 1805, the total number of households and farmsteads probably counted in the dozens. While some of the settlers could trace their claims to military bounties, some others could claim only an extralegal opportunity. An unknown number resided briefly before moving on without leaving any record. Others stayed long enough to sell their "improvements." Still others remained in hopes of gaining clear title to their "preempted" homesteads.[2]

Federal policy for the disposition of public lands had initially set a uniform price of $2.00 per acre. Apart from the relatively short-term balloon-payment feature of the contracts it made with major investors such as the Ohio Company, Congress did not provide for individual purchaser credit. Acting as a real estate wholesaler with land as its bulk commodity, Congress was also unsympathetic to squatters. By 1800, however, with the eastern portion of the Northwest Territory well on its way to becoming the state of Ohio, the name of the Territory's nonvoting Representative in Congress became identified with significant revisions of the original Ordinance. The Harrison Land Act provided a credit option by allowing purchasers to spread payment over four years. It also reduced the minimum size of saleable tracts from 640 acres to 320 acres. Essentially it defined Federal land policy for the opening of the land "between the Miamis" and the formation of Champaign County.[3]

Successful application of the Harrison Land Act was somewhat compromised by the earlier actions of John Cleves Symmes. Faulty maps, faulty optimism, and faulty opportunism had all been operative in Symmes' sales of tracts widely scattered throughout the area he claimed to have purchased from Congress. Salvaging what it could, Congress reduced and redefined the Symmes Purchase as the two fractional Ranges and the first three complete Ranges lying between the Great Miami River and the Little Miami River on the immediate north side of the Ohio River. Land "between the Miamis" further north of those five Ranges became "Congress" lands. Then, because Symmes had already implemented a survey system in a manner "nowhere paralleled in the United States," with survey Ranges lying east-west rather than north-south, Congress retained the Symmes system and extended it northward into the "Congress" lands. The resulting Federal land survey district usually named "Between the Miamis" comprises Ranges 4 through 15. The western two-thirds of Champaign County lie in Ranges 10 through 13.[4]

The eastern third of Champaign County lies in the Virginia Military District, characterized by the survey system known as "metes and bounds." Location of any particular farm, even in such legal proceedings as tax delinquency, was given in terms of a nearby watercourse such as Darby Creek, Treacles Creek, Mad River, and so on, instead of the Range, Township, and Section scheme used in the Congress lands. The disputed line of separation between the Congress and the Military survey districts became the occasion for a whole episode of state and congressional actions, including separate surveys in 1802 by Israel Ludlow and in 1812 by Charles Roberts. The legacy is that Champaign County and its neighbors on both the north and the south—Logan County and Clark County—were laid out according to the two most awkward land surveying schemes in the nation.[5]

The published record of the Federal land sold under the Land Act of 1800 and recorded at the Land Office in Cincinnati does not distinguish the settlement intentions or speculative motives of the original purchasers. Purchase and entry dates therefore provide a pattern of interest rather than a pattern of use or settlement. Three such interest patterns characterize the survey district "Between the Miamis" and the adjacent portions of the Virginia Military District. The first is a time trend northward. Lower numbered (southern) Ranges show entries earlier than higher numbered (northern) Ranges. This is merely another way of noting that Hamilton County (Cincinnati) was settled earlier than was Logan County (Bellefontaine). A second pattern is a clustering of dates. Some years saw more recorded entry activity than others did. One cluster was in the middle of the first decade of the 1800s, more than coincidentally close to an 1804 revision of the Harrison Land Act reducing the minimum purchase of Federal land to 160 acres. The cluster suggests something of a boom time both politically and economically.[6]

The interweaving of those first two land interest patterns, as well as the relevance of speculation practiced in military bounties, is evident in the 1810 Ohio State Tax Duplicate. As of that date, Champaign County still encompassed the lands of the later Clark and Logan counties. Within it, 249 "Taxpayers" claimed 396 parcels of land, ranging in size from a single acre to 1,666 acres. Locator information given in the Tax Duplicate points to three groupings. One group is of 188 parcels identified by Congress Land survey detail. A second group of 98 parcels has Military Land entry numbers. The remaining 111 parcels have a locator such as a creek, indicating location in the Military District. Each of the three groupings provides some information relevant to customs of land use.[7]

The Congress lands claimed by 121 named "Taxpayers" ranged in size from ten acres to 740 acres. Most of the parcels were in acreage multiples of eighty, with the largest cluster (51 parcels) around 160 acres indicating a settlement concentration time in the half decade following 1804. Most of these Congress Land claims were in Townships 4 and 5, that is, in what became Mad River and Urbana Townships in Range 11 and somewhat fewer in Concord and Salem Townships in Range 12. The record shows claim entries for Townships 4 and 5 in Range 13 further north, but all were assigned to William Ward, and may or may not have had occupants. The threat of wolves and panthers was still fearful, and the County Commissioners offered bounties for their pelts. The clustering of claims in 1810, in other words, was near the center of John Ogden's "trough," and was definitely thicker in the south, thinner in the north.[8]

Claims in the Military District included much larger tracts than was characteristic of the Congress Lands, but the relevant interpretive clue is in the ownership detail provided in the Tax Duplicate. Nonresident taxpayers claimed a third of the parcels (77), with half of those (33) assigned to the entrepreneurial surveyor and politician Duncan McArthur. In addition, almost all of the claims in the Military District showed a current taxpayer name different from the name given on the original entry. These were military bounties acquired as investment opportunities. When the nonresident taxpayers and the few resident taxpayers with more than three or four claims are removed from consideration, the remainder is a list of county resident taxpayers claiming acreages not significantly different in size from those found in the Congress Lands. Most were located along Mad River or Buck Creek or else along King's Creek or Darby Creek. Little evidence from 1810 indicates any settlement north into what became Logan County.[9]

The practice and the timing of making advantageous use of military bounties is illustrated in early Salem Township. In 1802, Isaac Zane was granted three tracts located along King's Creek, each of one square mile, nominally "in consideration of his having been taken prisoner by the Indians, when a boy, during the Revolutionary war, and living with them most of his life; and having, during that time, performed many acts of kindness and beneficence toward the American people." Four years later John Taylor came from Virginia to the King's Creek area. The record does not indicate the source of Taylor's finances nor of his terms of payment or his success in meeting them. The record only indicates that Taylor purchased 640 acres from Isaac Zane for four dollars per acre. Zane was turning his military service to profit. For his part, Taylor could justify the purchase price on the commercial possibilities of location. In 1810 he erected a gristmill, although the entrepreneurial venture was probably precarious in the short term because the number of land entries for the area declined in the years 1808–1810. A distant factor was a retrenchment of investor interest following the Jeffersonian Embargo of 1807, while much nearer was renewed Indian unrest, particularly associated with Tecumseh. Thus diminished the first wave of settlement in Champaign County.[10]

With the continuing passage of time, a second settlement wave is apparent and with it, also a third land purchase pattern. The War of 1812 was more than a marker. For some settlers such as Jess Johnson who had come to Concord Township in 1806, participation in the War of 1812 was a personal defense of home and hearth. For a very few, such as Joseph Vance, the war was the beginning of a lifetime of politics and public service. For many others, the war was a spur to economic activity in all the northern parts of the Miami Valley. General Hull's march northward through the area in 1812 implicitly defined the end of the frontier period in west-central Ohio. The commercial stimulus of soldiers in need of provisions lingered, as did some of those soldiers. One was William Sanford Rawlings. Recruited in Kentucky, encamped with Hull south of Urbana where he was impressed by what he saw, and later discharged back in Kentucky, Rawlings returned to settle in Urbana Township in 1814. Other adventurers were perhaps influenced by the near-explosion of travel and Western promotional literature of the day. All contributed to an increase in land sale entries in the years immediately following 1813. By the standards of the day, financial credit was generously available.

Optimistically in 1817, therefore, Joshua Howells laid out the hamlet of Christiansburg, in the southwest corner of Champaign County, on land he had entered some time previously. The patterns were clear, and clearly brief. In 1820, Howells' hamlet disappointingly numbered only six houses. He could not have seen it coming but, following the Panic of 1819, there was a significant falloff of land entries throughout the Miami Valley. Credit for the purchase of farmland simply dried up. Thus ended a brief second wave of settlement.[11]

While the immediate consequences of financial panic were undoubtedly painful for some farm families, a broader social measure finds positive elements as well. An 1822 sheriff's sale of three contiguous eighty-acre portions lying along Buck Creek south of the Champaign/Clark county line, initiated by the Urbana Banking Company, demonstrated how much an active financial infrastructure had developed. Another element was evident in the efforts by the County to collect delinquent land taxes. For assessment purposes, farmland was rated under one of three headings, with #1 considered best and #3 considered marginal. In late spring of 1822, Champaign County Auditor John Thomas published notice of tax delinquencies for the previous year. Of the forty-four properties in the May listing, all located in Congress Lands, the two rated as #1 were 160 and 166 acres respectively. The four entries rated as #3 ranged in size from 80 to 160. The majority of the notice was for the thirty-eight properties rated #2. This included two small plots of 2½ and 7 acres and two large plots of 320 and 323½ acres. Most were close to 160 acres. The separate notice of delinquencies in the Military District lands listed forty-two properties, all but five of them smaller portions of originally larger claims and none rated as #1 farmland. Heuristically presuming a county-wide uniformity of rating, the fact that eighteen of the forty-two properties were rated #3 (marginal) hints at some of the reason for the tax delinquency. Implicit here was the third land-interest pattern, for all these data together indicate that the ideal farm size, though not necessarily the most practical farm size, was a quarter section, 160 acres.[12]

By the time of the Panic of 1819, the Harrison Land Act of 1800 had governed federal land policy for nearly twenty years, adjusted considerably by Congress but without significant modification of principle. However popular it may have been politically, its installment purchase feature had resulted in widespread abuse. In an 1820 major overhaul, therefore, Congress abolished credit for Federal land sales. The offset was a reduction of the minimum saleable tract to eighty acres and a reduction of the official price to $1.25 per acre. For one hundred dollars cash, anyone could buy eighty acres of the available public domain. Federal land was still available in the Miami Valley, and the revised policy was a factor in settling the northern parts. When the village of Spring Hills in Harrison Township was laid out in 1826, the surrounding farms were among the smallest in the county, typically eighty acres. A handful of forty-acre farms represents the additional adjustment made by the Land Act of 5 April 1832, the last of the Federal land laws relevant to the settling of the county.[13]

The successive waves of migration into the Miami Valley, meanwhile, had provoked the political administrators of the day to refine western Ohio's county and township boundaries. The relatively large Champaign County initially carved from Greene and Franklin counties in 1805 segmented into Clark, Champaign, and Logan counties in 1818. The 1820 census enumeration showed 8,479 persons in the area that retained the name of Champaign. Most populace of the townships was Urbana, at 1,747, largely because of the 644 persons residing in the Village of Urbana. The second-most populous township was the almost entirely rural Mad River Township, at 1,345. The county's nine townships became ten with the creation of Johnson Township in 1821, eleven with the creation of Adams Township in 1827, and the definitive twelve with the creation of Rush Township in 1828. Nevertheless, the overall population increase to 12,137 by 1830 remained unevenly concentrated in the three south/southwestern townships of Jackson, Mad River, and Urbana.[14]

Mad River Township in particular reflected the migration and settlement patterns of Ohio's first decades. Oriented south toward the regional center of Cincinnati—the emerging "Queen City of the West"—most of its immigrants had come from or through Virginia or Kentucky. Some, such as the Weaver brothers, Christopher and William, had been born in the southeastern portion of Pennsylvania and as young adults had made their way through Maryland and Virginia to make a first home in Kentucky before moving on to Ohio. Others similarly from Pennsylvania and Maryland and Virginia and Kentucky joined them in the half-dozen years following the War of 1812. In the third wave of immigration in the 1820s, Mad River Township and its immediate neighbors on the east and west continued to attract. Then, as striking as the increase was how quickly the increase slowed. Following a small surge of immigration roughly midway through the 1830s, the Mad River Township population reached 1,894 by 1840. It also reached a plateau, although George Craig could not have known that when he surveyed the village of Terre Haute into town lots in 1838 "as a speculative experiment." The 1850 township population of 1,908 meant a net increase of only fourteen. For the next forty years, the township population would vary within about one hundred persons of the 1850 figure. In 1880, the village of Terre Haute was still barely 125 persons.[15]

The population growth pattern begs interpretation. The result of the early "waves" of immigration into the township was a filling in, up to the perceived capacity of the land. Once that capacity was reached, population density remained nearly constant for almost two generations. That represented a choice. Since the attraction of the land was for its agricultural uses, immigration slowed because other persons seeking land for the same goals no longer found it available in Mad River Township. And, unless one assumes a radical reduction in fertility, the natural excess of births over deaths was also compensated by out-migration. The young and the transient went elsewhere—"West," to neighboring Jackson Township, then to neighboring counties but more likely to neighboring Indiana and then Illinois and across the Mississippi River. Mad River Township, sooner than other parts of Champaign County, held a "pass through" status.[16]

Such portions of the immigrant tide as remained took up farming on "undulating" wooded land cross-marked by the many small creeks flowing mostly to the southeast. The 1820 census indicated 285 persons engaged in agriculture in Mad River Township. By the standards of the day, most of those persons were heads of households, presumptively male. If a spouse and two or three children are added to each of those households, nearly the entire township is accounted. The farms of those persons, like most farms in Ohio in the 1820s and 1830s, were diversified, partly by choice, partly by necessity. Some, perhaps most, could be described as "pioneer clearance" farms, for as of 1832 only one-fourth of the land had been cleared. Presumably also, a few farms were already on their way to becoming sentimentally remembered "old cleared" farms. The land was much like the gently wooded hill country from where most of the migrants had come; it lent itself to the farming technology they knew. The general description of American agriculture at the time, as phrased in the classic study by Percy Bidwell and John Falconer, fits southwestern Champaign County very well: "The outstanding characteristics of the farm economy of the early settlements were: (1) the *extensive* character of the enterprise, that is, the application of small amounts of labor and capital on large amounts of land, and (2) self-sufficiency, or production for consumption and not for sale."[17]

In 1820, Mad River Township was typical; it was much like any contemporary agricultural area west of the Appalachians. The census of Champaign County that year showed 286 persons engaged in "manufacturing," one-third of whom lived in the town of Urbana. Of the remainder, Salem Township accounted for forty-two, Goshen Township accounted for thirty-three, and Mad River held fourth place with twenty-seven. None of the other townships had even a dozen. Typical also was "the scarcity of trading-points," assessed in the Beers history as "a matter of great inconvenience to the pioneers." Of the nineteen persons in the county engaged in commerce, sixteen were in Urbana, two were in Mad River, and one was in Goshen. The farmers of Mad River Township were no more inconveniently situated than were any others in the county, and Cincinnati and Dayton were eager for their trade. Even as other options for trade became available, their effect was to confirm the agricultural character of Mad River Township. "Wheat Wanted" declared "J. & P. M'Cormick" in an 1826 newspaper notice. "The subscribers will pay the highest market price in cash, for wheat delivered at their mill on the West side of Mad River, on the road leading from Dayton to Urbana, seven miles east of Dayton."[18]

Measured against its contemporaries, Mad River Township was reasonably competitive, reasonably complete as a setting for rural life, and reasonably desirable. By approximately 1840, its farm families had achieved something of a balance between the productive potential of their land and their need for labor to work it. Apart from the small but steadily increasing quantity of consumer goods that required cash for purchase, and apart from their more serious need to pay taxes, they had relatively little incentive to improve the efficiency of their production technology. Their social and civic and religious needs were satisfied in the villages of Westville and Terre Haute. They were near enough the county seat of Urbana, the fledgling manufacturing center of Springfield, and the Miami Valley's regional hub of Dayton. They were not isolated in wilderness. In the absence of improved roads to any of those centers, they were mildly buffered, and free to be independent. Changes in machine technology affecting labor and changes in attitude and understanding affecting care of the land would come rapidly in the middle decades of the century, but they would not come as the initiative of this township. The lay of the land, an appropriately adapted productive technology, and a strongly integrated scheme of values had already dictated that choice.[19]

4.

Traditions and Revisions

By the standards of the day, southwestern Ohio's Miami Valley was a richly active agricultural region. Already by 1820, it had produced an estimated 250,000 bushels of wheat and nearly 500,000 bushels of corn (primarily fed to hogs). An 1826 assessment was that the boats descending the Great Miami and the Little Miami rivers each season carried agricultural produce—primarily flour, whisky, and pork—valued in excess of $100,000. Champaign County farmers were contributing to that total, and their potential future contribution was being enhanced by technical developments in farm implements. One set of developments related to soil preparation, another to harvest. Constraining the adoption of either set was the regional culture, revealed as an indicator of how farm land could and should be worked, and to what end.[1]

Consider first the notion that plows in their design and material represent understandings of function, of useful purpose. Choosing to adopt—or not to adopt—plows of new design or different material reflects an understanding of efficiency, of the contextual costs and benefits of changing the way the plowing function is accomplished. The common experience for the initial generation of white farmers in Champaign County was what they described as "pioneer" conditions, essentially wooded land. Because diversity in terrain and location within the county determined different needs, however, farmers in actuality exercised various standards of efficiency in assessing their implements. Then, as pioneer conditions diminished unevenly for everyone in the county, the pace of adopting innovative farm implements generally quickened. What showed in the 1820s and early 1830s were changes in plow design and material. What that implied were culturally constrained different measures of efficiency.

The first generation of settler-farmers in Champaign County had carried with it the agricultural technology of turn-of-the-century Virginia Piedmont, including the custom of plowing erosion-prone shallow furrows. The preferred style of plow for cultivating cornfields was the single-point shovel or horse-hoe plow with a wrought-iron share fastened to a wooden stem. A moldboard, if the plow was typically late colonial in design and if the soil was being prepared for wheat or other small grain, was made of wood covered usually with strips of metal. The already considerable resistance at the drawbar of such plows was increased when a rider sat on the beam to force-hold the share point in the soil, and even then, the resulting furrow was shallow and uneven. When drawn through recently cleared woodland by a pair of oxen, the wooden plow was likely to break at hitting large tree roots or to exhaust the farmer who had to "jump" the plow over any number of obstacles. This was not a very efficient technology, but the trade-off was that neither did it require much cash outlay to purchase or maintain. A farmer might well have a heavy moldboard plow for opening new ground and a lighter shovel plow for cultivating. Any local blacksmith, called on to repair the wood-and-iron implements, could just as easily manufacture similar items from local materials for a local market, as was the apparent practice in early Salem Township in the shop of Wesley Hughes.[2]

Numerous inventors, principally in Virginia and then in Massachusetts and New York, had addressed the problem of plow efficiency at least since the 1790s. Part of the problem was in plow design and part was in materials and therefore, cost. In 1797, the same year a white settler first made a home in the Mad River Valley, Charles Newbold of Burlington, New Jersey, obtained a patent for a cast-iron plow. The chief defect of Newbold's plow was its cost, for when it dulled or broke, the entire plow had to be replaced. David Peacock as early as 1807, and then New York's Jethro Wood more successfully in 1814, corrected Newbold's defect by joining together share, moldboard, and landside from separate castings. The result was a device with replaceable parts. Other contemporaries worked on the material in the share, the shape of the moldboard, and the overall handling. None of the metal plows was a commercial success prior to about 1820. Then fairly rapidly through the 1820s, during the time period of Champaign County's third wave of settlement, farmers in New England and the Middle states adopted metal plows in a variety of designs.[3]

Champaign County farmers were aware of these developments. Reminiscing in 1871, Aaron Gutridge of Goshen Township remarked on the changes from his boyhood and on "the fields that were plowed with long, wooden mould-board plows, then the cast plow." In the same volume of recollections, T. S. McFarland asserted that in 1819, William Werden of Concord Township was the first to introduce a metal mold-board for plows. A half dozen years later, Urbana's John Reynolds & Co. was an authorized retailer of "Jethro Woods Patent Ploughs," made by Joseph Ridgway in Columbus. In 1828, an Urbana blacksmith named William Downs announced that he had purchased the right of distrib-uting "Sweney's Ohio Plough" for Champaign and Logan counties. His notice explained that "The share is made of wrought iron, the land side of the same, properly steeled; the cutter is also made of wrought iron, with a steel edge." The notice is vague as to where the plows were actu-ally made. In 1832, David Parry was much clearer, announcing an Urbana Iron Foundry "at which will be manufactured Cast Iron Ploughs, Mill Irons, Wagon Boxes, and all kinds of Castings for machinery, &c."[4]

Sales of plows in Champaign County are unknown. The collective evidence is that county farmers were slow to adopt the all-metal plows. In the bottomlands along the waterways and wherever the soil was heavy, the cast-iron plows did not scour. The introduction of steel, unless it was of the highest quality and therefore the most expensive, did not change that experience. Wherever the forest cover was incompletely cleared, cast-iron plows were not sharp enough to cut through roots and were likely to break. Where the soil was sandy, the cast-iron wore away quickly. The familiar shovel plow, by contrast, had the advantage that it could be improved with added and better-quality metal without any obvious erosion of the user's cultural heritage—if a plow was needed. Cultivation of corn by hand-hoe was common as late as 1840.[5]

Not until the early 1840s, that is, not until the pioneer stage of farming was past, could the advantages of the new metal plows be exploited effectively in west-central Ohio. By then, they were increasingly available in multiple styles. Steel self-scouring plows were being made in nearby Troy by the T. Wilmington Company and by at least three firms in Cincinnati. The Urbana hardware firm of Weaver & Brothers advertised in 1845 that "We have on hand and for sale Cheap, Baker's Patent Ploughs" which were "well calculated for breaking up loose black soil and bottom land, as well as stubble, being so constructed that the mould board will scour and become smooth with a very little use." A newspaper advertisement in 1848 promoted steel moldboard plows in several sizes, with and without cutters, and in either right- or left-handed configurations, all available from Urbana's Erastus Sheldon. For those who could afford to pay the relatively higher purchase price, the best of the new plows cut through more diverse and more difficult surface soil conditions and they cut deeper, resulting in better drainage and less soil erosion. At least in theory, they allowed the cultivation of more land more intensively, often with fewer workers. Certainly they reduced the strain on the draft animals. As metal replaced wood, therefore, mules and horses began to replace oxen.[6]

The cast-iron plow with some steel components came into general use when it could be manufactured efficiently and marketed effectively. Despite the promotions noted above, that was something new, and in the 1820s and 1830s it was still waiting to happen. The farmer-producers of Champaign County were calculatingly practical. As long as there was land to clear, and as long as the new technology provided no particular benefit, reliance on the familiar heavy breaking plow, the wooden mold-board plow, and the shovel plow continued. That also meant that the labor involved in plowing did not decrease and that the relatively slow pace of acreage expansion held steady through the 1830s. While use of an all-metal and later an all-steel plow was a strong indicator of the farmer's increasing participation in a market economy as both producer and consumer, the evidence suggests another role as well—that of careful observer.

A second technical development came at the other end of the growing season, where participation in the nation's expanding market economy was even more evident in the use of manufactured edge tools such as sickles and scythes. Harvesting (that is, reaping, binding, and shocking, with threshing considered a separate process) was almost entirely handwork. Corn was picked by hand, and wheat was cut with a sickle, work that could be done indifferently well by either males or females. On slopes and among still-rotting stumps on newly cleared land, the sickle was the most efficient reaping tool available, despite the backbreaking pace of barely one acre per day. By the end of the American colonial period, another implement was changing that pace. The familiar long curved-handle walking scythe was fitted with a cradle, essentially a huge comb that lined up the stalks as they were cut and laid them down in a consistent direction, ready for binding. With a slight increased loss of ripe grain through what was called "shattering," a skilled adult male could now reap three acres per day.[7]

The cradle scythe was introduced into Ohio prior to 1830, and for another decade or so, both sickle and cradle were used in harvesting wheat, sometimes in the same field. Gradually the cradle superseded the sickle in general use, and remained the dominant reaping implement until the Civil War. Jacob Gardner, still living in Urbana in 1880 when John W. Ogden made his notes for the Beers history, was "the first one of whom we have any knowledge who made the making and repairing of cradles a regular business." W. J. Knight, looking back on a farm life that began in 1865, remarked that "Even in my own later day, a grain cradle was used to harvest grain in stumpy ground where a horse-drawn machine could not be used."[8]

Just as with plowing, the land and labor implications of this harvesting technology were constitutive of the agricultural ideology of the day. Farm grain productivity was set essentially by the number of persons able effectively to swing the cradle. If the average male adult worker could reap three acres per day, and if that male was part of a farm household containing at least two additional workers to bind, and if the optimal harvest time for wheat was about two weeks which hopefully included about ten good working days in the field, then this farm family/household could reasonably run about thirty acres of small grain. But, not much more—not without increased risk of waste or without increased supply of seasonal skilled labor. There is record from 1853 that in order to complete their harvest, some farmers in Champaign County hired extra workers from the dairy farms of the Western Reserve, but the most important part of that record is the year itself. Any significant use of nonlocal seasonal wage labor appears to have been atypical until there was extensive mechanization of the harvesting process. An early pre-mechanization witness to the absence of outside hired labor was young Calvin Fletcher who arrived in Urbana in June of 1817. The following summer, in a letter to his father back home in Vermont, Fletcher observed that "We began to harvest about the 1st of July. The Farmers all join together—men women & children collect at some one of the neighbours finish his harvesting & so around. At these meetings they drink a great deal of whiskey & it is not uncommon for them to fight. The Kentucky-ans & Virginians frequently have a piched Battle between each other."[9]

As hinted in Fletcher's account, skill was not uniformly distributed within the farming community, however willing the hands may have been. Some individuals were simply better able to handle the implements and were therefore in demand for exchange of labor. The nostalgic recol-lections in the later historic record indicate little supply of workers apart from the members of the neighboring farm families, all of whom had similar seasonal obligations. John Cawood's call for laborers in June of 1831 was only marginally exceptional. "I will employ from 10 to 25 hands, by the job or month, from this time to the 1st of June next," he announced. "Liberal wages will be given. Apply at the farm opposite Alexander Tay-lor's below the mouth of King's creek." The farm's location in the relatively level portions of central Concord Township suggests that Cawood had a significant part of his land in small grains, while the option of employ-ment through an entire year suggests a very local orientation. Neverthe-less, for the 1820s and 1830s, Cawood's newspaper recruitment notice was unique. Labor arrangements and recruiting, regardless of extent, were handled informally through personal networks.[10]

The actual elasticity of the labor supply in Champaign County during the early decades of the century is, at this distance in time, an unknown. In the tradition of general farming, one pattern is clear. Every farmer had land put to uses other than just grain farming—to pasture, to woodland, and to other crops such as corn, buckwheat, oats, and pota-toes. The terrain, the climate, and the agricultural expectations of the time enforced such diversification. The task facing every farm decision-

maker was to make an appropriately balanced assessment of the acreage
of corn that could be cultivated, the acreage of small grains that could
be harvested, and the acreage of woodland that could be cleared and
prepared in time for the next planting cycle. Wheat required its most
intense labor at harvest. Corn cultivation was never as intense, but it
demanded attention for a greater part of the year. Planting was handwork, requiring approximately a day's labor per acre, and prior to the
introduction of corn seed planters, twenty acres per laborer was atypical.
Thinning and cultivating was hoe-work, only slightly alleviated with the
use of the horse-hoe. The result through the 1820s was an optimum of
about ten acres of corn per adult worker, a figure necessarily parallel to
the optimal wheat acreage figure. Presuming some modest management
skill on the part of the average owner-operator, the need for labor was
spread through the entire year as a near constant, with the implication
that a stable, reliable, and even resident labor force was most efficient.
Furthermore, no one enterprise on a diversified farm carried a risk factor
that jeopardized the entire farm, financially or otherwise. Later, when
market forces pushed farm operators toward economies of scale, the same
family-centered diversification appeared less adaptive and, for some,
painfully conflicted. Nevertheless, through most of the antebellum
period in west central Ohio, even when an occasional seasonal labor
shortage was acute, the "family farm" was an adaptive expression of the
available labor resource. Furthermore, the new technology exemplified
in the grain cradle reinforced a culturally sanctioned gender- and age-
based division of labor. Even as it promised some increase in productivity, the grain cradle had the greater advantage of risking very little capital
and, for males, very little status. In its effect, the grain cradle set a baseline for agricultural demographics as well as agricultural productivity.[11]

5.

The Transportation Problem

The population of Champaign County was increasing; so also was the efficiency of some farm implements. More farmers were working more land and producing more wheat and more corn. In absolute terms, all the increases were modest but they do provoke a question: What did the farmers do with what they called "surplus" produce? From the early 1800s and on into the 1810s, what could they do with it? The answer was simple: Very little! The point was made incisively in a centenary retrospect by one of Ohio's most careful chroniclers of agricultural change, John H. Klippart: "The success of agriculture, from a financial standpoint, depends upon the facilities of reaching good markets." The farmers of Champaign County had few such facilities. There was, in the 1847 retrospective phrasing of Cincinnati lawyer Jacob Burnet, "no market." For the producers who needed or wanted outside markets, the problem was, in the 1838 perspective of Caleb Atwater, "a want of good roads, either by land or water, on which our home productions could be transported."[1]

The surviving detail supporting such assessments is consistent though disappointingly thin. John F. Mansfield's 1807 "Map of the State of Ohio" shows a road north from Springfield and terminating at Urbana, with no other routes leading to or from Urbana. In Springfield, that road branched southeast to Chillicothe and southwest to Dayton. William F. Gephart's 1909 study of "Transportation and Industrial Development in the Middle

West" is illustrated with numerous maps of Ohio that unfortunately depict a considerable amount of information not otherwise discussed in the text and not ascribed to any particular sources. They are therefore suggestive rather than definitive. A composite reconstructed "Road Map of the State of Ohio 1810" indicates only two state-recognized "roads" within Champaign County. One was the trail (essentially the later US 68) running south from the Greeneville Treaty line, through Urbana, to Springfield where it branched east (the later National Road), southeast (the later State Route 41 and a portion of US 35), and southwest (continuation of the later US 68). Very possibly this was the same trail described by William Patrick in 1881 as "a celebrated Indian trail from Old Town, then called Old Chillicothe, [which] ran through Urbana to Sandusky." The other "road" was a trail west from Urbana to Fort Greeneville (later US 36). Also shown on Gephart's map was a trail running southeast from Urbana (portions of the later SR 29 and SR 56 to London). Daniel Drake's 1815 book on Cincinnati included a "Map of the Miami Country" showing those routes, plus a route between Urbana and Troy (an unrealistically straighter line than the later SR 55) as well as several routes north from Cincinnati toward Dayton and Xenia. Gershom Flagg, writing from Springfield in November of 1816, described his very recent journey on the eastern portion of Zane's Trace to Zanesville and then to Columbus and finally by way of Urbana to Springfield: "we have not traveled more than 20 miles a day the roads being very bad." The descriptive word of choice used by other writers was "execrable," and any extended journey took days to accomplish. Calvin Fletcher's experience of going from Urbana to Cincinnati in April of 1819 required three days on the road. On the return, he rode the distance in only two days and wrote later to his father that "This journey never was performed in less time."[2]

More than merely transporting Ohio's "home productions," Caleb Atwater's "good roads, either by land or water" provided structure for the movement of people and information. Changes in structure necessarily implicated more than the volume and direction of commerce. Military, commercial, and political interests overlapped, perhaps even coalesced in concern. Jacob Burnet chose to understand the implications in commercial terms: "The farmer had no motive to increase the product of his fields." While that may have been true for some farmers, by the actual time of

Burnet's writing it could no longer be asserted so categorically. What happened during the thirty years from the mid-1810s to the mid-1840s was a "market revolution." That was possible, in turn, because of a "transportation revolution." In John H. Klippart's very practical phrase, "reaching good markets" became somewhat easier. Concurrent with the waves of settler migration into and through Champaign County were the successively overlapping improvements in interior transportation—steamboats on the Ohio River, barges on the Erie Canal in New York and on its imitators in the Ohio canal system, wagons on "improved" surface roads, notably the National Road, and finally the railroad. Although it all happened in less than a lifetime, it was experienced as unevenly incremental. Within the lifetime of any one farmer, consequently, the transportation "revolution" was an uncertain basis on which to reassess agricultural and economic motives. All did eventually, but not at the same pace.[3]

In a political sense, the transportation revolution began with the creation of Ohio as a state in 1803 and with the concern of Atlantic coast interests to connect commercially and militarily with "the Ohio country." Agreeing to the general route recommendations of an official study commission, Congress in 1806 authorized a "Cumberland Road" from Cumberland, Maryland, to somewhere near Wheeling, Virginia, that is, a surface road over the mountains providing connection between the eastward-flowing Potomac River and the westward-flowing Ohio River. In the spring of 1811, actual road-building began, only to be interrupted by the War of 1812. Nevertheless, what commerce and politics did not accomplish, the military conflict did indirectly by demonstrating the nation's military need for usable surface roads north from Cincinnati to and across the conflicted international border region. Champaign County, situated roughly halfway between Cincinnati and Sandusky Bay, was a beneficiary of related concern in the immediate post-war period, for the number and quality of passable trails serving the county began to increase. The most "natural" route ending at Sandusky Bay used a former Indian pathway following the Scioto River upstream to the very low Continental divide, and then continued downstream alongside the Sandusky River as it flowed toward Lake Erie. In the 1820s, that pathway would be invested with a high level of anticipation for its commercial possibilities as a canal route favoring Champaign County. In the mid-1810s, no one was imagining such a "Scioto Trail" canal and the route was instead improved by widening it enough to accommodate pack animals. This also allowed seasonally limited use of wagons.[4]

A transportation revolution had started, but just barely. Work on New York's Erie Canal began in 1817. A few months later, Ohio's Governor met with the Governor of Michigan Territory and with representatives of the Ottawa, Wyandot, Delaware, Chippewa, Potawatomi, Seneca, and Shawnee peoples to clear the remaining Indian title to lands north of Ohio's Greeneville Treaty Line, that is, north of what had been the 1805 boundary of the original Champaign County. Soon enough there would be settlers migrating into northwest Ohio, and soon also there would be economic pressures for better transportation linkage between the western port cities on Lake Erie (such as the newly founded Portland at Sandusky Bay) and the agricultural interior of the State. The agricultural producers of Champaign County would be affected both directly and indirectly. In the interim, the Cumberland Road (not yet called the National Road) would not be complete from Baltimore to Wheeling for another year. Cincinnati's Daniel Drake had just recently published his often-noted assessment that there was "not a single good road" in Ohio, and none in the Miami Valley that was passable at all seasons. With the year 1817 as a loosely convenient temporal focus, therefore, Caleb Atwater's commercially viable "good roads, either by land or water" need to be viewed from a perspective that begins very widely before narrowing again to rural Champaign County.[5]

Commercial traffic between the Atlantic seaboard and the West tended to take the form of a huge circuit moving primarily in a counter-clockwise direction. All the overland routes were limited in everything except political potential, and common to all was the brute problem of getting across or around the mountains. The number of "gateways" was limited. The Genesee Road west from Albany through the Mohawk Valley to Buffalo was favored by business interests centered in Boston and New York. This was the corridor with very promising Great Lakes connections. A second route followed along the Potomac River from Baltimore to Cumberland, then up Wills Creek and on to the Monongahela River and finally to the Forks of the Ohio at Pittsburgh, with significant military implications—it had been General Braddock's route in 1755. This was the route selected in 1806 to be the start of a "national road" because it was perceived, by some, as the route with the most flexible options for commercially servicing the entire Ohio Valley. So it was, unless one happened to be partisan toward Philadelphia and chose to take the Forbes, or Old Glade, Road west from Harrisburg directly over the difficult mountains to Pittsburgh. Or, unless one was already in the purview of Richmond and chose to travel by way of the Roanoke Gap and then northwest to the Ohio country or west through the Cumberland Gap on the Wilderness Road to the headwaters of the Kentucky and Tennessee Rivers. All those routes were already being used by cattle and hog drovers. Each of the routes was later tested for its east-west canal potential, and later they would become the routes developed competitively for trunk lines by the railroads. Significantly, in view of those later competitions, the geographic/geologic "shape" of west-central Ohio favored no one of those routes as its "natural" conduit from the east. All were used, particularly if users were able to incorporate the Ohio River or its tributaries.[6]

Until after the War of 1812, the bulk of admittedly very little commercial traffic on any of the trans-Appalachian routes moved almost exclusively one-way, from east to west. The exceptions, such as the eastbound droving of livestock, confirmed the general pattern. Travelling from Cumberland to Wheeling in October, 1822, William Blane encountered "vast droves of hogs ... going from the State of Ohio across the mountains to the Eastern States." Wary of sharing the rough roads with such droves, wagons returning east after having delivered their cargoes of valuable manufactured or processed goods could afford to carry some less valuable bulky and unprocessed western produce. Otherwise, commerce from almost anywhere in the Ohio Valley reached the east indirectly by going south toward New Orleans on "the Ohio-Missouri-Mississippi river trade axis." Transport by water was an essential component of normal commerce, and the orientation was necessarily downstream. The typical vessel reaching New Orleans was a flatboat or barge designed for one-way transit only. Even after the day when steam packets began to make relatively regular round-trips on the Mississippi, one-way water transport downstream, with transshipment to ocean vessels for re-export or more commonly for a loop around Florida and up the Atlantic coast, was still faster and cheaper than packing eastward back over the mountains. "Cheaper" was relative, for all the evidence indicates that river trips to New Orleans, while often exciting, were also extremely dangerous.[7]

6.

Making Do, With Roads and Without

During the decades immediately on either side of 1800, as settlers moved into the interior upstream along the smaller tributaries of the Ohio River, into areas such as Champaign County, their practical distance from major market connections increased. They became of necessity self-sufficient. Without a cash crop and ready access to viable markets, their integration in the national economy was minimal. Even when access to such markets began to improve, there were times such as following the Panic of 1819 and the sudden collapse of prices, when interior producers had no purchasing power because they had no acceptable circulating medium. They were, for short periods of time, and by definition, subsistence farmers, bartering locally for the few things they did not grow or make.[1]

The reality for a longer period of time—well beyond the pioneer period—was the exchange-based nature of the local economy. All of the merchants and service providers advertising in the Urbana newspapers indicated a willingness to receive "country produce" in lieu of cash. In 1824, for example, E. C. Berry announced that in exchange for carding and fulling at his Urbana Manufactory, "Sugar, Feathers, Ginseng, Beeswax, Wheat, Flax-seed, Wool and such other articles as can be disposed of without loss, as may hereafter be agreed upon, will be received at the market prices in payment." Even the newspaper itself could be subscribed with the delivery of a range of named commodities. In one appeal, the editor prodded his delinquent subscribers with humor, requesting "some oats, corn, and flour, as we stand much in need of these articles. We have a horse, a cow, &c. to feed; and we frequently eat a little ourselves, when we can obtain provisions." In another appeal he noted wryly that "Money will not be refused, for debts due this establishment."[2]

Few of Champaign County's earliest farmers actually lived along one of the better roads facilitating commercial activity. The minimal trails to the nearest gristmill could at best accommodate a horse or packmule. A bushel of wheat or corn typically weighs about sixty pounds, and one of the children in a family could ride a horse loaded with bags of corn to be ground for the family's home use. It was, in the recollections of S. E. Morgan, a wonderfully "perilous and adventurous journey" for "a boy just big enough to straddle" the "old family mare" to be entrusted with carrying a bushel of corn a mile and a half along "a zigzag, crooked forest road" to Taylor's Mill on King's Creek. There the miller might have kept a portion of the grain or flour as payment, or might have made an immediate exchange for the arriving grain with an appropriate quantity of flour ready at the mill.[3]

For any major market trip from a country mill, with packhorses each carrying three or four bushels of grain, trails better than a zig-zag crooked forest road were crucial, and the location of a mill was strategic to its success. As evident in the early maps, grain could be conveyed over established trails to Cincinnati or Dayton, or later to Columbus and Sandusky. Hauling grain to a nearby commercial market to negotiate for price as well as to vote, pay taxes, or purchase essentials was not likely a frequent experience. An undated memory in the Beers account of Adams Township noted that travel to Sidney or to Urbana was required to purchase "even the necessaries of daily life. An entire day was consumed in traveling to and from the towns just mentioned, and much valuable time was lost." Another recollected trip from Urbana to Cincinnati in 1815, hauling barrels of flour, took eight days. A dozen years later the situation was no better, at least in the month of February. Running short of ink, the editor of Urbana's *Mad-River Courant* was able to print only half a normal issue. "We are also out of paper, but expect both paper and ink soon," he explained. "The roads are so bad, it takes better than two weeks for a team to make a trip to Cincinnati and back."[4]

The questions of "how" and "when" to transport produce to market were not asked lightly. Few farmers had satisfactory grain storage facility, and even fewer could afford to hold their produce at home in order to take any advantage of off-season prices. In rounded numbers for the entire country, the overall portion of American farm produce not consumed within the local community and therefore available for commercial sale in 1820 was rarely more than about twenty per cent. In language of the day that lingered for decades, there was little "surplus," in Ohio or elsewhere. Not yet. Instead, and even profitably for a few producers, the influx of migrants—new farmers not yet productive on their own— consumed much of Champaign County's small agricultural surplus, and transactions were not likely to be in cash. Nevertheless, the typical debt-burdened farmer needed some cash, usually for taxes.[5]

One solution was to rely heavily on the local miller or village shop-keeper. Urbana merchant William Rianhard, for example, offered to "pay the market price in goods for any quantity of good, merchantable wheat delivered at Vance's Mill." Wheat was then processed into flour. Typically, five bushels of wheat went into one barrel of flour and at approximately two hundred pounds per barrel achieved a bulk weight reduction of about one-third. Barrels necessitated cartage by wagon, a task more easily accomplished by a strategically located merchant or miller's assistant than by a farmer not living along established roads. For the more entrepreneurial or adventuresome farmer with an appropriate wagon and team, Jonathan Harshman had a special inducement. In addition to paying "the highest market price in Cash, for any quantity of Wheat during the Fall and Winter season," he offered to "pay cash to those that deliver Wheat & for the carriage of Flour to Cincinnati."[6]

From anywhere in the Miami Valley, an overland trip to Cincinnati was ultimately constrained by the region's "downstream" orientation. Easily by the 1820s, and explicitly by 1831, Dayton was a focal contact point because of the relative condition of access roads, because of the grain dealers who had established business there, and because of the existence of several breweries and a market for barley. More importantly, Dayton was where flatboats were launched to float to the Ohio River—in normal years, a spring-flood phenomenon—until the 1829 opening of the Miami Canal. The cargo leaving Dayton was typically flour, bacon, and whisky.

While floating with the current may have required as many as six days to reach Cincinnati, flatboats were cheaper and safer than the wagon alternatives. The ultimate flow was toward the export market centering in New Orleans, where in the early years, flour was the most desirable commodity from the Ohio Valley, and flour was Cincinnati's most valuable product.[7]

Milled grain was the market norm, published as "the wagon price" of a barrel of flour arriving in Cincinnati. Where the commercial milling actually occurred is less clear. The advertisement by a Cincinnati firm in an Urbana newspaper, announcing that it had "just received an assortment of first quality Dutch Bolting Cloths, From No 0, to 9; and shall hereafter keep a constant supply for sale," implied that milling was widespread. So also did David Parry's sequence of Urbana newspaper advertisements announcing the making and repair of grist and saw mill castings. The nominal distinction between gristmills and commercial flouring-mills was never applied consistently. Typical of the many water-powered mills scattered throughout Champaign County, even in its blurred phrasing, was the 1828 announcement on behalf of Glenn's Mills on the Mad River west of Urbana, that "the grist mill, for manufacturing merchant flour," would be in operation by the first week in August. The overall implication is that milling occurred wherever water flow and fall were adequate, which also dictated where connecting roads were most likely to facilitate exchange centers.[8]

In very local exchanges, consequently, both wheat and corn had currency value. However, the demand for unprocessed product was limited, and bulk corn was unlikely to have been hauled very far. Corn was fed to animals and became either beef or "provisions"—pork, lard, hams and bacon, and other pork products—or it became whisky. No figures exist to indicate volume of milling and distilling or the number of persons employed in either task. The price of whisky held steady during the late 1820s, and whisky itself could serve as a medium of exchange. The census of 1820 showed three-fifths of the state's 552 distilleries located in the Scioto and Miami valleys, the leading corn-producing region of the state, and the Beers history indicates distilleries at or near most of the sites where mills were functioning.[9]

Corn sent to market in the form of beef or pork was especially characteristic of the southern and eastern portions of Champaign County.

The 1805 boundaries of the original Champaign County included the cattle rangelands located east of Springfield and oriented toward the Scioto River. Those rangelands are not representative of most of the land that makes up Champaign County. Nevertheless, suggestive of cattle-raising practice immediately following the War of 1812 was Daniel Drake's 1815 estimate that "the prairies of Champaign and Greene Counties furnished $100,000 worth of cattle annually." Approximately fifteen years later, James Rawlings, farming the south-central area of Urbana Township at the edge of that prairie range land, found his market for grain in Dayton but his market for livestock in Richmond, Virginia, "where it was taken on foot."[10]

Ohio farmers and stock-raisers usually did not themselves make the overland trips to the east but relied instead on cattle buyers and hired drovers, the livestock equivalent of merchants and millers. The financial risks were considerable. During the sometimes lengthy interval from when information was received at home to provoke a decision to sell, and the arrival of the stock at an eastern market, prices might well drop. The final physical condition of the animals was always a factor. So were the expenses (pasturage and some feed) incurred on the journey. A variety of establishments catered to the practical needs of drovers and their animals. An incautiously described "house of Entertainment for Teamsters, Drovers, and all other travelers" opened in 1834 at the "extremity of East Main street" in Urbana. The attraction of the "commodious" house was its "suitable stabling, a wagon yard, and convenient lots for the reception of cattle, hogs, &c." With similar conveniences in multiple rural settings, droving enabled a market outlet for interior producers.[11]

Again, therefore, participation in the market economy was not a conceptual problem; it was a practical problem. Clearly, there were "roads," but the problem for commerce was that when surface roads were dry enough to be passable for wagons transporting flour or provisions or whisky, the smaller waterways had not enough flow to float commercial barges. When the water was adequately high because of recent rains, hauling produce to those barges meant dealing with axle-deep mud. The contemporary perspective here is again Caleb Atwater's: "it might happen, and often did happen, that all the streams in the state of Ohio were up, at nearly the same time. The flood came, and with it departed such an amount of produce, that the market was glutted." The spring runoff, sometimes as a flood, would move quickly downstream in late March or early April, and within ten days might be over for the season. Since the autumn rise was never as high, the effect was a brief and common annual window of opportunity to sell the year's produce. Newspapers throughout the Miami Valley reprinted Cincinnati's newspaper reports about the condition of ice on the Ohio River in winter and the depth of flow in summer. An "Agricultural Report" appearing in Urbana's *Mad-River Courant* in the winter of 1824 ended with a hint of opportunism that all would have understood: "Our roads are yet passable, and we trust will now continue so till the spring rains break them up." The consequence of missing the opportunity was avowed retrospectively in the Beers history: "for many years the markets within reasonable distance scarcely repaid the labor of hauling."[12]

7.

New Connections, New Directions

For the nineteenth-century farmers who sought to market their "surplus" commercially, the transportation costs, measured in time and money and even in brute feasibility, had to come down. During the first third of the century, that did begin to happen, though initially only at some distance from Champaign County, and more effectively on water than on land. In 1811, the *New Orleans* inaugurated steam-powered water travel on the interior rivers of the continent when it journeyed one-way from Pittsburgh to New Orleans. Four years later, the *Enterprise* made the same journey and successfully returned against the current to Louisville. By the end of the decade the commercial implications of steam-powered river travel were redundantly clear. The great one-way downstream flow of North American commerce was altered in ways that the slow and expensive upstream keelboat trade had only minimally accomplished.[1]

For the small producer far upstream in the Ohio valley, the new steam technology provided little or no immediate cost benefit in shipping bulk commodities. Part of the reason was that steam-powered vessels were helpless to counter the seasonally long periods of low water above the Falls of the Ohio at Louisville. Brief summaries of "The Markets," appearing regularly in Urbana's *Western Citizen & Urbana Gazette*, and usually listing only Cincinnati prices, often began with a narrative comment such as the following, dated 25 December 1838: "Navigation being entirely closed both by river and canal, business of most descriptions, in the absence of supplies, is nearly suspended." The report of two weeks later portended well: "The river is now open and rapidly rising.—A number of boats are at the wharf taking in cargoes for the New Orleans and other western and southern ports, with a fair prospect of getting out without difficulty." The fickle river had other plans, evident in another two weeks: "There is but a small business doing in produce—the river having fallen so as to prevent shipments to any extent." Steam-powered watercraft of shallow draft and of traditionally low capacity operating above the Falls served a regional market on the upper third of the Ohio River, but until the construction of an adequate canal around the Falls, through traffic remained seasonal.[2]

Different from feasibility was cost. Freight rates did not begin to decline significantly until steamboat operators faced competition from the northern canals. Somewhat ironically, the volume of down-river traffic by flatboat actually increased through the 1820s as boatmen conveying bulk commodities could book one-way passage upstream for the return trip home from New Orleans, saving weeks of dangerous overland travel. Another potential gain from river steam transport was the opening of new markets for northern agricultural products within the South as the cotton economy expanded into the territories along the lower Mississippi River served by Memphis, Natchez, and Vicksburg. Attempting to cater to that expanding southern market on behalf of the Ohio valley, Cincinnati was the self-acclaimed "Queen City," most relevant to Champaign County farmers in its role as "Porkopolis." The first regular meatpacking house opened there in 1818, and hog drives decreased eastward as steamboat traffic increased southward. No longer was it as necessary to breed hogs primarily for their hardiness as travelers. Some attention could be given to breeding for the whims of the market—more or less lard, more or less flesh. Size began to matter. Visual evidence of the change throughout the Miami Valley was in the popular breed known as Big China, sometimes called the Warren County Hog, and from about 1835, in the nearly as large Berkshire. In effect, the steamboat was a stimulus to the swine industry in southwestern Ohio.[3]

Any more specific accounting of the benefit of river steamboats to farmers in Champaign County is difficult to measure because the mid-1820s saw near-simultaneous developments in several forms of transportation. Nationally it was a time of debate about internal improvements and the merits of Henry Clay's American System, on behalf of which Champaign's Joseph Vance was an acknowledged Congressional spokesman. While the states and the Federal government tried to find agreement on funding a lock-and-canal system around the Falls at Louisville, Ohio's General Assembly debated its own canal system, and both state and Federal governments considered extending the National Road west across Ohio from Wheeling. The editors of Urbana's newspapers through this period were for the most part staunchly pro-Clay, and they provided close detail of Congressional debates. They also reprinted less partisan articles from mostly eastern newspapers on particular road and canal projects. Progress of the canal being built across northern New York was an especially compelling interest.[4]

Consequently, even before completion of the Erie Canal in 1825, the Urbana papers were eagerly following the Ohio efforts to develop an all-water connection between Lake Erie and the Ohio River. From the very first proposal introduced in 1817, the issue of route was understandably prime, both politically and practically. In Urbana, the locally satisfying presumption was for a canal "about 20 miles from this place, between this and the Scioto river." The hope was that the Canal Commissioners would favorably ascertain the possibility of a connection with the Mad River itself. When the Commission's engineer determined that the summit above the heads of the Sandusky and Scioto rivers did not have enough water to feed a canal, and even more critically determined that the Mad River was another seventy feet higher than the Scioto summit, the matter was apparently settled that no canal would ever connect into Champaign County.[5]

Until interest in a Mad River canal connection resumed later in the decade, county concern with internal improvements focused almost completely on bridges and roads. Bridges served to connect both the near and the distant, that is, neighbors and markets. Therein was basis for some pique from county residents living due west of Urbana, whose exasperation was with a political process that seemed never to result in good bridges over the Mad River. The quality of roads was a more general public issue, although at times no less exasperating. In the background was the conviction, often stated directly, that in order to connect profitably to commercially significant waterways, viable all-weather roads were essential. "Reaching good markets," therefore, was a problem with obvious solution: make more roads and make them better.[6]

Through the first several decades of the state's existence, the Ohio General Assembly considered road-related legislation in nearly every one of its sessions. Among the most relevant actions was an 1809 law incorporating the first turnpike, setting the precedent for the state's official approach to overland transportation. The premise was politically simple, that road users should be the ones to pay for road maintenance, whether travelers on a toll road or farmers living adjacent to a township road. Farmers as the presumed beneficiaries carried the principal tax obligation for public roads. "Land holders will take notice," the County Auditor explained. The law required a tax based on one of three ratings of land quality, and allowed the tax to be paid by work. In effect, the owner of a 320-acre farm of mixed land ratings was obligated for the equivalent of three days of work. Such tax-work was an investment in self-interest, by which everyone would benefit. So it was said. Then, as each new piece of the developing infrastructure made all the other connecting pieces more efficient, the users would enjoy the benefits of additional road construction and improvement. That included several trails developed more or less concurrently in response to the economic and political changes associated with an increase of Lake Erie traffic. Hull's Trace north from Urbana to Perrysburg by way of Kenton and Findlay was made a post route in 1822. Champaign County travelers heading north could also take advantage of the Scioto Trail slightly to the east. Travelers connecting from the south used a route from Cincinnati to Xenia (later US 42) and Springfield.[7]

None of the new or newly improved roads was especially good. John H. James' trip by horseback from Cincinnati to Xenia and then on to Columbus in January of 1826 took the better part of four days over an "abominable" road, most of it through "forest," and mostly through mud caused by the winter rain. For the ambitious James (soon settled in Urbana), solving the transportation problem required his involvement in the Cincinnati, Lebanon and Springfield Turnpike Company, of which he was appointed Secretary in May of 1828. For Ohio's farmers who wanted to reach good markets, on the other hand, toll roads turned out to be a solution of conflicting visions, illustrated in Mad River Township. When population increases in the mid-1810s portended economic development and the need for better roads, township trustees laid out road districts and began state-regulated oversight of road maintenance by township farmers. Later, when the final wave of migration into the county gave hint of a more directly revenue-generating traffic, private organizers started the Urbana, Troy, and Greenville Turnpike Road to run from Urbana through Christiansburg (Addison) and on to Troy and Greenville. Neither population nor traffic reached anticipated levels, and benefits of the road were never commensurate with its toll rates. A road was eventually completed as a free tax-supported "turnpike," and it later became part of SR 55. The episode was not unique. Inconsistently maintained and of uneven quality, early turnpikes did not significantly reduce freighting costs.[8]

Optimistically widespread nevertheless, the anticipation that freight rates would drop was politically ascendant. Ohio's Governor in 1827 urged the people "to lay out" more roads in order for farmers to take maximum advantage of new through routes, a reference to Ohio's developing canal system. The Ohio & Erie Canal was to connect Lake Erie at Cleveland with the Ohio River at Portsmouth, and was to be the principal Ohio canal. A second canal was to accommodate the Miami Valley but with a northern terminus unspecified. Some decisions were still to be made. Because the commercial function of surface roads was to provide access to bodies of water—rivers, lake, and now also canals— more and better roads meant more and better access. Hence the Governor's urging. Champaign County newspapers followed the Canal Commission's continuing work, the ceremonies of 1825, and the engineering and other practical frustrations as portions of the system became available for use. For farmers who had provisions and grain to sell, the canals were enhancing the options inherent in the county's geographic setting. Here, too, some decisions were still to be made.[9]

Situated roughly midway between lake and river, Champaign County farmers were positioned to assess their options in practical terms. Their northern option was to haul produce by wagon overland to Sandusky. Lake carriers there would receive the produce and transport it to Buffalo and the Erie Canal or, after 1829, to receiving centers on Lake Ontario through use of the Welland Canal. The Beers history reports with some retrospective exaggeration that farmers of Adams Township in the late 1820s and 1830s made that hundred-mile journey several times each year, transporting wheat and provisions, each trip occupying ten days. Journeys remembered from several childhoods certainly took place. Their significance was not in their volume or frequency, however, but as an element in changing the overall pattern of the nation's internal grain trade. Sandusky and Cleveland, joined by Massillon, Milan, and Toledo, were competing for the produce of northern Ohio, Indiana, and Illinois because the urban population in the Northeast increasingly depended on the "West" to provide its agricultural food needs. The enabling prominence of the Erie Canal can hardly be overstated. The challenge of serving the eastern food market was taken up by dairy farmers in northeastern Ohio and by grain farmers in northeastern and north-central Ohio—and by some Champaign County farmers. Because Ohio's own canal system initially connected with Lake Erie only at Cleveland, most western Ohio farmers gained little. While the canal route north could be accessed at Columbus, and while Columbus merchants were advertising in Urbana newspapers for the region's grain trade, a wagon conveyance to Columbus was hardly more practical than going directly to Sandusky. More typically favored in the upper Miami Valley was the southern canal access in Dayton, even when Columbus might have a small price advantage. It was more practical and certainly more comfortably familiar, and flour exports to Cincinnati increased through the 1830s.[10]

The cultural heritage, the lay of the land, and the market infrastructure as it was locally perceived all oriented south. Just as with the introduction of river steamboats twenty years earlier, the canals reinforced existing Miami Valley patterns of agricultural activity. The effect was not entirely parallel, however. Decades of lobbying on behalf of improved state roads north from Urbana indicated a willingness to explore a northern alternative. Further witness to a changing orientation was in the very tangible commercial "imports" increasingly available from local merchants. More eastern merchandise, more manufactured items, more retail goods were available at lower costs and in better condition than ever previously. In 1822, prior to the canals, Urbana's Isaiah B. Heylin & Co. announced that the firm had "received from Philadelphia, and are now opening, at their old Stand, a large and general assortment of Goods." Also received "from Cincinnati" was "an assortment of Pittsburgh nails, window glass, sad irons, cotton &c." The intimation was that all the goods had come to Cincinnati by river for at least a portion of the transit, and had been hauled by wagon up the Miami Valley to Urbana. Two years later, Robert Wilson announced that he had "just arrived from the Eastern Cities" and was "now opening a large and extensive assortment of Dry Goods, Groceries, Queensware and Hardware; all of which he has purchased with Cash, and is determined to sell for the same, or approved produce." "Eastern Cities" was a loose reference to Philadelphia, explicitly so in an 1825 ad placed by Wm. Rianhard & Co., and sometimes to Baltimore, explicitly named in an 1826 ad placed by J. Reynolds & Co. Even goods shipped from New York with a Miami Valley destination were likely to have been routed through Philadelphia and/or Baltimore. That changed with the opening of the Erie Canal. "Eastern cities," when used later in the 1820s, included New York and implied a canal route. The announcement in 1831 that Urbana's Barr & Hunt had "just received from New York, a general assortment of Fall & Winter Goods," marked a clear transition. Dry goods merchants now made a point of advertising that their goods had been purchased in "New York."[11]

The effect for farmers was a general rise in commodity prices. A Wheeling newspaper editor claimed in 1831 that "Twelve years ago, wheat was worth but thirty one cents a bushel, along the borders of Lake Erie; now it is worth seventy-five cents." Other grain price estimates, both contemporary and later, were similar. Nevertheless, because the quality of connecting roads to the lake or river-based grain collection centers remained a problem, the benefit for Champaign County farmers was still modest. That may explain why all the commercial transitions of the 1820s, while noted locally with interest, were held at a dispassionate distance ever since the Ohio Canal Commission opted against an extension canal near or through Champaign County.[12]

Detachment changed when the commercial consequences of the Miami Valley canal began to be apparent in the greater Dayton area. In

March of 1829, *Mad-River Courant* editor Martin L. Lewis exploded indignantly: "The time has come when the people living in the Mad-river valley ought to feel something of the spirit of improvement, which is going ahead in the land. As yet they have received no advantage from any road or canal made within the state, and all the improvements now commenced will profit them but little when finished." This was not exactly true. He was campaigning for "a canal [to] be made from some point near Urbana, to Dayton, so as to afford us the means of transporting our surplus produce to market, and bringing our merchandize from market." Clearly expressing the valley's customary southern orientation, a petition making the same call circulated through the community. Gratifyingly in January of 1830, a general bill extending the Miami Canal north from Dayton also authorized a Mad River survey.[13]

Well before any survey results were announced, the editor of Urbana's short-lived *Country Collustrator* assessed "The Prospects of Champaign" rather differently than did Lewis. Urging his readers to spend "a few moments in the consideration of affairs, belonging, in a manner, exclusively to our own county," Wilson Everett offered a cautionary assessment of improving farmers' access to "an attainable market."

> We live in a section of country fertile by nature, and capable of being improved in fertility, by art. Owing, however, to the absence of large streams, and to the non-existence within our limits, of mineral ores and deposites [sic], we cannot become in any great degree a manufacturing people; for those in possession of such natural advantages will thereby be enabled to supply us with their products much cheaper than we can create them within ourselves. But while they do this, we, through the fertility of our soil, are enabled to grow for them provisions at a cheaper rate than they possibly can. All, we think, will admit that we are an agricultural people, and this being our situation, it behoves [sic] us to take such measures, as at the least expense, will enable us to originate those articles which are our staples, and on the sale of which depend our own support and prosperity.[14]

Here was an agenda without hyperbole, sympathetically presenting itself as a kind of reasonable self-analysis, even self-criticism. Yes, new connections and newer orientations were altering the practice of agriculture. Steam-powered riverboats had expanded the incentives for producing corn and hogs. Canals were providing new incentives to produce wheat and flour. Precisely, therefore, here also was insistence on facing honest limitations as the necessary basis for fulfilling aspirations. We are what we are, "an agricultural people."

For probably most of Champaign County's small farmers making their important family decisions, Everett's assessment was a redundancy. The short-term effects of changes in the nation's transportation systems tended to confirm rather than change who and what they were. Furthermore, despite the promotional rhetoric of both editors, a nascent willingness to produce for the eastern markets was still seriously constrained by the practicalities of access. The final canal-related effort to ease that access ironically only served to expose a potentially divisive element within the county's putative rural identity.

The effort began during the winter of 1838–1839 when a canal engineering assessment recommended tapping the Mad River as a form of water insurance for the Miami Canal extension. County support for the measure was conflicted because the assessment included estimates of significantly reduced flow and decreased waterpower downstream from where the Mad River was to be tapped. Apparently trying to soften the negative impact, the Canal Commission noted that a slight extension of the feeder, presumably into West Liberty, would bring it to an intersection with the proposed route of the nascent Mad River & Lake Erie Railroad. The response of Urbana's civic leadership was vigorously self-interested, not only in its support of the overall project but also in its efforts to route the feeder into Urbana instead of West Liberty. Whether intentional or not, the apparent disregard for the negative impact on rural life further downstream exposed a rift along the county's town/country social fault line. Meanwhile, confronted by political maneuvering of all interested parties and their competing expert analyses, the General Assembly ultimately took no action at all. A canal extension into Champaign County was never built, and more importantly, it was never needed. The Grand Canal Reservoir in Mercer County, later known as Grand Lake St. Marys, proved sufficient for northern canal-related water demands. The canal extension itself was soon almost irrelevant. By 1845, when the completed Miami Canal Extension reached the Maumee River at Junction, railroads had become the new transportation factor for the farmers of Champaign County. The summary of canal traffic for 1851, the zenith year of the Miami & Erie Canal, showed the change. The canal's southern terminus at Cincinnati received ice, flour, whisky, corn, oats, pork and bacon, sugar, wood, paper, lumber, and iron. The northern link at Junction received coffee, sugar, laths, and lumber. Unprocessed grain, particularly wheat, is not mentioned, despite the evidence from other sources that the producers in west-central Ohio were sending steadily increasing quantities of bulk grain to market. By 1851, a railroad passing through Urbana, not a canal, carried Champaign County's grain north. And, whatever else the new connections implicated, the county's central town was exercising a decided new role.[15]

8.

Urbana

With each decennial census enumerating more people in an ever-expanding territory, the statistical population center of the United States moved steadily westward. Specific occupations and uses of the land changed, tracing their respective time-trails across the map. Agriculture in the form of general farming with wheat as a cash crop moved from New England and the Middle Atlantic seaboard into New York and Pennsylvania, leaving behind an increasingly specialized farming and a more pervasive commercial and then manufacturing business concentration. Into the Ohio Valley, and west and north across the states of the Old Northwest Territory, the plow and the water-powered mill displaced the ax and hoe. Steam and industry followed. However much this presumed sequence was romanticized, it was a factor in the nation's political self-consciousness, serving as a goad to "progress" and a righteous judgment on those who stood as obstacle in the way of the nation's "manifest" destiny. Sequence momentum also gave contextual significance to the trades, crafts, and industries established to serve local needs while simultaneously prompting new perspectives. Thus, as the potential service area for each industry expanded, the producers of farm commodities tended to look south and east for their markets, while the producers of farm implements tended to look in the opposite directions for theirs. The patterns of innovation and adaptation within the Mad River

Valley may not have been unique in the history of North American agriculture. Nevertheless, they were not entirely typical. For a few years during the middle decades of the century, Champaign County and especially its central town of Urbana were at the nexus of everything vibrant and innovative in matters agricultural.[1]

In 1805, when Champaign County was partitioned from Greene and Franklin counties, Joseph Vance, Sr., father of the future Governor, opportunistically made his home in the new county and, "in his capacity as surveyor, laid out the town of Urbana" and named it. Col. William Ward, who held a patent for the land, had selected the site allegedly on the criterion of geographic centrality with its potential as a county seat. A half dozen years later, the impressions of fifteen-year-old William Patrick, freshly arrived from New Jersey, were of oak and other "full growth timber" reaching all the way to the Public Square, with much "wet prairie" along the flow of the town branch. Jervis Cutler's 1812 topographical description of Ohio mentioned Urbana as containing "about sixty houses," noting also that it was "rapidly increasing in inhabitants." That included a thirty-year-old John Reynolds who in 1803 had settled west of Mad River and who in 1807 removed to Urbana where he established the town's "first mercantile house of any importance."[2]

A dozen miles to the south was Springfield, very similar to Urbana, and after the separation of Clark and Champaign counties in 1818, also a county seat. The waterpower potential of the site in Springfield where Buck Creek joined the Mad River was greater than anything upstream, but Urbana's hinterland held prospect of better farming. In 1820, the first year Urbana appears in the census record, the town had an imprecisely documented population of 644. Ten years later it claimed an official population of 1,103, nearly the same as Springfield's population. No one anticipated the greater economic effect that the unfinished National Road would bring to Springfield. Instead, canals were the factor accounting for Urbana's official net loss through the 1830s of thirty-two residents while Piqua, directly to the west and located along the newly opened Miami Canal, gained 993.[3]

Location was only part of the story, for Urbana's first sowing during the 1810s and 1820s had attempted to replicate what a proper town *should* be, and moving through the locale was a very slight breeze of gentry air.

Thus, in addition to merchandizing, milling, making and repairing, socializing, educating, and worshiping, a variety of formal institutions were initiated that reflected more than the town's ambitions as a county seat. A newspaper briefly in 1812, a bank in 1814, a couple of hotels, a social lodge as early as 1809, an agricultural society—all were tried and in most cases had difficulty surviving the personal efforts of the founders. Although it was not unusual in its imagined future significance, its nascent social structure was inconsistent with the actual population density and the transient nature of the town's early population.[4]

In the decade following the boom and bust of canal enthusiasm, Urbana experienced a second sowing. The town population began to increase, effectively doubling to an 1850 figure of 2020. Sources of growth again included emigration from the same Middle Atlantic and Upper South communities that had provided the start-up generations of settlers. How long those distant extended family networks continued to facilitate chain migration into and through Champaign County is not clear. No less relevant and no more precise numerically were other sources of growth that included both individuals and family units residual from canal and railroad construction in the state. So it was that the John H. James household was pleased with a succession of Irish immigrant domestic helpers, and in 1852, the Irish Catholic community in Urbana was sufficiently viable to require the services of a priest. Not everyone was pleased. In the prejudices of the day, an expanded Catholic presence was at best a mixed blessing. In October of 1856, some kind of Saturday night altercation, described in the newspaper as a "riot," took place near the Catholic church. An Irishman died from a blow delivered by an investigating Marshall. In reporting the incident and the subsequent inquest, the newspaper sided with the Marshall and against "the Irish doggeries in our midst."[5]

Population growth also occurred by "natural" means. As the immigrants had children, the proportion of immigrant to native-born declined. Because the census records prior to 1850 do not list names of all members of households, the enumerations of 1850 and 1860 are peculiarly suggestive. The inferred pattern is that the initial immigrants, settling as farmers primarily in Union, Goshen, Mad River, and Urbana townships, had multiple children. As of mid-century, typically one adult child per each of those first families was residing on the original land claim. In some families, adult siblings or first cousins resided on nearby farmsteads obtained through a combination of purchase, rent, and marriage rather than through partible inheritance. Other siblings either moved into town or left the county. The census records of both 1850 and 1860 indicate that in each of the county's townships, family names clustered spatially. Township meetings, village schooling, and religious gatherings had the distinct "feel" of being extended family events.[6]

All of these demographic variations were evident in the Jacob Minturn family. Originally from New Jersey, Jacob and his immediate family migrated from Virginia down the Ohio River to Cincinnati and inland to Butler County, Ohio, in 1802. They were preceded, accompanied, and followed by former New Jersey and Virginia neighbors (surnames Baker, Clark, Jones, Lafferty, McLain, Runyan) with whom they were intertwined by marriage. Jacob's eldest son, Barton, married Hannah Jones before they left Virginia, and their first child, Jacob, was born in Ohio in 1803. In the spring of 1804, the Jones and Minturn families removed to near the Buck Creek headwaters where some portions of their extended family/community had already settled. Barton's second son, Edward, was born there in 1805. When Hannah died in 1806, Barton married her sister Esther and in 1807 had a third son, Smith. The next year, Barton's own sister, Elizabeth, married Daniel Jones, the brother of Hannah and Esther. A parsimony of honorific name selections leaves a confusing genealogical record. It also serves as witness to the strength of extended families in everything from the erection of log houses on neighboring farms to the sharing of financial risk in innovating agricultural practice. A few years following the death of Esther Minturn, Barton sold his farm-related possessions and moved into Urbana. Already living in town since about 1830 was his eldest son, Jacob, well established as a machinist in the business of making and repairing farm implements. Approximately a decade before Barton died in 1866 at the age of 87, his youngest son Smith emigrated from Ohio for the "West." The several original Minturn farmsteads in Union Township became the heritage of Barton's middle son Edward and his cousins, some of them named Jones.[7]

The first generation of immigrant settlers had come from somewhere else to create farms and a town where none had existed. Now, as the first native-born generation came to maturity, institutions and enterprises attempted in Urbana in the 1840s could draw on a far more extensive and far better-reinforced network of social and economic relations than had been possible previously. It was well on the way to being a "settled rural community," perceived by its residents as being more populous than the census enumerations actually confirmed. Optimistically enterprising and comfortably stolid—that was Urbana in the 1840s and 1850s.[8]

The assessment reflects the sometimes uncomfortable duality of Urbana. From a geographer's perspective, it was a "district trade center," providing the "indispensable" services making nineteenth century agriculture possible. From the perspective of town-dwellers themselves, the centrality of Urbana made it the obvious and natural setting for the marketing and display of farm products, for the exchange of farm ideas, and for the manufacture and sale of farm implements. When any of these town-centered activities required increases in county-wide taxes or provoked changes in customary farm practice, however, "indispensable" was a matter of perspective. Urbana was a town with its own priorities. This is not to hint of animosity but rather of occasional overreach, of a presumptive insensitivity. Editor Wilson Everett's affirmation in 1831 that "we are an agricultural people" was a cautionary guide. Repeatedly over the years, Urbana's civic boosters needed additional reminders that farmers and their interests could never be taken for granted. When they were, anything town-sponsored was likely to be challenged. Loyalty to town-initiated institutions was never automatic.[9]

For the most part, the surviving record of selective memories and anecdotal evidence indicates that county residents believed they were entering a new stage of their history. What most marked the stage was improved surface transportation, essentially the railroad. For everyone, changes associated with the railroad were not just seen; they were felt. Quite simply, the significance of the railroad was huge.

9.

The Prospect of a Railroad

The railroad came to Champaign County from the north. During the decade when Ohio's canal routes were being contested and lobbied, Sandusky business interests hoped their fine harbor on Lake Erie would be the northern terminus of the Ohio Canal system. For lack of adequate water between Columbus and Sandusky, canal engineers instead recommended Cleveland as the system's lake terminus. The Sandusky interests therefore had to explore other options. As early as 1826, Eleutheros Cooke of Sandusky proposed a rail connection south to Dayton. Two years later an unsigned notice appeared in Urbana's *Mad-River Courant*, stating "that application, will be made to the Legislature of Ohio, at their next session, for a law to incorporate a company...to construct a rail road from some point on Lake Erie, near Sandusky Bay, so as to intersect the National Turnpike road east of Mad-River." The same notice also proposed "a company for the purpose of constructing a Rail Road from the navigable feeder at Columbus to the navigable feeder on Mad-river of the Ohio and Miami Canals." Both proposed companies were seeking to connect bodies of water by rail rather than canal, and both proposals implicated Champaign County. By the time an east-west rail line connecting Urbana with Columbus was built, a Mad River feeder canal was no longer needed. None of that was anticipated in the 1820s as county newspapers irregularly but frequently reprinted articles featuring developments in *both* railroads and canals.[1]

When a bill to incorporate a railroad with its northern terminus at Sandusky was introduced in the 1830 session of Ohio's General Assembly, the legislators did not act. Guarding their limited funds, they were reluctant to provide state financing for the still dubious endeavor of railroading. With no prospect of direct state aid for a railroad and apparently feeling defiant of state canal dispositions, therefore, the Sandusky interests requested a charter again in 1831. The goal was clear: "to secure the facilities for conveying to market, the surplus produce of our country." Attendees at Champaign County's public meeting on the matter agreed without dissent. Charged with carrying that agreement into the next round of intercommunity negotiations were five delegates—four Urbana attorneys, plus General Joseph Vance. Regardless of its town or country expression, all of the support for the proposed railroad was premised on the fundamental axiom that railroads served primarily local needs and objectives. Similarly premised were objections such as the fear that a railroad would displace or obstruct essential surface roads. The appointment of local farmer James Dallas as one of the new railroad's commissioners gave credibility to the county's agricultural interest in the project. Nevertheless, driving the entire venture was the more-than-local prospect of connecting western Ohio more directly with markets in New York. Canals were demonstrating the possibilities, and railroads provided a supplementary dimension. Significantly if also provocatively, all twelve of the Ohio railroads chartered in 1832 were oriented for north-south traffic, ultimately connecting to water in both directions.[2]

Among the twelve was the Mad River & Lake Erie Rail Road Company. As detailed in its charter, the line was to connect Sandusky and Dayton by means of a route through Springfield, Urbana, Bellefontaine, and the vicinities of Upper Sandusky, Tiffin, and Lower Sandusky. Agents all along the proposed route were authorized to solicit subscriptions for capital stock, but the actual opening of the books was delayed, at first for two weeks, and then for an additional two months, as various parties aired concerns about competency in the survey of the route. The editor of Urbana's newspaper seemed hardly able to admit relief when progress was finally evident. "For some time we had doubts upon this subject—the success of the rail road—they are now removed," he wrote in November of 1833.[3]

Organizational structure of the company took shape with considerable local consequence when stockholders met in Urbana and elected
Joseph Vance as President and John H. James as one of twelve Directors.
The Directors then selected James, chief officer of the Urbana Bank, as
Treasurer. A year and a half later, on 17 September 1835, a grand ground-
breaking ceremony in Sandusky stimulated expectation that construction would proceed steadily southward, but company stock was frustrat-
ingly slow to sell. Despite public reminders to shareholders to pay as
promised, adequate financing to continue construction was a constant
problem facing John H. James, President of the line from 1837. Problematic also were issues of land use in farm country. For some owners of
farms along or even near the proposed rail route, location was a sales
asset. Other property owners, despite newspaper editorial castigations,
resisted any incursion of the railroad onto their lands.[4]

Progress was fitful. Consequently, the honor of being Ohio's first
functioning railroad defaulted to the Erie & Kalamazoo, a thirty-three-
mile line running northwest from Toledo to the town of Adrian, Michigan, beginning in 1836 and initially using horse-drawn cars. Two years
later, four railways opened for traffic in Ohio, and one of them, the Mad
River & Lake Erie, using steam locomotion from the outset, is usually
noted as the "first" steam railroad in the state. Commercial runs of gradually increasing distance south from Sandusky began with sixteen miles
to Bellevue. With "bright prospects," the "citizens of Champaign" anticipated the beginning of construction between Urbana and West Liberty.[5]

Despite James' efforts at provoking "a more vigorous prosecution of
the work," the line did not reach Urbana until an additional decade
passed. The principal reason was the national financial depression following the Panic of 1837. Lasting until 1843, the effect on all the new
western railroads was to force a "virtual collapse" for lack of capital and
credit. With near-regularity, newspapers carried both cajoling and
threatening notices of stock installment payment dates. Equally constant
was the nagging boosterism of Urbana's Joshua Saxton, whether surreptitiously in the form of front-page reprinted articles on the farmers' critical need for roads, or more optimistically direct as in 1841: "The prospect
of connecting Cincinnati and Boston by a continuous rail road communication grows brighter every day."[6]

Financing of the railroad was local, and more than money was involved. Much of the company's financial business passed through the Urbana Bank. When rumors about the bank's solvency spread, some local merchants expressed their confidence by publicizing willingness to take Urbana bank paper at par. Long-term and intertwined personal and business relationships, optimistically expanded enterprises, and always the final collateral of land were implicated as litigation proceeded on a new scale. The evidence is incomplete, some direct and some circumstantial, with one complex situation serving as illustration. In December of 1842, the railroad lost a suit over some property in Urbana, and the sheriff sold the property at auction. As part of the same or a closely related set of actions, Urbana merchant and local investor William Rianhard filed for bankruptcy. The following month, the sheriff gave notice of a sale of 628 acres of land in Pretty Prairie belonging to Henry Vanmeter (himself a former Champaign County Sheriff), taken to satisfy the claims of merchants Henry Weaver and William Rianhard and the Clinton Bank of Columbus. Vanmeter in turn filed counter claims against the Columbus bank. That bank, meanwhile, gave public notice of its claims against Joseph Vance.[7]

Late in 1842, presidency of the railroad passed acrimoniously from John H. James back to Joseph Vance. Vance intimated that James had mismanaged railroad funds. Both Vance and James suffered financially, evident in sheriff's sales of property of each. The Urbana Banking Company was placed in receivership, and the interaction of railroading, banking, personalities, and county identity dominated the pages of the newspaper through 1843. James attempted to resume his law practice, and he spent much of the 1840s trying to extricate himself from the financial entanglements railroading had wound around him. The public had quite enough, and at the 1843 annual meeting of stockholders, turned out most of the old Directors, elected new officers, and moved company offices from Urbana to Bellefontaine. Newly elected Director on behalf of Champaign was farmer Samuel Keener.[8]

As funds and management allowed, meanwhile, construction of the railroad continued southward, and usage of the completed portions for both freight and passenger traffic was promising. Extension to Tiffin made that city the most convenient transshipment point for some Champaign farmers, and the market reports in Urbana irregularly mentioned Tiffin prices. The best indicator of the volume of agricultural traffic heading north was the grumbling about the condition of the wagon roads leading to Tiffin.[9]

National financial recovery meant that by 1844 the railroad had regained sufficient promise to attract investors. The significant difference was that the new interest was less personal and less likely to be resident in one of the towns or farms along the intended route. Investors had approached the General Assembly for a loan, or at least the willingness to guarantee a loan. The result was an arrangement by which the state gained an ownership stake in several struggling railroads. The result also was a prod to the Mad River line and its southern neighbor/competitor, the Little Miami line, to coordinate their plans to achieve a through line between Cincinnati and Sandusky. The new fiscal stability in turn provided basis for the two lines to send an agent to Boston to obtain sufficient capital (purportedly half a million dollars) to complete construction. Large-scale, nonlocal investment was already evident in controlling transportation developments elsewhere in antebellum America, and this would be the pattern of the future. Because locally subscribed shares still had installment payments due, however, Urbana editor Joshua Saxton's frequent defenses of "Our Railroad" were vigorous and sometimes feisty: "The Road will be made, and its enemies will find that they bite against a file in opposing it."[10]

In late spring of 1845, the same editor dared to express his optimism that the line could be completed to Urbana and in operation by midsummer of 1846. Similar hopes were apparent in the contracts to bring the Little Miami north from Xenia to Springfield, the anticipated connection point between the two lines. By August of 1845, trains on the Little Miami were making regular runs between Cincinnati and Xenia, and in August of 1846 reached their goal. The Mad River & Lake Erie was less successful in meeting its goal. Not until 30 March 1848 did the first passenger train enter Urbana on the finally completed line from Sandusky. Some kind of inaugural passengers-only round-trip pleasure excursion (for a fare of $5.74) between Urbana and Sandusky occurred at mid-May. Construction of the final fourteen miles between Urbana and Springfield was completed in August, "and on Tuesday evening [29 August 1848] the first regular train of cars passed through [Urbana] from Sandusky City to Cincinnati." The Mad River & Lake Erie official record rounds off the date of reaching Springfield as the first of September.[11]

From the vantage of seventy years later, the personal issues were no longer germane and the 1917 Middleton history of the county was close to gleeful (despite being inaccurate) in marking the date of the first through train as "a red-letter day." Since that date, "Urbana and Champaign County have been in touch with the markets of the world." The more prosaic assessment expressed in the company's Annual Report for 1848 was of "a great increase of facilities for through business" to the Ohio River. The Mad River & Lake Erie Rail Road had successfully linked the state's two defining bodies of water, accomplishing by rail the principle intent of the canal system. For Champaign farmers, the Mad River & Lake Erie had become more than a prospect for improved overland transportation. It had made them part of a phenomenon that was changing all of the United States.[12]

10.

Changing Prospects

The inexpensive transport of bulk agricultural commodities was the goal, the attraction, and the concern of the railroad. Over several decades, that was also its effect, with some human passenger-related changes apparent much sooner. When completed, the rail line reduced travel time between Cincinnati and Sandusky from days to a company estimate of fifteen hours. The price of such timesaving, at least for John H. James in the early years of the line, was in having to endure the foul smells and cramped posture of democratically close quarters.[1]

For farmer-producers throughout the Mad River Valley, the railroad multiplied the freight transportation options, and all of the options were exercised during the half-dozen years centered on 1850. Grain could be hauled by wagon to Cincinnati, Columbus, Springfield, Dayton, Piqua, or Sandusky, or to Urbana and the railroad; the direction of shipment could be either north or south. Hogs could be driven to Cincinnati or to Dayton or to some other nearby packing house, including one such enterprise in Urbana, where barrels of provisions would have been prepared for shipment either by wagon or by rail and again either to the north or to the south. Cattle could be driven to the same packing centers, destined for either northern or southern transit, or to London in Madison County for inclusion in the overland market there. It was all a motivating perspective, explicitly anticipated by editor Joshua Saxton: "We congratulate the people of the Madriver Valley upon the speedy completion of this great thoroughfare, which will secure them the advantages of a northern and southern market." For the farmer-producers themselves, all that really mattered was the price paid in either Sandusky or Cincinnati and the relative cost of getting to either location. Local wisdom was that "the northern market is always better than the southern," which the weekly listing of market prices seemed to confirm.[2]

Hints of efficiencies yet to come were ambiguous. Beginning in the first week of April 1849, the Urbana newspaper listed the arrival and departure times of the mail. For the east-west "cross mails" destined to and from cities such as Delaware or Troy or Piqua, no railroad carriers yet existed. The Ohio Stage Company compensated with its interim service passing through Mechanicsburg and Urbana and continuing on westward. Other evidence of limited rail service was in the constraint of climate: "On Tuesday last [10 April 1849] the cars commenced running their regular spring and summer trips between Sandusky and Cincinnati." The significant news in that second week of April was that "The Lake is now open to Buffalo."[3]

Ambiguity notwithstanding, the nation's expanding interior transport systems were already changing the relative simplicity of a ground-level perspective. What editor Saxton had described as "northern and southern" markets were actually two major trade complexes, a lake complex to the north and a river complex to the south. The ports on Lake Erie were successfully drawing the grain trade northward, although by the time the Mad River railroad line finally reached Urbana, Sandusky's economic challenge to the port of Cleveland had peaked. To the west and northwest, completion of the Wabash & Erie Canal across Indiana in 1843 connected Ohio's northern Miami Valley with much of northeastern Indiana and southeastern Michigan. All three areas were thus connected with a Lake Erie outlet at Toledo. Not only did Toledo, in about a decade, leap into first place as Lake Erie's principal grain port. It also showed the expansive direction in which the nation's grain belt was developing. Young Chicago, further west and still a water-oriented port on Lake Michigan, was a phenomenon beginning to happen. To the south, meanwhile, and by a combination of canal and rail connections that included the Little Miami Railroad, Cincinnati was attempting to maintain its queenly status and increase its client area. Other towns and cities all along the Ohio and Mississippi rivers were making similar overtures within their own service regions. As both the northern lake and the southern river trade complexes continued to expand right up to the Civil War, it was ironically obvious from even a short historic perspective that both routes were dependent on the emerging railroads to provide overland feeder transport.[4]

It was a dynamic and perhaps foolishly optimistic time, despite local assessment that war with Mexico was unsettling the market and reducing the price of staple commodities. Even strongly phrased local Whig opposition to the extension of slavery did not offset the widespread flush of nationalism that accompanied territorial expansions and the discovery of gold in California. The still novel but immediately practical telegraph was bringing such news almost instantly, it seemed. Before the end of 1848, a telegraph company was formed to connect Cincinnati with Sandusky by means of wires strung along the Little Miami and the Mad River railroads, reaching Urbana in August 1849. The possibilities associated with railroads were boundless as Ohioans heard proposals for extending rail connections from St. Louis all the way to California's gold fields, or at least from Cincinnati to St. Louis. And, just as important as the railroad's geographic extension was a shift in railroad imaging. Promotion initially presenting the railroad primarily as a feeder to a lake or river connection was now boosting every small line as a link *in* the nation's vital "through" rail network, or more modestly as a link *to* such vital networks. There were many such small lines. Ohio's first railroad charter had been granted only in 1830. Over the next decade, the Mad River & Lake Erie Railroad was just one among seventy-six additional companies receiving charters for railroads in Ohio, and more charters followed. Few resulted in any significant track mileage, and their combined total mileage in 1850 was only 575, but the convenience of using a census year as a marker is misleading. Within their state's borders, Ohioans were supporting the nation's largest proportionate increase of railroad track mileage ever, with an antebellum peak in 1854. By the time of the 1860 census, Ohio was nationally in first place, with nearly three thousand track miles. Contributing to the state's total track mileage as well as to the newer images of railroad function were the three lines crossing Champaign County.[5]

As detailed above, historic priority goes to the north-south Mad River & Lake Erie, already having difficulty in retaining its share of the agricultural freight transportation market.[6]

A second line, the Springfield, Mt. Vernon, & Mansfield, was built in the southeast corner of the county beginning in 1851. Running diagonally northeast-southwest through Union and Goshen Townships and the town of Mechanicsburg, it was soon renamed the Springfield, Mt. Vernon, & Pittsburgh. As they had done with the Urbana Stagecoach Company two decades earlier, local residents again risked their money. In the background was encouragement from promoters in Springfield who had been competing with southern and western Champaign County interests for rail connections to Dayton and Columbus as well as to Cincinnati and Cleveland. Wonderfully understated was the summary newspaper comment reporting an 1858 incident in which agents of the Springfield, Mt. Vernon & Pittsburgh attempted physically to impede Mad River & Lake Erie traffic until certain concessions were granted: "Some considerable excitement exists." The Beers history only hinted at the strain of the development campaign and its aftermath: "The people of Goshen Township voted $25,000 in aid to the road, and later some litigation was had, but seems to have been decided favorably to the road, after an outlay of nearly as much more in the legal test." Neither the scheme nor the dissatisfaction was unusual.[7]

The county's third rail line ran directly east and west. Envisioned as early as 1836 by some of the same local investors and promoters involved in forming the Mad River line, the Columbus, Piqua, & Indiana was incorporated in 1849. The plan was to build east from Piqua through Champaign County to Urbana. At the same time, the Urbana & Columbus Rail Road Company would build east from Urbana toward Columbus. The scheme was contingent on local financial support, including direct investment by the County in the capital stock of the two rail companies, a proposal rejected by the voters on its first ballot appearance. When resubmitted to the voters in the spring of 1850, the authorization barely passed. Arguments in favor had emphasized "accommodating the Farmers of the respective vicinities with a convenient market for everything that grows in the soil, and opening up a handsome trade for the towns," but the vote distribution confirmed that Urbana interests were

decidedly not synonymous with those of the whole county. Adams
Township was overwhelmingly unfavorable, and Mad River Township
voters rejected the measure at the ratio of four to one. The eastern
segment was completed in September of 1853, a depot and warehouse
building was erected in Urbana, and soon, "a fair business between
Columbus and Urbana" had developed. Track work west continued concurrently, and the first train to travel from Columbus to Piqua passed
through Urbana on Monday, 16 October 1854. Securing "the advantage
of an eastern market at all seasons of the year," the line gradually
extended to Indianapolis, and the first regular through train from
Columbus to that city was on 4 April 1859.[8]

The differing geographic orientations of the railroad tracks signified
more than the crisscross pattern they made on a county map or the rival-
ries they reflected. The Mad River & Lake Erie line ran north from
Urbana to Sandusky where it struggled to compete in the rivalry for the
grain trade being played out among the lake port cities. Along with multiple physical improvements in route and roadbed, the line made arrangements with rival railroads, resulting in somewhat cheaper and certainly
faster transit eastward. The effect was a viability due less and less to Sandusky's role as a lake port and increasingly to its role as a connecting rail
terminal, evident in the late 1850s in a new series of Urbana newspaper
advertisements placed by Sandusky commission merchants. Since the
county's diagonal second line had connections from Mechanicsburg to
the strategically situated port of Cleveland, Mechanicsburg became the
relevant rail depot for the eastern third of Champaign County. The railroads had decentralized some of Champaign's significant economic
activities, implicitly admitted when Urbana's principal newspaper began
to include Mechanicsburg prices in its weekly market listings. Not surprisingly, Mechanicsburg's Goshen Township voters were not warm to
the prospect of using their tax dollars for the support of the proposed
east-west Piqua line.[9]

Halfway between Cincinnati and Sandusky and nearly halfway
between Cincinnati and Cleveland, the farmer-producers of Champaign
County experienced the competition among the grain centers as generally advantageous for pricing. Whether measured in time, distance, or
trouble, north or south made little difference. The county's third rail line,

coming from the east, exposed a dynamic that did make a difference. Some commodities—such as grain and flour—were almost completely diverted from water transport to rail transport. The reason? From the Atlantic coast, a handful of consolidating and emergent trunk rail lines were pushing west, pursuing ever-extending direct rail connection without any need for transshipment by any interior waterway. The goal was as obvious and anticipated as it was explicit. By the early 1850s, three of the trunk line systems were seeking connections to the lines passing through Champaign County. A cursory historic overview contextualizes the changing status of county railroad interests and the commercial prospects of the farmers who supported them.[10]

Downstate New York interests, eager to eliminate transshipment through the Erie Canal, chartered the New York & Erie Railroad in April 1832, to travel from Piermont on the Hudson River through New York's Southern Tier of counties to the shore of Lake Erie. Despite financing difficulties similar to those experienced by the Mad River line in Ohio, and despite some issues of ineffective management as well as a defiantly nonstandard wide track gauge of six feet, the Erie was the first railroad to make direct connection between New York City and Lake Erie. Erie's announced intentions for a broad-gauge road crossing Ohio diagonally from Cleveland to Cincinnati were eagerly reported until delays in execution provoked increasingly laconic local newspaper coverage, relieved occasionally by "good news." Just as with each of the other transportation linkages entailing a potential route through Urbana, public meetings ("A large and enthusiastic gathering of our citizens took place at the Court House on Saturday evening last...") adopted resolutions touting the location of Urbana as the "garden spot" of Ohio, and committees were formed "for the purpose of devising a plan or plans to make sure the passage of the Broad Gauge direct route" would be through Champaign County. The relevant Erie affiliate, the Franklin & Warren (renamed Atlantic & Great Western in 1855), persuaded potential investors in Champaign County to take up $100,000 of company stock in return for making Urbana a point on its route. Frequent reports as early as 1854 asserted that the work was under contract.[11]

Within the northern and central portions of New York State, and servicing the hinterland of the Erie Canal as well as competing with

each other, were numerous short-distance railroads, known collectively
as the Central Line. With the economic threat of the New York & Erie
clearly in view, several of those lines consolidated in 1853 to become the
New York Central. Then, like the Erie but from its own western terminal vantage near Buffalo, the New York Central also looked toward
Cleveland and the possibility of completely eliminating Lake Erie water
transshipment. As seen from Urbana, the likelihood of a northern Ohio
linkage was assessed positively.[12]

The third eastern trunk originated in Philadelphia where the local
financiers were determined not to be left behind either by New York to
the north or by Baltimore to the south. When the Pennsylvania Railroad
reached the Ohio River at Pittsburgh in 1852, it entered the competition
for the regional trade in grain and provisions as well as coal. Its greater
relevance to the agricultural lands of west-central Ohio was its orientation due west across the Virginia panhandle and its negotiation (some
thought it mere flirting) with a half dozen eastern Ohio railroad companies. Through one of those companies, the Steubenville & Indiana,
the Pennsylvania secured linkage to Columbus, and in 1857 the Steubenville & Indiana began advertising itself as the Pittsburgh, Columbus, &
Cincinnati. This was the line connecting with the Columbus, Piqua &
Indiana, not only giving the Pennsylvania Railroad an east-west connection across Champaign County but also giving basis for the popular
designation of the entire complex of Pennsylvania affiliates in central
Ohio as the "Panhandle."[13]

The arrival dates of the eastern trunk lines in Ohio only hint at the
bigger story of the "third phase" of North American railroad development. Not just the Pennsylvania but all the trunk lines were making
arrangements with smaller Ohio lines—agreements to construct connections for transfer, agreements for rates and/or subsidies, and sometimes
agreements involving ownership and management. By the time the Erie
established its presence within Champaign County, the four lines crossing the county provided all-rail linkage to nearly every city and significant
town anywhere in the northern half of the United States east of the Mississippi River and to much of the rest of the country as well. The War that
began in 1861 only demonstrated what was already proven in the grain
trade, that the railroad had taken on "more than local significance."[14]

Both the "more" and the "local" were expressed in diverse and diversely felt patterns of consequence. One pattern would superficially seem to belie the direct interest of farmer-producers in the railroads. The people most immediately invested in railroads lived not on the farms but in the towns. It was a very self-aware interest. Prematurely in 1836, Abraham Burke opened a "Rail Road Hotel" in Urbana where he was "prepared to accommodate the traveling public, in a style which he flatters himself will be satisfactory." Intending to exploit the commercial possibilities that Urbana would have "by reason of its Rail Road facilities," Joseph B. Baker relocated his dry goods business from Westville to Urbana in 1849. Other merchants began using the association of railroad sights and sounds rather than canal or steamboat images to promote their wares, as in Stadler & Brother's 1848 boldface newspaper notice that "Locomotives arrived!! And by them a large & general assortment of New Goods."[15]

More generally, the rising number of processing enterprises, specialty occupations, and service industries—all related to agriculture but not directly involved in working the land—were visible primarily in the activities themselves, mostly in the towns. One was the construction and use of grain storage warehouses along the track lines. These were owned or managed by "Forwarding and Commission Merchants," an integral part of the local business community. Two such warehouses were built in Urbana along Mad River & Lake Erie tracks the same year rail service was effective. So considerably felt was the new presence of the railroad that a summary of the first year's traffic volume—published initially in the *Urbana Citizen and Gazette*—was included in the County's 1849 report to the State Board of Agriculture. The further evidence provided by newspaper advertisements suggests some rapid transitions. In 1848, three Sandusky forwarding firms, a Cincinnati firm, and a Springfield firm with its own Cincinnati orientation all placed the first of their many notices in Urbana's *Citizen*. Soon there were notices on behalf of other firms, and what was new about the notices was a frequency and an intensity in their appearance, suggesting a scale of operations different from anything previously common in canal transactions.[16]

For the farmer-producer, transaction with the railroad facilities necessitated very little initial change in customary production methods. Greater was the change in attitude and ultimately in long-term produc-

tion decisions. The railroad was solving some endemic problems such as
the lack of any extended storage facility on the typical farm and the con-
sequent practical need for seasonal wagon trips of several days' duration
to distant collection centers. Farm produce still had to be hauled by
wagon from the farmstead to the rail depot, but a round-trip could be
accomplished within a single day's daylight hours as long as the one-way
distance was no more than about half a dozen miles. This was possible
partly because of the proliferation of railroad lines and partly because of
the technology and economics of steam locomotion. Until about 1870,
the usual fuel in Ohio was wood, perceived as less expensive and less
corrosive of engine fire-boxes than the available sulfur-laden bituminous
coal. Since the earliest steam locomotives required frequent regular stops
for fuel and water, the reasonable spacing of those stops took account of
local wagon hauling distance. "Stations" developed at roughly the interval of a standard township or its double, that is, every six or twelve miles.
Then, as the railroads settled into their respective routes across the
county, the towns and villages along all the routes each attempted to
serve as the favored rail connection site for the farmers in its vicinity.
While neither the time nor the risk of overland hauling can be quanti-
fied precisely, the availability of numerous railroad grain stations reduced
the cost of both time and risk. The farmer-producers of Salem Township,
for example, needed no sophisticated economic advisers to help them see
the obvious benefit of being able to haul a load of grain a few miles to
West Liberty rather than the forty miles to the canal connections in
Piqua or Sidney or three times that distance to Sandusky. Canals had
previously changed the farmers' economic matrix by bringing the transportation portion of production costs under eastern market prices precisely at a time when eastern demand was pushing prices upward, stimulating the expansion of commercially oriented agriculture. The railroad
did not alter the dynamic except in degree. For farmer-producers not
accustomed to keeping the kind of financial records later economists
would have liked, the advent of the railroad simply meant a conveniently
close market connection.[17]

The market connection itself consisted usually of nothing more con-
spicuous than a rectangular trackside building. The later term "elevator"
was not yet common, and the grain warehouses of the 1850s did not

emphasize verticality, nor were they single-purpose structures. They were designed for the collection and storage of farm produce such as wool, the sale of farm implements, the seasonal slaughter and packing of hogs, and in some instances the milling of grain or sawing of lumber. Built to accommodate the threshing customs of the day, the earliest warehouses in the county had little provision for weighing and measuring grain, except in limited quantities and with much physical handling. The threshing machines of the day directed grain by chute into a bin or hopper for measuring and cleaning. Later models directed the cleaned grain into bags, and a threshing crew usually included one or more baggers. Grain would arrive at the warehouses either as filled sacks carried by all-purpose farm wagons, or as loose bulk grain in the boxes of somewhat smaller and more tightly floored grain wagons. The grain must have been in bags when William D. Enoch delivered his newsworthy single wagonload of wheat to Jacob C. Kizer's warehouse in West Liberty in September of 1871. Drawn by four horses, the wagon contained just over 210 bushels, weighing 12,610 pounds, not counting the four men riding on top of the load. The quality of road conditions could not have been at issue.[18]

As evident in the Enoch news item, the handling of grain changed through the 1850s and 1860s with the installation of outdoor scales. The North Lewisburg warehouse of Audas & Miles, for example, was a building eighty by twenty-five feet, two stories high. Located in anticipation of traffic on the A. & G. W. Railway, the facility included a pair of Fairbanks' Hopper Scales and Sink capable of holding about four hundred bushels of grain, as well as another Fairbanks' 4-ton Stock Scale. A one-story addition to the main building, forty by twenty-five feet, contained a ten-horsepower engine used for elevating grain, shelling corn, or other similar tasks. The farmer drove his loaded wagon onto the scale where it was weighed, unloaded, and then weighed again. Alternatively, grain was emptied from bags or shoveled into the bin of a hopper scale connected to an elevating device to move the grain into a second-floor storage bin. In the case of corn, which might have been husked but not shelled, the wagon contents were first shoveled into the receiving bin of a sheller. Although small capacity corn shellers were readily available for sale, the warehouse provided a convenient option.

Steam power, when mentioned in warehouse descriptions, referred to the powering of shelling and grinding devices and only secondarily to elevating devices.[19]

Rail transport of grain was mixed in format. General-purpose boxcars could be loaded with bags of grain, individually carried into place, a practice maintained as long as grain sales were by "sample" rather than by grade. From the early 1850s, the same general-purpose boxcars could be equipped with "grain doors," close-fitting half-doors which allowed loading the car with loose grain shunted into the cars by gravity feed from the elevated storage bin comprising much of the second floor of a warehouse. The various storage units were dangerously open. In 1871, an eight-year-old boy died when he fell into the bin from which grain was being drawn off into a rail car at the I. B. Thomas warehouse in Kennard.[20]

Apart from the convenience features for grain farmers, most of the agriculture-related effects of the railroad became apparent only over a period of years. One of the earliest to show was some reorientation of the county's hog raising. An important market had been the many distilleries located along the Miami River, particularly in Dayton. The distilleries would buy the animals, fatten them cheaply on the mash left over from the brewing process, and then sell the animals to the slaughterhouses. A year after the arrival of the railroad, the farmers' new option was assessed by Joseph C. Brand: "Nearly all the hogs fit for market, up to this time, have been shipped alive to Sandusky, thence by steamboats to Buffalo, and then by rail road to Boston, at prices to the farmers here by a shade less than the Cincinnati market." Brand's phrasing is suspiciously overstated, for the railroad company's annual statement for the period coinciding with his report recorded the transport total of only 844 live hogs. Nevertheless, particularly in the comment on price convergence, Brand was explicit that eliminating the costs of driving animals overland for any distance was a gain. Within a very few years, single trains were transporting as many live hogs as the Mad River line had reported for its entire year of 1849.[21]

More generally for both grain and livestock marketing, a major effect of rail transport was to locate the point of sale closer to home. This in turn stimulated improvement of connecting roads, and turnpike companies were chartered for each of the main roads radiating out from Urbana. A more accessible market encouraged sales of smaller numbers of animals at more frequent intervals with greater certainty of pricing, which therefore put raising of stock more nearly on a cost accounting basis than had ever been possible when dealing with drovers. Stock did not now need the extra or intensive period of corn feeding that preceded a drive across the Alleghenies, and the producer could choose to grow less corn or feed more stock. The county's tradition of diversified general farming was thereby encouraged as grain production and animal production could each be evaluated for profit on a regular basis. The railroad, still sufficiently novel in 1851 to be singled out as explanatory, had changed the incentive pattern: "The easy access to our city markets, by railroad, has raised the price of all marketable commodities, so that our farmers are realizing profits heretofore entirely neglected, because unrewarded."[22]

As the customs of produce-exchange and self-sufficiency were left in the past, costs overall became more transparent. Individual farmer-producers, possibly even the majority, experienced positive gain and genuine improvement in their way of life. A nuanced effect for everyone was a dual orientation, usefully imaged in terms of compass geography. County farmers continued to live and to work in a world that was traditionally oriented north-south while being challenged, constrained, and commercially integrated into a world that was fundamentally oriented east-west. A railroad map of the county thus becomes a metaphor for a worldview. The railroad itself, regardless of direction of travel, was carrying away as much grain and other commodity as county farmers could produce. How, then, to produce more?[23]

HUSSEY'S
REAPING MACHINES.

CERTIFICATES.

These Machines cut faster & cleaner, and are more substantial than any other now in use. They cut fallen Grain, & are most admirably adapted to cutting Clover for seed.

HUSSEY'S MOWING MACHINES.

These are an invaluable Machine to Farmers having a large quantity of Meadow lands.

Gatling's Premium   Grain Drill,

The most simple & best adapted Machine for sowing Grain in use. See small Bills.

CRAWFORD'S CLOVER HULLER

Which hulls Thirty bushels of seed per day, ready for market.

☞ The above Machines are manufactured at the Machine Shop of the subscribers, in Urbana, Ohio. Certificates will be furnished to persons wishing to purchase, or any information desired.— Orders should be sent in as early as possible.

All kinds of Job Work done to order.

MINTURN, ALLEN & Co.

URBANA, O., March, 1851.

Citizen & Gazette Print, Urbana

1851 advertising broadside for Hussey's Reaping Machines. *Courtesy the Ohio History Connection.*

II.

Reapers

How to produce more? The answer within the agricultural technology of the day was to run more land. Production was measured in bushels. Such factors as weather, soils, and management skill obviously resulted in sometimes extreme yields, both low and high, but in the aggregate statistics of record, overall yields—bushels per acre—did not appreciably change until after the Civil War. Up to that time, farmers had more bushels to sell most readily by working more acres. Presuming they had land available, however, they still had to deal with the limits of their own human energies and the efficiencies of their technology. The solution was to increase their efficiency, to change their agricultural technology, to increase farm labor productivity through the use of horse-powered machinery. The strategy put Champaign County at the heart of America's agricultural inventiveness for about two decades in the middle of the century and very much at the center for a smaller portion of that time.[1]

The most practical problem facing grain farmers was the normally brief time in which to accomplish the various harvesting tasks. A calculated sequence was essential. The general order was mowing, raking, reaping, and threshing. Mowing hay, while arduous with a scythe, could be finished discretely, interfering little with the ongoing but intermittent cultivation of corn. The cut grass, however, needed to be cured, gathered, and stored—jobs that required much labor and sometimes many days when other tasks were also demanding attention. Winter wheat was normally ready for harvest by the first week of July. A midsummer harvest might well come due precisely when labor was needed to make hay. For the earliest farmers in the region this was not a problem because they put up little hay as long as they had wooded pasture land on which their cattle could forage and browse, but that practice was changing. They also tended to sow their winter wheat in the cultivated cornrows about the time of the corn harvest. This was efficient when using the sickle for reaping, but reliance on that implement was changing as well.[2]

Once grain was "reaped," that is, cut and gathered in some fashion, the preliminary result was shocks of tied bundles of grain left in the fields for some drying or curing time. The shocks were later gathered to a barn or threshing floor where the grain was shelled from its head or "threshed" in the narrow sense of the term and "cleaned" by being "separated" from the straw and "winnowed" from the chaff. Each of these operations was a separate hand process. About evenly distributed throughout pioneer Ohio were the two threshing techniques of flailing and treading. Both entailed spreading out the cured grain bundles on a clean hard surface such as the floor of a threshing barn. A flail was a long wooden handle with a shorter wooden beater attached at one end usually by a leather thong. The skill of flailing was in swinging or flicking the handle in such a way that the beater struck the bundles on the floor with enough force to separate the grain from the stalk and the seed from its hull. The technique was as physically tiring as it was ancient, yet despite the frequent need for a worker to stop for rest and for raking, it could be accomplished by a single individual. Treading was equally ancient, and while significantly less tiring, it was also significantly less efficient. Usually in a somewhat larger work area than required for flailing and therefore not always under the cover of a barn roof, one or more animals were driven repeatedly around the interior of the room or yard to trample or tread on the bundles. Treading required more workers, minimally an animal handler and a raker, although an adult and a child could manage. Dirt and debris from feet and the near-inevitable addition of animal waste made treading less clean. Southerners tended to tread, Northerners tended to flail, but beyond family history and local custom, the determinants in Ohio were scale and pressure of time. A small harvest was likely to be flailed; a larger harvest was treaded. Despite its greater waste of grain, treading continued as a practice because it entailed no new capital investment. And, as an instance of conservative adaptation, it could easily be combined with mechanical help in cleaning. According to one record, the first fanning mill in Champaign County was used in Jackson Township about 1835. Most likely, that mill was hand cranked. Threshing was labor intensive but could be left until winter when workers were not needed in the fields.[3]

With even minor changes in any of these practices and particularly with any attempt to increase output, the apportionment of time and labor needed adjustment. In the late 1820s, adjusting the mowing-raking-reaping-threshing sequence took the form of interest in "some cheap labor saving machine to perform the thrashing operation." Machines which complexly combined the processes of beating, separating, and winnowing, and which were driven by increasingly complex power sources from hand cranks through horse powers to steam engines, were commercially developed over a period of about forty years. To the average farmer, the central concerns were efficiency and capital outlay. The first to use threshing machines were the farmers living near the major population centers. A few Cincinnati-area farmers were using threshing machines by 1828, and within three years, at least two different machines were available for purchase through agents in Champaign County. Among the named endorsees of "Clark & Stark's Patent Thrashing Machine" was a relatively young Jacob Minturn.[4]

The historic record does not indicate the extent of threshing machine sales, nor does it indicate the extent that hired labor accomplished the threshing process. John Thomas, of Salem Township, gave newspaper notice in 1834 that he had purchased "Luman Cooley's patent and best improved Thrashing Machine, for wheat and clover seed," and that he was prepared to accommodate "Farmers of Champaign county." Such promotion of custom threshing service was as atypical as it was indicative. The purchase of machines and the hiring of harvest labor in Champaign County increased modestly through the 1830s, while for the small-scale farmer who had a place to store shocks of grain until winter, the flail remained cost effective. Inventive effort had meanwhile taken up a different part of the mowing-raking-reaping-threshing sequence in prospect of a more pronounced impact on labor productivity. That interest became the horse-drawn mechanical reaper.[5]

Mowing grass and reaping grain are conceptually similar tasks, and may involve the same implements. Witness the scythe alternatively with and without an attached cradle. Initial efforts at mechanization of the cutting—which date from the mid-1820s in both England and the United States—were intended for both grasses and grains. All of the machines used horses for motive power although some were pulled and some were pushed. All were geared to take mechanical power from a wheel rolling on the ground, although the number of supporting wheels and their size and placement, as well as the simplicity and efficiency of the gearing varied. All had a cutting bar with some kind of oscillating knife but the length of the bar, the size and shape of the cutting edges, and the adjustability of the bar varied. Some of the machines had a reel to direct the grain into the cutters, and some had mechanical rakes to pull the cut grain off the machine. Some were essentially mowers, some were reapers, some were adjustable as either, and some were even combined reaper-threshers. Some provided for the principal operator to ride on the machine, while the rest required all workers to walk. Most required a minimum of two horses and two workers, and several required more of each. And, until the machines began to be widely exhibited and advertised for sale, the makers asserted strong statements about their independent inventive imaginations and exclusive patent rights, even as they surreptitiously and piously borrowed from their competitors. Such was very much the case between the makers of the two most successful machines of the 1830s and 1840s, Obed Hussey and Cyrus McCormick, neither of whom—despite their respective partisans—truly "invented" the mechanical reaper. Hussey's original mechanical contribution was probably the greater as nearly all machines adopted or adapted his cutting bar, but McCormick's combinations, promotions, and production and sales volume were undeniably influential. The interest here is the Champaign County connection.[6]

Cyrus McCormick's personal ties to Champaign County were meager and indirect at best. He grew up on the family farm near Walnut Grove, Virginia, where his father Robert had tinkered unsuccessfully since the mid-1810s with making a mechanical reaper. Supposedly with no other models than his father's failed attempts, Cyrus, twenty-two years old, made a machine that successfully reaped several acres of grain in the 1831 harvest. There were local witnesses, as there were again the following year. For lack of interested buyers and for other personal concerns and family financial pressures, the reaping machine was set aside.[7]

Obed Hussey, in contrast to Cyrus McCormick, was a New Englander, a Quaker, and a sometime seaman. Forty years old in the winter of 1832–1833, he was living in Baltimore where he had the use of workspace in the agricultural implement factory of Richard B. Chenoweth and where he made both drawings and models of a mechanical reaper. During late winter or early spring, he removed to a farm near Cincinnati, where he completed a working prototype of his reaper and demonstrated it on 2 July 1833 at the Hamilton County Agricultural Society Fair. In December, Hussey received a patent for his invention.[8]

Supposedly, neither Hussey nor McCormick knew of each other's machines until news of Hussey's patent stimulated McCormick to file his own claim in 1834, alleging priority because of the 1831 field test. The Hussey machine was heavier and more rigid. The draft horses pulling it tired more quickly, particularly since the gearing required a brisk pace. The initial McCormick machines were lighter and more functional on uneven surface conditions but were more liable to break. The type and position of the cutting knives of the respective machines differed initially. Probably the biggest practical difference was that the Hussey machine laid the cut grain on a platform from which a rider on the machine raked the gavels off to the rear. While the McCormick machine similarly laid the cut gavels of grain on a platform, its raker walked and pulled the gavels to one side only, out of the way of the machine's next pass through the field. The Hussey machine tended to work more efficiently in heavier grain but also always required two to four more workers than did the McCormick machine.[9]

The real difference between the McCormick and Hussey machines was that McCormick sold no machines during the 1830s. Beginning with the sale of a single reaper in 1833, by contrast, Hussey made manufacturing arrangements in various parts of the country and sold about forty-five machines through the 1830s. Traveling and exhibiting his machine in the Genesee Valley area of New York, in the Miami Valley north of Cincinnati, and in several other farm states as well as back in Maryland, Hussey was his own promoter and distributor. Quality of manufacture was uneven, and so was the critical response.[10]

The competitive pace quickened in 1839 when McCormick revived his interest in his own reaping machine. In the phrasing of the McCormick biographer, the "First War of the Reapers" was on. Both men made adjustments in the design of their respective machines and thus at any given time there were multiple versions of each machine being made by various licensees. Two additional factors, which McCormick soon understood with greater acuity than did Hussey, were the absence of quality control when oversight of manufacture was by a licensee, and the necessity for operator knowledge of the most effective uses of the machine. Both inventors sought to widen their market areas throughout the northern wheat producing regions. For McCormick that included the far-sighted and very risky decision to locate production in Chicago while maintaining some scattered locally licensed manufacturing as a transition until centralization became complete in 1851.[11]

Again contrastingly, Hussey continued his completely decentralized production arrangement with machine shops throughout the country's farming communities. Among those arrangements was one with Jacob Minturn and Gideon Allen of Urbana, Ohio. The sources are thin and include some circumstantial detail. In 1844, Philander B. Ross of Urbana purchased an interest in the Urbana Woolen Factory, becoming partner with John Reynolds. The following spring, the firm apologized to its customers and the public for its "considerable embarrassment, from not getting machinery in operation as soon as we expected." Rectifying the past and pre-empting future trouble was the information that "In the Basement of the Factory is established a machine shop, for the building of Woolen Machinery, &c." Expanding the "&c." was the offer to build a variety of tools and implements for potential farm use, including "Double boxed portable horse powers and threshers."[12]

At some time not clear in the record, Jacob Minturn and Gideon Allen became associated with the Urbana Factory's machine shop, probably shortly before the Hussey reaper's first Champaign County demonstration in 1846. Rezin C. Wilson and William S. Taylor, neighboring farmers in Union Township, had jointly purchased a Hussey Reaper and had it shipped from Baltimore. Nothing has surfaced to indicate how they came to make the Hussey purchase other than the probability of personal connections to farmers in Hamilton County and/or Hussey's promotional tours through the Miami Valley. By the standards of the day, Wilson's "very large farm" was "admitted to be the best and largest wheat farm in the county," and he used the Hussey machine to reap about a hundred acres of wheat. Taylor's "nearly" one hundred acres of wheat was only slightly smaller, and his multiple business interests and public service as County Surveyor gave visibility to his investment in the experimental harvesting machine. For multiple reasons, the Wilson-Taylor harvest generated considerable attention. Among the witnesses was neighbor Samuel Keener, who later that year provided the county response to an interrogatory from the newly organized State Board of Agriculture. Question: "Have any considerable improvements, within your knowledge, been introduced in your county during the past two or three years, in the modes of farming or the kinds of farm crops, implements or stock?" Answer: "Hussey's reaping machine, worked by horse power, was introduced in this county during the past harvest, and some two or three hundred acres wheat cut with it. It cuts the grain without waste, and leaves a short even stubble. It employs nine men and four horses to work it, and cuts upon an average 12 to 15 acres per day."[13]

An indicator of the loose autonomy within which local licensee-manufacturers worked was evident in Keener's further comment: "The man who sits on the [Hussey] machine, to pass the grain off the platform, works very hard, and to great disadvantage, from the position in which he is obliged to sit. Machines are now being made in Urbana, our county town, to order, by a machinist who promises to make them that they will pass off the grain to the binders for any size sheaf that may be desired, thus superseding the necessity of a man on the machine for that purpose." The maker was announcing his intent to alter and improve a patented design. In its own day this was not at all inconsistent with the payment of a license fee to Hussey of $10 per machine. Nor was it inconsistent with widespread practice among the manufacturing licensees of various implements. This was one of the chief ways that design flaws were captured, corrected, and ultimately appropriated by the larger manufacturers and even original patent holders.[14]

The unnamed machinist was Jacob Minturn. Gideon Allen shared
the work with Minturn, but their workshop location for 1846–1847 is not
confirmed. The only certainty is the sequence and the intimation from
Keener that responses to the Wilson-Taylor harvest were favorable
enough to result in the custom-order production by Minturn and Allen
of approximately two dozen machines in time for the 1847 harvest. Then,
in preparation for the 1848 harvest season, a published notice informed
"the farming public" that the firm of Minturn & Allen had "purchased
the exclusive right . . . to make and vend Hussey's celebrated Reaping
Machine for this part of the State." The work was to be done "at their
shop in the Basement story of the Urbana Factory." The firm made
approximately fifty machines for the 1848 season, and about the same
number the following year. Prospects were good enough to entice some
local investment. On 25 September 1849, Urbana businessmen Jacob
Kauffman and James A. Nelson joined Jacob Minturn and Gideon Allen
in announcing that they had "associated themselves together, under the
firm of Minturn, Allen & Co., for the prosecution of the business of
Machinists, in its various branches." Temporarily limited to the scale of
production possible within the Urbana Factory basement, the firm was
praised by newspaper editor Joshua Saxton for "having secured an eligible site upon the railroad, where they intend, as early as practicable, to
erect suitable buildings, with the most improved machinery, to be pro-
pelled by steam power, they will soon be able to compete with any similar
establishment in this part of the State." By March of 1852, the new 40x80
building was finished, with its machinery powered by a thirty-horse
power steam engine built by Minturn and Allen themselves. In the same
vicinity along the railroad near the depot were the equally new steam
mill of Colonel John H. James and the slightly older barrel factory of
Gwynne & Sheffield, both operating "full blast."[15]

Specifically promoting the manufacture of "Hussey's Reapers,"
Minturn, Allen & Co. solicited "all kinds of Job Work in their line," and
indicated that besides its Mowers and Reapers, the firm also made
"Gatling's Premium Grain Drill." Wheat drills were to planting what
the mechanical reaper was to harvesting, and in the 1840s and 1850s generated almost as much interest. According to Samuel Keener, a mechanical horse-drawn seeder was first used in Champaign County in 1846,

the same year the horse-drawn reaper was introduced. Most likely that seeder was Pennock's Wheat Drill, developed by Samuel Pennock in 1841 and locally manufactured by Hull & Smith of Dayton. By 1850, some Champaign County farmers were also using the seed drill patented by R. J. Gatling of North Carolina, available from Leffel & Runyon of Springfield until the franchise was acquired by Minturn, Allen & Co.[16]

In the annual fall exhibitions for 1850, the Gatling Wheat Drill made by Minturn and Allen took prizes at both the Champaign County Fair and the Ohio State Fair, accolades that were immediately and regularly featured in newspaper advertisements for the firm. That winter, the firm made a "highly finished" Gatling Wheat Drill for the inventor himself to take to England for exhibition at the World's Fair. The following summer of 1851 they built another demonstration model of the Gatling drill for the New York firm of Henderson & Kitchen, intended for exhibition at the New York State Fair. Presumably, this was the machine that received a Gold Medal award at the American Institute in New York City that year. Multiple advertising notices appearing simultaneously in the weekly issues of the Urbana newspaper evinced a new confidence in self-promotion. While the Urbana firm did follow custom and publish endorsements from local farmers, it showed no reluctance to the use of advertising hyperbole—"These Drills will recommend themselves." Neither was it reluctant to exploit novelty advertising, such as the attention-getting sketch of a grain drill in a notice printed vertically within its column.[17]

Apart from confidence, a gimmick to attain or even maintain commercial visibility was apparently felt necessary. Mechanical seeders had quickly lost their novelty, and multiple manufacturers and their local agents offered competing implements. With their Gatling Wheat Drills priced from $50 to $85, "according to neatness and mechanical finish," Minturn, Allen, & Co. were competitive with the industry average price of about $70. Evidence of how near and aggressive that competition could be was the promotion of "the best wheat drill in the world" by Westville-area farmer Newton H. Harr. In 1857, Dayton alone had four firms that together manufactured nearly three thousand grain drills.[18]

By the time of the 1854 State Fair, according to William Vance, wheat drills of all makes were "in pretty general use" in Champaign County. No numbers were reported, but the farm sale notices from about this time forward typically included wheat drills if implements were itemized. The farmers who purchased them were finding them cost effective, most persuasively for the amount of seed they saved. More importantly, the drill was not an implement in isolation, and its ready adoption was powerfully indicative of the systemic interconnectedness of changes in the small grain culture complex. Most visually obvious was a change in the selection and appearance of the fields. Drills received their name allegedly because they made military-like rows of plants at regular intervals in contrast to the irregular patterns that resulted from broadcast sowing. Seed-rows and the machines making them were most practical on even-surfaced ground, as were all the horse-drawn machines used in the cultivation and harvesting of those rows. One necessary consequence was greater preparation of the soil surface, and that meant a greater interest in horse-drawn clod crushers and harrows. Jacob L. Kintner's 1851 endorsement of the Gatling drill, reprinted from the *Louisville Courier*, was tellingly significant not only for what it hinted of a regional market but also for its practical admonition to remove stumps from the field.[19]

The cradle scythe still had its own necessary place within the complex. A reaper's first pass through a field of grain required a pathway, cleared in advance by using a cradle. And, although the entire new horse-drawn machine complex was marked by the steady migration of wheat culture from the smaller hillside acreages to larger more level fields, not all fields put to small grain were conveniently level. Neither an anomaly nor an anachronism, handwork with a cradle was the preferred method for reaping oats or buckwheat growing on hillsides. Judging from Urbana newspaper ads in 1852, the anticipated field trial of mowers and reapers planned for Springfield later that same summer seems not to have signaled a worrisome change in the local retail hardware business for cradles.[20]

The reasons for adopting reapers or other horse-drawn machinery were entirely practical. Cost and availability were simply two of the factors made more manageable by the near-explosion of new firms offering mostly similar competing machines. Among the efforts timed to take advantage of the expiration of the original Hussey and McCormick patents was a reaper designed by Andrew J. Cook of nearby Enon and briefly manufactured by the short-lived Urbana firm of Goble & Stuart. Attempting to counter any overreach by the new enterprises was a new intensity of reaper-related patent infringement litigation. Obed Hussey, in a newspaper notice, warned all persons against purchasing and using any machines "embracing principles for which I have a Patent, without any authority from me, and in violation of law," and added that "Minturn, Allen & Co., of Urbana, have the right for Ohio for making and vending the above Machines."[21]

Recognizing publication of the Hussey authority as a narrowly regional advertising ploy, the question follows: Did Ohio farmers buy and use the Minturn-made Hussey reapers? The answer within Champaign County is: Yes, but only slowly at first. Up to about 1850, the total number of mechanical reapers sold and put to use in the entire country was rather small. Hussey's own claim was that 358 machines were made under his name during the period 1840–1849. Minturn & Allen accounted for about a third of that aggregate. From the testimonials later collected for reprinting in Follett L. Greeno's 1912 *Obed Hussey Who, of All Inventors, Made Bread Cheap*, all of the named county adopters farmed in the flat-to-gently rolling land that forms the central core of the Mad River Valley. If the geography of the county and the Hussey production figures are then cautiously interpreted in favor of a local market accounting for perhaps half of the Minturn & Allen production, approximately fifty to seventy-five Hussey machines were in use by 1850. The Champaign County report to the State Board of Agriculture for that year noted summarily that "Our farmers are using Huzzy's and McCormick's Reapers, to very great advantage in saving wheat and labor." The phrasing implies McCormick was the principal Hussey competitor, and by the time Minturn and Allen began production in their own new building, that competition had significantly intensified. McCormick machines were available for sale from the Urbana warehousing firm of Mosgrove & Wiley, and Dayton's E. Thresher & Co. regularly advertised in Urbana for the variety of agricultural implements it manufactured. In preparation for the 1853 harvest season, Springfield's Warder & Brokaw promoted its manufacture of the New York Reaper, and Newton Harr had taken on the Champaign County agency for "Manny's Adjustable Combined Reaper and Mower."[22]

Minturn and Allen managed competition in part by relying heavily on their local credibility. "In reference to our Machines, we say to the farmers, as we have said heretofore," intoned one ad. "We make no charge for a machine, until it has been tried and satisfaction given." Presumably, the Hussey testimonials were also necessary. Nationally, McCormick was outproducing and outselling Hussey and all other competitors, building a total of eight hundred machines for the 1848 harvest and about fifteen hundred for the harvest of 1849. The concentration of production in Chicago had succeeded in introducing some quality control, and the McCormick machine finally developed a reputation for reliability. The result was evident in the droll Report of the Committee on Farm Implements at the 1851 Ohio State Fair. Noting that multiple firms were making reapers, the committee reported that the McCormick and Hussey machines were rated superior to all others, but between them "the committee are *divided in opinion* as to which is to be preferred, and *no premium is awarded*." Two years later the report from Champaign County to the State Board of Agriculture again stated that Hussey and McCormick "Reapers and Mowers are in general use throughout our county." The mention of a Hussey reaper in an estate or farm sale was more a confirmation of "general use" than of particular brand loyalty.[23]

In short, familiar integrity carried a shrinking advantage. Critically effective, therefore, was competitive demonstration, some quite international and some very local. The field trials held as part of the 1851 World's Fair in England provided enormous publicity for McCormick. Back in Ohio the outrage on behalf of Hussey was almost as great, and the sympathies of the Urbana *Citizen* were repeatedly evident in its reports of the English trials, at least the ones that were decided in Hussey's favor. Closer to home, field trials of mowers and reapers were a prominent feature of the still novel Ohio State Fair. The 1852 event, hosted by Springfield, reflected the extent of implement manufacture in the Springfield-Urbana-Dayton area. Nine reapers and three combined reaper/mowers demonstrated before a crowd of two thousand people. Gold Medal went to "Densmore's Self-Raker," made in Springfield. Silver Medals went to Minturn, Allen & Co. for each of its Hussey entries.[24]

More than merely demonstrating the many engineering improvements made in the previous three or four years, the State Fair field trial and its counterparts elsewhere in the country showed the mechanical reaper to be a useful, reasonably reliable, and cost-saving machine. They also offered a view of the changing world of farm implement manufacturing. At an 1853 "Trial of Reapers" held at Wooster, Ohio, the distinctive new feature noted as either present or absent among the reaper entries was "self-raking." Ball & Aultman of Canton, Ohio, had the Hussey entry, a sign that Obed Hussey had made more Ohio arrangements than just with Minturn, Allen & Co. McCormick in Chicago and the newer enterprises in Brockport and Buffalo, New York, and in Canton, Cincinnati, and Springfield, Ohio, among others, were specialized factories rather than general-purpose mechanical shops. As much as his resources allowed, Obed Hussey pursued patent infringement litigation, but following the end of the 1848–1852 experimental period, his major role in implement manufacture ended. His reaping machine, when well-made and properly used, performed well, but neither it nor its inventor was sufficiently adaptable to accommodate the uses now being found for it. Most generally available as a combined reaper and mower, and at a typical price of $115, it was a practical investment for the farmer who could afford no more than one machine. The majority of reaping machines in use from about 1850 to the end of the Civil War met that multipurpose standard. Nevertheless, the Hussey machine was fundamentally a mower, in competition with other mowers such as the machines of William F. Ketchum. Hussey successfully sued Ketchum for patent infringement but conceded the larger contest when he sold his invention to the same firm. By then, McCormick was aggressively contending with one of his own former licensees, the Brockport, New York firm of Seymour & Morgan, which in turn had a licensee in the firm of Warder & Brokaw of Springfield, Ohio. The agricultural implement industry was entering a phase that would carry it through the Civil War. Was there still viable place for a small, locally oriented manufacturing enterprise?[25]

It could not have been obvious in 1847 when Minturn and Allen were just beginning to make reaping machines how much would change in barely six years. The small firm's exhibit of a Hussey reaper in the 1853 Ohio State Fair was very well reviewed, especially the firm's "very splendid and perfect piece of workmanship." The sobering reality was that fine craftsmanship was insufficiently competitive when every other aspect of the business from design to marketing to litigation was volatile. Personal issues could also enter the mix, and the silences in the public record invite speculation. Through the entirety of 1854, and continuing through the first week of March 1855, the Urbana *Citizen* carried brief ads for Minturn, Allen & Co., one for Wheat Drills and another for Mowers and Reapers. Absent was the braggadocio characterizing the firm's previous promotions. Through March and April, the ads themselves were absent. In May 1855, appeared a single small ad by Minturn, Allen & Co. for its Mowers and Reapers. In an unusual statement, editor Saxton called attention to the ad, almost as though he was reintroducing the firm to the community. The new ad again ran weekly through June and July and into August, but with the issue of 17 August, it was finally and permanently absent. At the Champaign County Fair held during the first week of September, Minturn, Allen & Co. received first premium awards for both its reaping and its mowing machines. Later that same month, and very out of character with its other regular ads for patent medicines, the firm of Kauffman & Nelson published a one-line notice: "We will sell Gatling's celebrated Drills at $30 each." The half-of-normal price indicated a clearance sale. Something was happening within the business partnership. The only public information was finally announced in mid-November. As of the fifth of that month, the firm of Minturn, Allen & Co. dissolved, "G. A. Allen having sold his interest to Jacob Kauffman and James A. Nelson. The business will hereafter be conducted in the name of Minturn & Co." Gideon Allen disappeared from the record. No Urbana-made farm implements were exhibited in the 1856 Ohio State Fair. In view of the published "request" from Minturn & Co. for payment of debts for repair work, sales of new implements may have been low as the firm reorganized itself. In his mid-50s and for whatever complex of reasons, Minturn himself was already pulling away to re-center his efforts in a small family retail business in Urbana. On the first of July in 1857, the State Board of Agriculture sponsored a "great trial of reapers and mowers" at Hamilton in southwestern Ohio's Butler County where Minturn & Co. exhibited a Hussey Improved Reaper. That appears to have been the final Urbana/Minturn/Hussey entry in any Ohio State Fair.[26]

The years 1857, 1858, and 1859 in the county and in the nation were extremely complex in matters both political and economic. The newspapers gave much attention to "the latest from Kansas," to fugitive slave issues, to war in Europe, and to the political ventures of such Ohio figures as Thomas Corwin and Salmon P. Chase. Less explicit attention was given to national monetary and more general economic issues. One exception was when the *Urbana Citizen and Gazette* was itself impacted. Noting "the hard times and great scarcity of money," the editor/proprietor extended the time for closing accounts with the paper and repeated an interim willingness to accept wheat and corn in payment of all claims. Such willingness to carry local accounts had very serious implications, for a consistently high percentage of the newspaper gave public notice of Sheriff's sales that arose from claims for outstanding debts. Every issue of the *Citizen* contained record of litigation involving county agricultural leadership, often with single individuals simultaneously plaintiff in one case and defendant in another. Usually by the time litigation was initiated, real property was the focus, but the underlying issue was credit overextension and insolvency. Urbana's Agricultural Store changed hands in 1857 and again in 1859 when first Alonzo Bennett and then co-owners R. G. Jamison and John T. Zombro were unable to satisfy their creditors. A common theme in the litigation was that the defendant had been an endorser for someone who had failed to meet obligations, apparently the problem for the warehousing partnership of Mosgrove, Wiley & Winslow. The editor's account could only hint at the scale and extent of interconnected financial affairs: "In this operation quite a large amount of valuable property has changed hands in this community within the last few weeks."[27]

Jacob Minturn was in a similar situation, or his financial partners saw it so. The firm gave notice that effective the first of August, 1859, the partnership of Minturn with Jacob Kauffman and James A. Nelson would dissolve. The stated motive was straightforward: "that there may be a settlement of the Notes and Book Accounts due the firm, many of which are of several years standing." Did Kauffman and Nelson have some of their other moneys invested directly or indirectly in either the Agricultural Store or the warehousing operation? Certainly they had consistently exercised prudence in their business affairs. Was the weather a factor? For once, the weather was not a facetious excuse. Across the northern agricultural zone from the Miami Valley to New York, an unusual killing frost the first week of June 1859 was compounded by an equally unusual absence of rain for almost the entirety of June and July. For some farmers, the prospect of having enough of a harvest to meet even normal financial obligations was bleak. Perhaps Kauffman and Nelson simply decided it was time to reconcile all outstanding accounts. To the casual observer, their retail business in Urbana was no different from any time in the past.[28]

In view of the above, the small newspaper notice one year later was a surprise. Minturn & Co. offered "improved Reapers or Mowers" at a new lower price but with the same guarantee of satisfaction it had offered in the past. The following week's newspaper provided context. William O. Downs, Agent for Whiteley's Champion Reaper and Mower announced a Reaper and Mower Trial, to be held on the farm of Abraham Harr a little north of Urbana, and everyone was invited. Modeled on state and county contests, the privately sponsored event was unabashedly a marketing ploy. The timing seemed right. The national credit crisis had not yet completely resolved itself in 1859, but by the middle of 1860, economic and agricultural optimism both seem to have been high. A larger acreage had been planted to wheat than in the immediately preceding years, and the crop was ripening well a little earlier than usual. In the field trial, the consensus winner was the Ball machine for the way it handled both mowing and reaping. The nine local farmer-judges clearly favored the cost saving represented by a good combination machine. This would account in part for the only other detail in the report of the Hand-Raker competition, an equally strong consensus commending the Minturn Hussey entry. Notably absent in the published report was any mention of McCormick. Silence may mean that a McCormick machine was present but did not perform well. Silence may also mean that McCormick had no current local promoter to replace the failed Jamison & Zombro Agricultural Store.[29]

Precisely in such aspects as the presence or absence of a McCormick competitor, the 1860 field trial of reapers and mowers gave focus to a set of questions that historians ask today and which contemporaries would have considered quite appropriate. Did the mechanical reaper increase labor productivity, and did it allow for the harvesting and sale of more bushels of grain? In the broad view of the history of the US economy, the answer is unequivocally Yes to both questions. When the same questions are asked with reference to a specific locale, the answers again are Yes, but with a caution for detail. An assessment from multiple perspectives is therefore in order, beginning with another look at Samuel Keener's 1846 report to the Board of Agriculture. Keener described the Hussey reaper as cutting twelve to fifteen acres per day. That may have been an optimistic assessment, although Keener was usually a very reliable witness. More directly significant to cost accounting was Keener's statement that operation required four horses and nine men. Because of the tiring drag of the machine, no single team could sustain the work pace for an entire day. Two teams, and thus four or more horses, worked in relief shifts. The duty assignments of the nine operators are not entirely clear. Minimally, one person (not necessarily an adult) guided the team by riding one of the horses, one or more rakers took turns on the machine itself, and the remainder (possibly including some women and older children) raked, bound, and shocked the cut gavels lying on the ground. The gains were in the pace set by the reaper and in the elimination of three to four skilled cradlers. What had previously taken three or more people ten days to accomplish could now be finished in two days, theoretically enabling an equivalent number of workers to reap nearly five times the acreage. The costs were the capital investment in the reaper and the maintenance of multiple horses. Reaping by machine was not necessarily cheaper. The question of who purchased and used the new machines therefore begs a particular kind of answer.[30]

A major determinative was the availability and cost of farm labor. Antebellum opinion in the North was that labor was in short supply, often phrased in absolute and uncritical terms. Variously attributed to the attractions of industrial work in nearby cities, wage-labor opportunities in the "West," or even gold fever after 1848, enough of Ohio's farm-skilled labor force had emigrated from the farms to make harvesting a problem. Uncertainty about labor availability when it would be needed in the seasonally intense harvest time was for some operators the key element in the decision to invest in a mechanical reaper. It was not coincidental that the *Ohio Cultivator* in 1847 mentioned gangs of workers from the Western Reserve traveling as far south in Ohio as Champaign County to follow the harvest season north. That was during the same

year locally made reapers were first used in Champaign County. Samuel
Keener's 1848 accounting of the costs involved in raising wheat included
references to "board of hands" in both harvesting and threshing. Some
of the difference made by the machine was that it allowed the farm
manager to hire a less skilled and presumably less costly labor force. The
reaper was well received in Champaign County in part because it met a
genuinely felt need.[31]

A rather different factor takes account of the stereotypical but justifi-
able reserve of the small farmer as investor in innovation. Over against
that stereotype was an equally relevant and equally soft stereotype, antebellum America's fascination with machines and the presumption that
machines meant progress. By the time the McCormick enterprise was
centered in Chicago, reaper quality had improved and durability was a
recognized and valued feature. On these criteria, Minturn and Allen
workmanship could hold its own in direct competition. The mechanical
reaper was well received in Champaign County because it was well made.[32]

A third factor is scale. How many acres of wheat were minimally
necessary to justify the purchase of a reaper? A 1966 study of farms, labor
costs, and machine prices in 1849–1853 calculated the threshold at 46.5
acres. Finding that figure too optimistic, another study ten years later
found that the acreage threshold for cost-effectiveness was nearly one
hundred acres in the period 1849–1853, dropping to eighty acres in the
period 1854–1857. Because production and sales records indicate that
many farmers did in fact buy and use mechanical reapers in the 1850s,
the question then becomes, How did they overcome the serious threshold barrier? With results reflecting the cultural milieu of Champaign
County, the answer was that many farmers participated in shared contract arrangements. Rezin Wilson and William Taylor were atypical in
their scale of operation and they were the innovators, not the imitators.
Nevertheless, they were neighbors in Union Township where the settlement patterns, family custom, and social networks were already in place
to make cooperation a strong option. The same was true in nearby Salem
Township. Working within his own extended family network was Joel
Funk, who in 1854 hosted a public sale occasioned by the recent death of
a member of that network. The sale announcement included the phrase,
"the half of a mowing machine," meaning one-half an ownership inter-

est in the machine. Sharing the costs of expensive equipment was not unusual and would recur through several decades.[33]

Cooperation was even more relevant in the pooling of a related resource. Horse-drawn implements require horses. The evidence from the County Fair and other similar horse shows in or near the county was of a substantially increased attention to larger draft horses. Increases in the overall horse population without parallel increases in the human population also indicated the rapid adoption of a variety of horse-drawn implements and a substantial new capital investment in draft animals. However, not every farmer would have owned multiple working teams, as evident in farm estate sales that included small, usually even, numbers of horses. Neighborly and/or family cooperation would have been essential. This is the key to interpreting Samuel Keener's assessment of Hussey reaper use.[34]

A way of life involving the sharing of key resources entailed finding a workable balance among duties and dreams. A farm with twenty to thirty acres put satisfactorily into small grain could not immediately or rapidly expand its small grain acreage very much, even if the owner-operator had land available. Such land, more than likely, was in woodland, in pasture, or in corn cultivation. With this kind of situation in mind, a third study revisited the entire issue of antebellum labor productivity. The investigators found that in 1859 only about three percent of northern farmers had sufficient acreage devoted to small grains to justify a reaper profitably. By factoring in the mowing features of the most commonly sold combination reaper-mowers, the threshold was lowered enough to account for the known number of machines operating at the time. Those antebellum farmers who could see a profit in purchasing a reaper, did make such a purchase, whether singly or jointly, and more likely than not, the reaper of choice was a combination mower/reaper of the types entered in the 1860 field trial. That also means that the vast majority of the nation's farmers, most of them on relatively small acreages, did not purchase the new reapers. The mechanical reaper was most often found on the larger farms.[35]

The production unit structured to make the most effective use of the reaper, and in some ways most in need of the reaper, was the family-centered farm. Reasonably viable using an older harvesting technology,

and normally adequately balanced for labor resources, the farm with
twenty to thirty or perhaps more acres in small grain had basis for a cash
income but not enough to justify purchase of a reaper. However well
received the reaper was in Champaign County, the majority of the
farmer acquaintances of Jacob Minturn could not afford to buy one of
his machines. At the same time, they did know about the machines and
perhaps could even begin to adjust their farm operations for the day
when buying a reaper was a financial option, probably also dreaming of
being able to use the reaper on additionally acquired land.[36]

12.

Improving the Land

The goal was quantity, producing more of whatever would sell. While quality was always a recognized value, particularly in relation to livestock, the perceived market valuation of small grains put the emphasis on quantity. The term that conveniently blurred the finer distinctions between quality and quantity—as well as the changing valuations of each—was "improvement." "Improvement" implied an investment in the future and carried positive connotations and much ambiguity. In civic affairs, it could imply changes in corporate welfare visible in residential building and business expansions. Newspaper editor Joshua Saxton could crow that "The spirit of improvement is abroad in this community, if we may judge from the number and extent of the contemplated enterprises in which some of our citizens are about to embark." In farming, it implied careful management, the latest technique in tillage, selective breeding, higher yield seeds, innovative machinery, and of course a final result in higher market prices. This was the sense of the term in the 1847 interrogatory included in a circular sent out from the Ohio State Board of Agriculture: "Do you think the farmers of your county are making any perceptible improvements in their mode of farming, their implements of husbandry, the quality and management of their domestic animals, *or in the education of their children?*" [emphasis in original]. One might understand this attitude as *intensive*. The contrastive attitude was *extensive,* and for farmers it meant doing most simply whatever was necessary to put more land into production. The relevant distinction then became "improved land" and "unimproved land." More improved land meant more produce from the land.[1]

The relationship between acreage and overall volume of produce was self-consciously explicit, as in Samuel Keener's 1846 assessment: "The yield of the wheat crop, the past season, will scarcely reach an average of 15 bushels to the acre. The Crop, however, will probably be larger than of any former year, owing to the quantity of ground seeded." Some increase of the quantity of ground for seeding could be accomplished by reapportioning the various crops within an existing tilled area, and such a tactic would be more characteristic later in the century. Through the first half of the century, the goal of putting more land area into production normally meant cultivating land not previously tilled. Almost always that entailed clearing the forest cover or draining the wetlands. The active phrase for this was "improving the land." Never completely distinguished from other value-adding activities that included breaking sod, building fences and additional buildings, and preparing the soil for planting as much as time and topography allowed, improvement by clearing and draining was a continuation of pioneering activities. A measure of the distance from actual pioneer days was the increasing array of specialty equipment available for improvement activities, as in the locally made S. P. Castle's Stump and Grub Extractor.[2]

Newspaper farm-sale notices provide the evidence for how contemporaries described and valued their efforts. The language, even when idiosyncratic to individual persons or situations, was highly conventional and patterned. The most seriously relevant detail concerned total acreage and the proportion of it cleared for cultivation. "Clear" did not necessarily mean plow-ready. An 1827 sale notice for the farm of the late Abijah Ward stated that "Said farm contains 318 acres, one hundred acres of which is under improvement." Occasionally the ambiguity in "improvement" was clarified slightly. When Moses M'Ilvain offered his farm for sale in 1830, he described it as containing "400 acres under a good state of improvement," adding that it was "well adapted to raising stock." In other words, much of the land was nearly clear of timber but whether for reasons of soil or of terrain or of remaining timber was not under cultivation.[3]

When land descriptions specifically mentioned the tree cover, further information could be inferred. A notice emphasizing an orchard was likely to communicate a hilly terrain with potential for pasturage. A similar implication accompanied notices that included the phrase, "well timbered." While the phrase could mean that much work was still to be done, the pioneering sense of tree-clearing urgency was absent. Instead, "well timbered" could connote a potential resource for fuel, construction, and possible sale. Unusually rich in detail for a newspaper sales notice but entirely consistent with the size of the farm and the seller's visibility in Champaign County was Henry Vanmeter's 1839 announcement. Situated on Buck Creek in Union Township, his farm contained "about 628 acres, nearly one half of which is prairie, (partly meadow land, the balance in pasture) about 160 acres of Plow Land, under a high state of cultivation; the residue clothed with excellent timber; the whole enclosed with good fencing." Indicating a willingness to divide the property, Vanmeter asserted that "The soil is not inferior to any in this part of the country, and well watered with never failing streams and springs." A concluding two-word sentence cryptically referred to recent financial embarrassments within the county as well as to the farm's location in the Virginia Military District: "Title indisputable." Four years later when the equally prominent Joseph C. Brand offered his farm for sale, the notice gave evidence of Brand's sensitivity to the priorities of a potential purchaser. Also located on Buck Creek, the farm contained 160 acres, with another detached fifty acres of timber. The primary tract was "all enclosed," with "About 130 acres cleared, of which 15 acres are in meadow, and the remainder first quality of wheat land." Yes, there was plenty of clearing still to be done, but "The farm is in a high state of Cultivation, and would suit a purchaser wishing to proceed at once to farming advantageously."[4]

Brand's mention of enclosure was significant. "Improvement" by fencing was the visible sign and measure of good farming, keeping out more than keeping in. There could be no improvement in livestock if a breeder could not prevent unwanted animals from sexual access to the breeder's own stock. Fencing could be a serious matter. George Bowers in 1831 was prepared to pay a reward of five dollars for the arrest of persons who even attempted to pull down any part of the fences surrounding his blue grass pasture. Thirty years later the issue was widespread enough to provoke the State Board of Agriculture to seek a law "rendering the owner of horses, hogs, sheep and cattle running at large, liable for all damages they may do on the lands of others, without regard to the character of the fences enclosing such lands." The last phrase was witness to the difficulty and the costs inherent in constructing and maintaining adequate barriers. Consequently, well-installed fencing was a sales advantage.[5]

With some variations as illustrated, the relevant distinctions were simply stated: total land area, acreage under cultivation, area enclosed, and area remaining timbered. The result, evident in a slight change in the sale notice cliché used by the end of the 1840s, was "a well improved farm." For some sellers of well-improved farms, an additional measure of their success in clearing land was the greater attention they were able to give to quality of buildings. David M. Barnet's Urbana Township farm of 163 acres was "all under fence, and in a high state of cultivation—80 acres cleared," and included "a good new dwelling house, two stories high, put up of the best materials and finished in workmanship style."[6]

A less personal measure of "improving the land" was in summary statistics. The census for 1850 reported 147,267 acres of improved land, and 108,564 acres of unimproved land in Champaign County. By those figures, the proportion of unimproved land in the county was 42%. The 1853 figures compiled by the State Auditor included slightly more refined information. Of the county's total acreage in 1853, 102,761 acres were "arable or plow land," 55,125 acres were "meadow or pasture land," and 112,143 acres were "uncultivated or wood land." The first two categories together made up "improved" land, totaling 157,886 acres relative to the 112,143 acres of "unimproved" land. Six years later, the 1859 County report to the State Board of Agriculture listed 267,746 acres of taxable land, of which 116,906 were designated plow land, 47,824 were meadow or pasture, and 102,316 were uncultivated or wood. That later proportion of "unimproved" was thus 38%, down four points over six years. Those few data do not of themselves indicate a trend, but other assessments provide complementary support. A State Board of Agriculture tabulation determined that the 42% of Champaign County described as wooded in 1853 had shrunk to 31% in 1870. Because the white farmers did not continue the Native American practice of burning the prairies, some portions of the county reforested naturally, but the long-term trend was a steady increase in the absolute acreage brought under cultivation as well as in the taxable value of that land. The process was uneven, paralleling what was happening throughout the nation. The creation of new farms primarily in Illinois, Indiana, and Wisconsin achieved a statistically phenomenal expansion of improved acreage in the 1850s. Ohio was seventh in the rank ordering on that scale. At the same time, existing farms throughout the established agricultural regions also increased their improved acreage. Expansion by extension was the operative principle and remained so in the Northern states continuously through the 1860s and beyond.[7]

Removal of the forest cover was the initial and visually most obvious means to improving the land. A more problematic issue was water control. Critical to all agricultural activities, water was in excess at some locations and in demand at others. Reassuringly, clichéd references to "never failing" springs and streams signaled adequate water. The opposite problem of too much water was never even hinted. The astute potential buyer might have inferred a flood plain location or the presence of wetlands from minimal information such as the nature and extent of the forest cover. Otherwise, only familiarity with a specific area and a generous allowance for seasonal excesses prepared the new farm operator for dealing with the problem. Some areas were simply too wet to farm.

Wherever financially feasible, farmers dug ditches to remove excess water. Ditching had improved several portions of Champaign County by 1824, and for Urbana by that date, ditching had become economically and politically essential. When the town was first laid out with its four principal streets radiating in the cardinal directions from the central square, "Scioto street (running east from the square) was a wet, spongy prairie as far out as the Eichelberger hill." Known as Dugan's Prairie although it was most likely a fen, the land seasonally flooded, with enough residual moisture year round to support both fish and water fowl. According to the Beers history, the General Assembly in 1825 authorized John Reynolds to drain the prairie, "which he accomplished in a short time at heavy expense."[8]

Ditching was as effective as it was expensive, and both the benefit and the cost were realized by individual farmers who had other demands on their time as well as on their money. Entrepreneurially addressing farmers "having swamps, sluices and prairies, that they wish to have improved," therefore, a half dozen "citizens of Cable" formed a Ditching Club in 1860 to contract for ditching. The effectiveness of ditching was complemented and enhanced by the use of drain tiles that became readily—but not cheaply—available beginning about 1850 both in the United States and in England where it was specifically associated with "higher" farming. In 1860, David Kenfield of Woodstock was making and selling at least three sizes of drain tiles. Although drainage seems to have been of widespread interest, and although limited "underdraining" was practiced in a handful of Ohio counties including Champaign, tiling was a feature of the post-Civil War period. For the most part, the first two generations of county farmers avoided investing in the wetlands and instead dug their ditches and laid their drain tiles along primary roads, action that displaced the financial and administrative burdens onto County Commissioners and Turnpike Company Managers.[9]

More affordable improvement was to be found in the advice widely proffered and somewhat successfully followed for "deep plowing," sometimes also "subsoil plowing." Numerous inventors and promoters offered an array of implements for such purposes. The Urbana firm of Reynolds & Ross—the same John Reynolds who had drained the prairies east of town—consistently carried a diversity of plows, as did Alonzo Bennett's Agricultural Store. Little evidence of actual practice of deep plowing appears until after the Civil War.[10]

Samuel Keener's 1848 estimate was that "About two-thirds of our lands have been redeemed from the forest, and wet prairie, and the county is now generally in a good state of cultivation." Over the next dozen years, the "good state" provoked diverse assessments, in part because redeeming the land was never a finished task. Once the forest cover was removed and the excess water drained away, repeated cultivation tended to diminish whatever potential the land had previously contained. To the white settlers, the fertility of the best soils throughout the Ohio River Valley, like so many natural resources, had seemed inexhaustible. The irony was that land, the most definitive standard of wealth for the farmers, was also the farmers' most wastefully exploited resource. "Improving the land" by ever-widening extension could not be sustained indefinitely. Some minimal practice of *intensive* farming was essential.[11]

Champaign County farmers were no different from the vast majority of their contemporaries. In the State Board's *Annual Report* for 1848, Samuel Keener observed that in his county there were "very few, if any farmers who manure their lands regularly," and that "it would be difficult to find a single individual, who makes it a business to attend to his barn yard with a view to the accumulation and preservation of manure." County farmers were not ignorant of manuring, crop rotation, and the related practices that would have reduced or reversed soil depletion. In the often-opinionated efforts of newspaper editor Joshua Saxton, relevant information culled from various sources promoted rotation of crops and limited fallowing, or provided information on soil care and soil chemistry. An 1852 communication "To the Farmers of Champaign County" from "A Farmer" suggested that county farmers could themselves write for the column on such topics as "the best mode of manuring ground." None did until near the very end of the decade. Instead, county farmers—at least some of them—learned from each other's experience in other ways. In September 1859, Salem Township's Simon E. Morgan was confident that "The old idea of the inexhaustibility of the soil, is giving way." Less optimistic was "W. H." who in February 1860 concluded a detailed description of his own manuring of a worn-out field by sounding a warning: "Deep plowing is good; but depend upon it, enriching by clover, or some kind of manure, is essential, and the sooner we make the experiment the better."[12]

Attitudes were changing. So also were some land use customs. Nevertheless, work habits, cultural expectations, market priorities, and the availability of fresh land always somewhere in the "West" defined the dominant pattern. The Introduction to the Agriculture volume of the Eighth Census expressed the prevailing view: "Land is abundant and cheap, while labor is scarce and dear." Improving the land by adopting intensive efficiencies was countercultural. Even its advocates were inconsistent. The result at ground level was an element of intentional and loosely calculated exploitation. Neighbors could dream of farms *both* bigger and better.[13]

13.

Organizing for Improvement
An Agricultural Society

"Improvement," despite or even because of its inconsistencies, was desirable. Because this implicated everything about farming and farm life, a shared effort was essential, and the commonly available model for collective organization was an agricultural society. By the standards of a later generation, an agricultural society was an imprecise undertaking. In its own day, it was much like other contemporary reform impulses. Self-selected organizers, acting with benevolent self-interest, presumed that public demonstration of better ways to practice agriculture would inspire emulation. Desirable in part simply because of the opportunity for genial social interaction, the favored venue was an agricultural fair. With achievable results on display, the financial rewards of improvement would be obvious and self-legitimating. Everyone in the community would benefit, with the individual exhibitors of improved breeds, higher-yielding seeds, and more efficient implements enjoying some degree of social reward. Experience exposed multiple tensions in these expectations. Even to begin was an exercise in perseverance. As an indicator of shared and changing ideas about agriculture, therefore, the Champaign County Agricultural Society and its fair were as useful to contemporary participants as they are to the historian today.[1]

Apart from the high-minded and short-lived society formed at Marietta in the late 1790s, the beginnings of agricultural societies in Ohio date from the late 1810s. Citizens of Cincinnati formed a Society for the Encouragement of Agriculture and Domestic Economy in 1819. The name conveyed its purpose. In 1824, efforts at forming a similar society in Springfield met with "little encouragement." Three years later a cooperative endeavor centering in Urbana began with greater promise. The stated intent "to cause to be ascertained and practiced, the best mode of breeding animals, and preparing them for market" expressed a practical commercial interest. Regular meetings and an annual fair were announced, but beyond the organizational sessions, no other meetings seem to have occurred. More successfully that year, a new Hamilton County society formed in Cincinnati. This was the organization that sponsored Obed Hussey's first demonstration of his mechanical reaper in 1833. Also in 1833, Ohio's General Assembly encouraged all counties to establish agricultural societies. The legislation, little more than a gesture, did not obligate county commissioners to provide any funds, and it made no provision for any statewide coordination of activities and information. A number of societies were created. By 1841, all but half a dozen had disappeared.[2]

Grandiose plans, formal but underfinanced organizational structures, brief periods of activity, and multiple experiences of resuscitation and rebirth—such was the characteristic profile of the agricultural societies formed during the 1820s and 1830s. Champaign County matched the profile when in September of 1838, once again a Champaign County Agricultural Society was formed. John W. Ogden's attempted reconstruction of the membership and activities was admittedly incomplete and certainly contained some errors. Even so, three patterns were evident in the selection of officers and managers. One, the leadership included persons, such as lawyer John H. James, secretary through most of the society's brief formal existence, for whom farming was both a profit-seeking investment and a gentlemanly enterprise. Two, the family names represented the first and second generations of economic and civic leadership in the county—Vance, Ward, Minturn, Reynolds, Vanmeter. President William Vance was brother of the Joseph Vance who was then nearing the end of his single term as Governor of Ohio. Three, although

Ogden asserted that all parts of the county were represented, the leadership was centered in Urbana and Urbana Township (James, Keener, Reynolds, Showers, Ward) and the adjoining Union (Minturn, Vance, Vanmeter) and Salem (Enoch) Townships. That all of the leaders had some visibility throughout the county may be inferred from farmer Henry Vanmeter's status as the county's elected sheriff.[3]

A fourth pattern may be illustrated by Samuel Keener, and that is the farmer as innovative manager. Keener's attention to detail was meticulous, and he was exceptional in being able to compute to the penny his average cost per acre of producing wheat in the mid-1840s. A contemporary assessment lauded Keener's intelligence and taste as expressed in the layout of his residence and the surrounding gardens and orchards and fields, adding that "if Mr. Keener is not what would be called a hard working man with his *hands*, he makes good use of his *head* in directing the labors of others." Forty years later, J. W. Ogden favorably remembered Keener for what Keener did "for the development of a higher farming,...both in the introduction of thoroughbred stock and in his system of agriculture."[4]

The role of innovative manager especially fit the Urbana members of the society, persons who owned land that they may have enjoyed working personally but that required extensive use of hired labor. Distance from the daily drudge of family farming, and the social and financial resources making it possible, was particularly expressed in such persons' support for improvements in livestock. At a sale in Chillicothe in 1837, John H. James and Joseph Vance jointly bought a "Durham" bull for over $1,400 and brought it to Champaign County for breeding, allegedly the first effort in the county to attempt such a level of quality. A month later, James bought a heifer for nearly the same price and for similar purposes, and the Vance brothers paid over $1,500 for a blooded cow. The interest was in improving the local beef herds. Dairy would figure later, although not necessarily entailing a change of breed. Indicative of similar investments in stockbreeding, William Ward's "Public Sale of Blooded Stock" in September of 1838 included mostly "Horses, of Blooded Stock" and one full-blooded Durham bull.[5]

The timing of the Ward sale was hardly coincidental. A few weeks later, the Champaign County Agricultural Society held its first exhibition and Fair on the farm of John Reynolds on the north side of Urbana. The date was 24 October 1838, and as remembered by J. W. Ogden, much of the display actually took place in town, where the central square had already been serving as the site of a more-or-less regular farmers' market, regulated by town ordinance since 1827. "The horses and stock lined the fence on North Main, beyond the town limits, and the Court House yard was covered with the varied products of the farm." A less-than-county-wide support for the exhibition may be inferred from the newspaper's chiding of area farmers for their reticence to show their "fine" horses. Awards went to mostly familiar names: Ward, Vance, Reynolds, and Muzzy for horses; Vanmeter, James, Vance, Cartwell, Reynolds, Keener, and Kenaga for cattle; Keener and Vance for sheep; and Ganson for hogs.[6]

Regional interest in the value of agricultural societies, meanwhile, began to coalesce around the felt need for some kind of state-level organization. A December 1838 meeting in Urbana, open to all county farmers, selected delegates to an "Agricultural Convention" to be held that month in Columbus "to take into consideration the propriety and utility of constituting a State Agricultural Society." Not surprisingly, the persons selected were Samuel Keener, John H. James, William Ward, and now former-governor Joseph Vance. The convention resulted in the lobbying that led in 1846 to "An Act for the Encouragement of Agriculture," the chief feature of which was the creation of the Ohio State Board of Agriculture. Officially formed to advise the legislature on agricultural matters, the Board began to collect information from the counties and to offer premiums "for improved varieties of domestic animals, agricultural productions, implements and machines, and from time to time as the funds of the society permitted, premiums were offered for essays on subjects intimately connected with practical agriculture." Publication of the statistics, recommendations, awards, and essays began with the *Annual Report* for 1846 and continued regularly until the state's overall administration of agricultural concerns was reorganized in 1913.[7]

The interval of years marked at one end in Champaign County by the organizational enthusiasms of 1838 and at the other end by the establishment of a State Board of Agriculture was characterized by much distraction associated with the national depression that began in 1839. The Urbana portion (the majority) of the local Agricultural Society leadership

was preoccupied with the financially precarious Mad River & Lake Erie
Rail Road and then also with the investments of the Urbana Bank. Optimism and social harmony were in short supply. One casualty was the
barely re-established Agricultural Society. In May of 1839, the members
of the society met to elect officers and transact "general business." Presumably, that included planning the next fair, but the surviving record
does not indicate that any fair was held in either 1839 or 1840. Nearby
Springfield did host an annual meeting and exhibition for the Clark
County Agricultural Society in 1840, and the featured guest speaker
delivering an address to the society was "John H. James, Esq., of Urbana."[8]

At home there seems to have been something akin to organizational
desuetude. In mid-August 1841 "the farmers of Champaign county, or
such of them as are in favor of reviving the Agricultural Society of
Champaign county," were requested to meet "to devise measures for that
purpose." A meeting was duly held on the twenty-eighth of that month,
and as an indicator that the meeting was itself a salvage event, Joel Funk
and Joseph C. Brand were "appointed" Chair and Secretary. Recognizing that properly organizing the society would require it "to revise the
old or adopt a new Constitution," and seeking a generous attendance and
a proper attitude, society proponents delayed further action for two
weeks and solicited Joseph Vance to prepare an address on "the history
and science of Agriculture." When the society convened on 25 September 1841, Vance was elected President, though his tenure was clearly
honorary. In view of the nearly three-year hiatus in society activity, the
familiarity of other leadership names may have represented some effort
at retaining or recovering social and economic normalcy.[9]

Nevertheless, the motivating purpose in the tenuous 1841 reorganization of the society was to hold an agricultural exhibition. Inauspi-
ciously, the Managers had to reschedule their announced planning
meeting in order to recruit a "general attendance," and the announced
fair itself had to be postponed by a week, to 28 October. Editor Saxton's
endorsement of the fair was halfhearted, and he did not attend. Other
than a spare listing of premium awards submitted for public record by
Joseph C. Brand, the only contemporary printed comment was in a
"communication" from "Triptolemus," who combined enthusiasm for the
recent event, generous optimism for future similar events, and plenty of

advice. Farmers were urged to "turn their attention more to a *better breed of horses*" because it costs no more to raise a horse worth $100 than to raise one worth $30. Similarly commending the Berkshire breed of hogs, "Triptolemus" concluded with urging every farmer to join the Agricultural Society.[10]

A year later, Secretary Brand issued a more formal call for public support. At the open meeting held on 8 October, the incumbent officers and managers were re-elected. By resolution, "the annual exhibition of stock and other articles" was to "be held at the usual place of exhibition near Urbana, on Friday, the 28th." To add further qualitative interest, the Managers invited Urbana businessman I. A. Bean to deliver an address prior to the opening of the exhibits. Managing to capture the spirit of gentlemanly competition among several of the society's leaders, "good order and good feeling prevailed," wrote Secretary Brand. The gentrified atmosphere also carried its explicitly gendered distinctions, as when "The Society then voted a premium of two dollars to Mrs. Elizabeth Hitt, for a domestic Shawl, which was not only comfortable to wear, but beautiful to the eye. Let our Ladies all 'go, and do likewise.'"[11]

At least from the perspective of Joseph Brand, the society's 1842 fair was successful. The following May and again in his capacity as secretary, Brand announced a meeting of the Managers to make arrangements for the 1843 "annual exhibition." No record survives to indicate whether any planning session actually took place. The annual exhibition did not take place, nor was it resumed for several more years. Some hint of the preoccupying and continuing local financial stress was evident in John H. James' 1844 auction of cattle. The published listing suggests that the sale was substantial: three Durham Bulls, twenty to thirty cows, twenty steers, and some valuable heifers and calves. Once again, the sponsoring Champaign County Agricultural Society effectively ceased to exist, reviving only after formation of the State Board of Agriculture.[12]

The catalytic feature in the 1846 legislation was the provision of a guide for financing. The result was a reactivation of several dormant societies and the creation of many new ones. Editor Saxton was sufficiently impressed by the new State Board to editorialize his encouragement: "The advantages of a well regulated Agricultural Society are too well known to need an argument in their favor. Who will take hold of it?" No one, it seems, was yet quite willing. Instead, among the first of the new societies to be formed was the Clark and Madison County Agricultural Society. The linking of those two neighboring counties demonstrated the community of interest in the cattle-raising practiced along the National Road. While substantial portions of Champaign County loosely shared in that interest, the more compelling community among Champaign farmers was defined by the diversified farming practiced along the Mad River. In October of 1848, therefore, editor Saxton again tried to rouse the relevant self-interest. Provoking him was the number of agricultural fairs being held in nearby counties and specifically the recent successful district fair at Xenia. "We are inclined to think that the stock and productions of Champaign will favorably compare with those of any other county in the State, of its size and population; and if we had a well organized Agricultural Society, we believe its annual Fairs would demonstrate this fact to the satisfaction of all." The farmers of Champaign County were still not persuaded.[13]

Action of the State Board now provided the decisive stimulus with its announcement of a statewide fair to be held in Cincinnati in September of 1849. Printed promotions circulated many months in advance, and although an outbreak of cholera in the host city forced a late cancellation of the event, the planning had its effect throughout the Miami Valley. That fall, a Champaign County Agricultural Society was once again reorganized.[14]

The details are thin. The absence of newspaper notice of impending and scheduled meetings suggests that the initial arrangements made in December of 1849 may have been informal and perhaps quite cautious. The leadership group as later reported to the State Board of Agriculture looked deceptively much like the leadership of the county's previous society. William Vance of Union Township was President. Smith Minturn, also of Union Township, was again selected to serve as Vice President. John H. Young, a thirty-six-year-old attorney living in Urbana and operating a farm technically within the town limits, was designated Secretary. Treasurer was Daniel Snyder, Jr. of Mad River Township, the son of a recently deceased and much respected farmer of the same name. The first public notice of the "new" society appeared in May of 1850 over the name of the Secretary: "The members of the Champaign Agricultural Society, and the friends of the Society from every part of the County, are requested to meet at the Court House, in Urbana, on Saturday the 11th day of May inst. The object is to enlarge the association, and to make some arrangements with a view to the Fair of the coming fall." A follow-up meeting was called for the 15th of June, with Secretary Young asserting that "The Society is increasing rapidly." More bluntly admonitory was editor Saxton: "We say to every farmer, go and join the Champaign Agricultural Society."[15]

The interest, the focus, the purpose, and the rationale underlying all the activity was the intent to hold a fair. The details were reported in the *Citizen*, as much for promotional propaganda as for the record, as the managers prepared lists of premiums, designated judges, and made the other necessary arrangements. Set for the week immediately following the rescheduled first Ohio State Fair, the county exhibition gained from the timing. Whether for the novelty of the attraction or for other personal loyalties, but certainly not for the initially inclement weather, the crowd assembled for the fair was large and interested. A new spirit was evident in the call of Society membership to the regular annual meeting to be held on 29 November, when the incumbent officers and two of the five managers were re-elected.[16]

With the 1851 agricultural and exhibition season in view, an institution began to take shape. The leadership of the society met to set judging categories and premiums, and to designate appropriate judges for each category. Noteworthy for its evidence of State Board influence and encouragement was the documentation required of grain producers who hoped to claim bragging rights for their crop yields. In October, "Our Annual Agricultural Fair" "came off" as planned. The first of the two days was primarily concerned with the animals exhibited, as previously, on the John Reynolds farm north of town. Other articles were exhibited in front of the court house on the second day. Editor Saxton was droll in noting that with "a large number of our farmers, from all parts of the county," in attendance, "A commendable spirit of rivalry was manifested in all departments." Before the year was out, plans began to form to lease or purchase a permanent location for future county fairs. By the middle of the following year, the pattern was firmly in place as the managers met to take up "the important business" of preparing for the 1852 "Third Annual Fair."[17]

In the optimistic estimation of the State Board's Corresponding Secretary, the "rapid improvement" in agriculture that followed from the organization of societies was evident "in every county in the state," and was due specifically to their sponsorship of annual fairs and festivals. Possibly. County fairs were often of major local interest and were definitely an indicator of change. Any consequential influence of agricultural societies on agricultural practice is questionable, however. Certainly in its earliest years, the role of Champaign County's Agricultural Society as an agent of change was expressed largely through the personal examples of its leadership. Each year that leadership included at least one new name but dominantly there was repetition of names achieved in part by casual rotation among offices. The position of secretary regularly went to someone residing in the town of Urbana, either a lawyer or a merchant who owned farmland or whose family owned significant acreage in the county. In several cases, active older men retained a leadership role as elected managers.[18]

Four additional patterns are evident in the leadership rosters. One, Urbana, Union, and Salem Townships provided the bulk of the initial leadership, but Mad River Township was soon contributing a share. Into the mid-1850s, Johnson Township was also represented, but Goshen, Harrison, Jackson, Rush, and Wayne were consistently underrepresented. Two, the age profile of the leaders differentiated two generations, senior and junior, suggesting that the junior generation was being prepared intentionally, almost apprentice-like. In successive leadership rosters over a decade and a half, numerous instances of fathers and sons or uncles and nephews carrying similar if not identical names blur the clarity of which generation was the formal leader. Dallas, Funk, Pence, Smith, Thompson, Vanmeter, Wilson. Perhaps it did not matter.

The third pattern was that agricultural leaders tended to be leaders in other matters as well. A number of county farmers sat on the boards of directors of the railroads crossing through the county. The same individuals, together with other farm leaders, were also instrumental in the administration of turnpike companies. Much the same group of farmers commonly served as deacons or elders in their respective churches, several served as justices of the peace in their respective townships, and current or former military rank as an officer was always acknowledged socially. John Earsom of Union Township was "Deacon Earsom." James Dallas was "Judge Dallas" for having briefly held appointment as an associate judge. John H. Young was always introduced as "General Young." A few held or at least sought elected political office. Obituary evidence adds a related element. In the cases of those farmers such as Rezin Wilson who died in the maturity of their age rather than from illness or accident in their working prime, the tribute language contained little hint of elitism and much of role model. Such leadership by example was a form of peer review, a more democratic form of the impulse toward agricultural improvement than was emanating from some agricultural societies of the day. The result was that the agricultural leadership in both its narrower and wider expressions was not typical but it does seem to have been self-consciously representative.[19]

Underlying all these forms of social deference was one common and overwhelmingly significant trait. Leadership by example was most usually demonstrated on the county's larger farms. Size mattered. A theme, unrelentingly consistent in the extracts from the agricultural press reprinted in the Urbana *Citizen*, was the value of small farms. Emphasis varied, sometimes stressing manageable workload, sometimes excoriating foolish acquisitive ambitions. It offered an idealized image of the yeoman farmer, enjoying the blessings of good soil and clean open air, on land that was workable by the yeoman and his immediate family and was of course debt-free. It was sentimentalized in the epigraph to the *Citizen*'s Agricultural column, "He that by the plow would thrive, Himself must either hold or drive." It was a theme that was absolutely *not* expressed by the agricultural leadership of Champaign County. The opposite was true. Leaders were associated almost normatively with larger than average acreages.[20]

Wealth in antebellum rural America was measured in land. According to one assessment of 1860 census data, "To be wealthy in this egalitarian society of historical tradition was to be a middle-aged, native-born, white, literate, male farmer." In a related study, the same analysts also argue that "Big farms were more profitable per dollar invested than small." Owners of the larger holdings were more able to take advantage of innovations that would in turn yield greater profits. Essentially this describes the leadership of the Agricultural Society. Of the thirty-five current and former officers and managers alive in 1860 and reporting a figure for the census query of real property value, only an Adams Township representative operated a farm smaller than the county average of eighty acres. In thirty out of the thirty-five cases, the farms were at least double the average acreage, some by several times that amount. The interrelation between land wealth and agricultural leadership was further enhanced by the practical significance of the settlement pattern of extended families. Extensive intrafamily cooperation was a means to extend and/or coordinate land holdings, giving some persons the benefit of more extended holdings than they individually could have claimed. The Rawlings brothers who operated adjacent farms in Urbana Township and the Minturn brothers who operated nearby farms in Union Township were like the several farmers named Black in Wayne Township, Funk in Salem Township, and Pence in Johnson Township. The result of all such ties was a set of families recognized by their contemporaries as good managers, partly because they owned or managed larger-than-average acreages.[21]

Scale of operation was presumptive evidence of skill. Prize-winning yields or an increase in assessed monetary value of farm holdings then served as confirmation. The public endorsees of the Hussey reaper were substantially the same farmers receiving awards at the county fair for exceptionally high yields of wheat and corn variously in 1851, 1853, 1855, and 1859. State Board Secretary John H. Klippart, in an 1859 tabular summary of such awards, called attention to the skills presumptive in those statistics when he surmised that "soil and climate or 'season' are not alone essential in producing a good crop, but that culture has perhaps an equal influence." The contemporary view of Samuel Keener contained a judgment that not everyone endorsed: "I am forced to remark that we are falling off in the ratio of increase in population, with many other counties, which is attributable to the large size of farms, and the prevalent desire among many of our farmers, to invest their profits in lands adjoining them, until many covet 'the cattle on a thousand hills.'" Keener's consistently careful record-keeping was based on his own ownership (in 1838) of two farms totaling approximately 450 acres in Urbana and Union Townships. Whether Keener considered his own scale of operation large is unknown, even though his reported acreage in 1838 was already three times the size of an average Ohio farm as computed for the 1850 census, and four times the average Champaign County farm size in 1860. A few months before Keener died in February 1854, he sold his farm property. The sale was remarked by the Urbana newspaper, not primarily because Keener's farm in 1853 consisted of seven hundred acres, but because in the time Keener had owned the land it had appreciated from about $15 per acre to its sale price of $35 per acre, at a time when the average appraised value of an acre in Keener's Township was $23.74. The messages were clear. Keener's skills exemplified management of expanded holdings while also improving their value, thus accomplishing both bigger and better.[22]

14.

Geography, Generation, and Gender
Union Township, 1860

Land to own and to farm, that was the desire. In Champaign County in 1860, many individuals did own at least a small portion of farmland. Equally true by that date, if not earlier, was the difficulty of increasing a small holding into something larger. While a steady appreciation in the price value of land impacted all land owners, the purchase price of land may not in itself have been the most important limiting factor. The socioeconomic structure of agriculture in Champaign County was tiered. Some individuals and families operated on a scale not typical of their neighbors. In the best of American traditions, those individuals and families did not form closed social groupings, but to the extent that the settler generation and its heirs welcomed their kindred and married among themselves, some social barriers to outsider individual advancement did exist. It was possible for a young farmer to start small and to dream big. Realistically it was also necessary for such a farmer to consider other options. With a bank of data from the census records to give substance, and with the hindsight that includes the imminence of Civil War, 1860 is a convenient and pivotal year marking a culmination of whatever dynamic demographic principles had been operative through the previous two generations. Population schedules allow an inferential construction of some of those principles, while a more narrative approach to selected examples provides additional insight into the underlying cultural characteristics of midcentury rural Ohio. The key issues were land tenure and its control, the extent and the prospect of land ownership, and the shape of an evolving agricultural society. Detail from a representative township provides illustration.[1]

Union Township has a topography sharing all the features characteristic of Champaign County. In consequence, its diversity of farm lands and uses were equally characteristic. The handful of arrival/purchase dates included in the Beers biographical sketches conform to the immigration surges described elsewhere in this study, and its historic demographic profile mirrors the region's majority farm population. Most of the named initial settlers came from Virginia, and "With one or two exceptions," were Presbyterian. The early exceptions tended to be Methodist, as were many of those who came in the later waves. The census records show a continuing draw from Virginia, Kentucky, Maryland— with the slight difference that Pennsylvania and New Hampshire have greater prominence in the later antebellum years. In the considerable antebellum shifting migration throughout the Miami Valley, especially between Clark and Champaign Counties, social identities were determined more by the families who comprised near communities than by the need to transact legal business in either Urbana or Springfield. Bonds of loyalty echoed in place designations such as "the Mt. Pisgah neighborhood" or "the Pretty Prairie." When the editor of the *Ohio Cultivator* visited Champaign County in 1846, he described the northern portion of Union Township as "a neighborhood of good farmers, and farms of the finest quality of land."[2]

The 1860 Federal Census of Union Township was carried out during the second and third weeks of July and resulted in enumerating 1,681 persons, grouped into 293 Households, and whose occupation categories are given here in tabular summary form. From among the 1,681 enumerated residents, a selection was made as follows: 1) All heads of household, regardless of gender, occupational listing, or property ownership. 2) All persons shown with an occupation. 3) All persons claiming some real property. The result is a database of 603 persons.[3]

Occupations in Union Township, 1860

Blacksmith	8
Blacksmith Apprentice	2
Butcher	1
Carpenter	13
Carpenter Apprentice	1
Clerk	1
Conductor	1
Cooper	6
Dairy	1
Dept US Marshall	1
Domestic	17
Engineer	1
Farm Hand	138
Farmer	161
Farmer & Gardner	1
Gardner	1
Grocer	1
Hotel keeper	1
Laborer	127
Lawyer	1
Mason	2
Merchant	3
Miller	2
Peddler	1
Physician	4
Plasterer	3
Potter	2
Pump maker	1
Sawyer	2
Shoemaker	5
Shoemaker & Farmer	1
Student	3
Teacher	3
Wagon maker	5

Union Township was a farming community. Of the 521 persons listed with an occupation, 164 farmers (including the one dairy) and 138 farm hands together comprised the overwhelming majority of occupations. Not all farmers were heads of household, but the 150 who were heads comprised half the total number of heads. Farmers and farm hands together also accounted for 115 of the 181 claims to real property, a proportion that is deceptively low. Most of the females who claimed ownership of real property but who are listed without an occupation were in households that included at least one farm hand and/or a male farmer without land. About a dozen of the forty-five persons listed with other occupations appear very likely—from the size of the claim, the occupation or trade itself, or the composition of the household—to have been farm owners carrying on a related trade or business. In other words, close to 150 of the 181 claims to real property in Union Township appear to have been claims to farmland. Most of the remaining claims were in dollar amounts smaller than the smallest farmer claim.[4]

The modal farmer in Union Township in 1860 was a white male head of household, born in Ohio. The median farmer age was 44, the median claim to real property was $3,000, and the median claim to personal property was $600. Such a modal farmer was William Chance, born in Ohio, age 44, claiming real property worth $3,480, and claiming personal property worth $1,500. Chance had no other persons in his household claiming an occupation, meaning that he had no sons over the age of fifteen and no resident farm hands. His farm probably consisted of about 120 acres. His personal property, which was of higher value than average, almost certainly indicates an investment in livestock and/or in farm machinery. In either case, he would have had to hire some help for at least part of the year.

Beyond these criteria of age and property claims, three other criteria reveal several patterns that together express much of the dynamic of midcentury Ohio farm life. One criterion is land ownership itself, a second is the place of the farmer in the household, and the third is gender. The three criteria overlap decisively.

Of the total set of 164 persons identified as farmer, 112 claimed real property. That leaves over fifty farmers, nearly one-third of the total set, working land they did not own and farming by tenancy of some kind.

Those landless farmers must then be seen in relation to the persons who did claim land ownership. When all 181 real property claims are ranged in descending rank order, a disparity in land wealth is strikingly obvious. The highest figure overall is $54,400 and the lowest figure claimed by a farmer is $440. Within that range, and with the exceptions of a shoe-maker, a carpenter, a farm hand, a hotel keeper, and a sawyer, all of the 125 real property claims valued at more than $1,000 were made by farmers, or by females (thirteen) with no stated occupation. No land-owning person who claimed the occupation of farmer owned real estate valued at less than $440. One farmer claimed $440 and two other farmers each claimed $500 worth of real property. All other farmers claimed land worth a minimum of $1000 or they claimed no land at all. Of the twenty-six nonfarmers owning real property valued at $400 or less, only one was a farm hand. The remaining twenty-one who were listed with an occupa-tion were in a trade such as carpentry or were listed as laborer. The black-smith owning $250 worth of land was certainly not financially dependent on the produce from that amount of land. Neither was the physician who owned land worth $850. Presumably the other dozen or so persons with nonfarm occupations but owning land worth $500 or more were similarly working their land with at least some hired or tenant labor.[5]

The farmer resident of the township with the largest wealth in land was William Vance. Born in Kentucky, William Vance as a young adult had social connections but relatively little wealth of his own, although he did join with his brother Joseph in the purchase of some expensive breeding stock in 1837. That same year, he married Clarisa (Clara) Crain who in 1834 had been widowed and left with a "large tract of land." The 1838 Champaign County tax duplicate indicated that Vance was working 590 acres of land while claiming in his own name land worth only $1,707. By the 1850 census, Vance was claiming real property valued at $30,000, some in Union Township and some in Salem Township. Land was both the basis and the measure of wealth, and it could be a commodity in its own right as Vance bought and sold parcels of farmland scattered through the county. What made such transactions possible were a favor-able marriage and the customs of coverture.[6]

The legal heritage of the United States was the English common law, which understood marriage as obligating a woman to perform household services for a husband who was obligated in turn to provide her support. The presumption, most developed in Blackstone's *Commentaries*, was that the *feme covert*, a married woman, had no legal standing and no economic or political independence outside her marriage or apart from her husband. Prior to 1848 in Ohio, "the unmarried woman of lawful age" enjoyed some minimal legal property rights. When she married, she lost her independent property rights. If she had previously owned land, the practical possession of that land and any rents and profits deriving from it passed to her husband. Land was to be managed, if not actually owned, by a male, theoretically in the interest of his dependent spouse and children. If that male should die and thereby leave his widow and children without support, the custom of dower rights specified that the widow was entitled for life to one-third of her deceased husband's estate, again with the presumption that the bulk of such estate was in land. Because a woman's future life support was vested in land, neither her husband in his lifetime nor his estate executor following his death could sell his land without her permission. This was reflected in a phrase occasionally appearing in estate sale notices: "subject to the widow's right of dower."[7]

Because the law was neither uniform nor consistent, a woman's property rights were ambiguous and uncertain, and the Crain/Vance situation illustrates one cluster of the ambiguities. Lewis Crain's farm estate, at his death in 1834, passed in its entirety to his widow. Crain's will specified the condition that she remain single. In the event of her remarriage, the whole of Crain's personal and real estate would pass to his three children, Lucinda, James, and Louisa, in equal shares. When the widow did remarry, her new husband became the temporary manager of her land. William Vance was legally entitled to all the benefits and profits that he might derive from the land but he could not dispose of it at will; it was not his. The land itself was in its own legally awkward status because of the children, all minors. Resolution in January 1839 took the form of a public sale of "the well known & extensive farm, on which the late Lewis F. Crain, dec'd resided during his life-time, embracing much of the best portion of the Pretty Prairie, together with other lands, about six miles south-east from Urbana, containing altogether 509½ acres." The entirety was "to be sold subject to the Widow's right of dower." The surviving record does not indicate how Clara exercised her right, but management of some portion of her land apparently fell to Vance. He was in effect acquiring wealth through his marriage.[8]

William Vance was one of the five Union Township persons alive in 1860 who had been an officer or manager of the Champaign County Agricultural Society. The second largest landowner, Robert Woods, age 59 in 1860, was not one of the other four leaders but his interest in Society issues can be presumed from his membership in the earlier 1838 Society. Woods had then been a relatively recent arrival in the county, having migrated from Virginia in 1832 and having bought his farm the next year. Obviously he had done well. The third largest landholder, Jacob Vanmeter, age 68 in 1860, similarly was not an official leader of the Agricultural Society although his son Joseph was. These several official and unofficial Agricultural Society leaders, together with the other surviving members of the earlier 1838 Society, all have in common that as of 1860, each was the claimant of an extensive or highly valued area of land, head of his household, and farmer, and none was younger than forty-three. As of 1860, no one from Union Township in agricultural leadership was a tenant or financially dependent except within a family context. Land, leadership, family, and generation were much interrelated.[9]

The significance of family, that is, the significance of access to land wealth by reason of birth and inheritance, is illustrated by the several farmers named Cheney. Benjamin Cheney's 1860 real property valuation of $11,120 placed him twenty-fifth in the descending order that began with Vance. At thirty years of age, Cheney was the youngest of the farmers claiming land valued in excess of $10,000, too young to have acquired that much of an estate other than with an advantageous head start. Generation and lines of descent are not entirely clear. An earlier Benjamin Cheney and his three brothers had migrated to Champaign County in approximately 1808. At the time of his death he claimed about two thousand acres and eight children. Some of the estate was distributed among those children, but it was the fifth in birth order, Jonathan, who inherited primary responsibility for the home farm. In 1860 and at age forty-three, Jonathan claimed land valued at $17,350, which made him fourteenth in the land wealth ranking. In his household were his five sons with ages from sixteen to twenty-three, all identified as farm hand. Ten years earlier, when the 1850 census was taken, Jonathan's household also included his younger brother, twenty-year-old Benjamin, identified not as a farm hand but as a farmer. Obviously named for the pioneer settler, the younger Benjamin clearly benefited from the extensive land claims of that first generation. In 1860, his own family was too young to provide sons for farm help, and his household included two farm hands named John and Henry Little, aged eighteen and twenty-seven. Twenty years later, the Beers history described Benjamin Cheney as someone who dealt "largely in cattle, with which he is very successful," and who was at that date operating a farm of 296 acres. A third Cheney, this one named Samuel, was forty in 1860. His claim of land valued at $20,350 placed him tenth in the rank ordering of Township property owners. The census record does not show whether any of Samuel's claim was his by partible inheritance of the earlier Benjamin's estate, but Samuel's one son, age eleven in 1860, was named Jonathan, suspiciously in honor of a father's older brother by that name. Benjamin and Jonathan and Samuel were all skillful and aggressive opportunists. Even more importantly, all three were the beneficiaries of similar traits in the generation that had preceded them. Most important of all, each was an independent farmer and head of his own household because for them that was a possibility.[10]

For others the possibility was less clear. The fourteen persons identified in the census as farmers but who were not heads of their households together express a rather different dynamic not captured as a pattern quite as clearly by any other criterion. That dynamic is the fact of mortality. The aging process, the risk of life-limiting injury, and the truly unexpected death of an adult in the prime of life were ever-present realities in the farming enterprise. All of the fourteen farmers who were also not heads were of young or middle adulthood; and with one partial exception, they were members of households in which the nominal head was senior by at least one generation. There are three variations of this situation. One was exemplified by Thomas Cartmel, who at age twenty-nine was a farmer, claiming real property valued at $2,000. The nominal head of the household was Nathaniel Cartmel, who at age fifty-four was presumably father of Thomas but who was identified as a farm hand. The inference is that the older man, even with his small land claim of $400, was injured or disabled in some fashion and was dependent on his son, the obvious farm manager. The second variation is different from the first primarily in the continued role, even if only nominal, of the senior male in the household. Daniel Roberts was eighty-six years old, a farmer, and worth $4,860 in land. In his household was his son Hugh, who at age forty-four was probably the relevant decision-making farmer even though he claimed no land of his own. Also in the same household was Hugh's son, Daniel, who at eighteen was the farm hand.

The third variation is that of farmer in one of the six households headed by land-owning females who clearly were widows. Their status again calls attention to the "Married Women's Property Acts" movement underway in the United States. Following the action of Mississippi in 1839, Ohio in 1846 was among the handful of states that adopted legislation protecting women's property from debts incurred by husbands. Two years later, New York's Seneca Falls Convention gave visibility to multiple related issues, and the New York Married Women's Property Act became the test and the foil for subsequent, mostly piecemeal, state actions throughout the North. Among the consequences was an unsuccessful effort to write female suffrage into the 1851 Ohio Constitution. More successfully in 1861, the Ohio General Assembly debated a Women's Rights Bill. Champaign County's representative provided detailed notice on the bill's content and progress, but when the bill finally became law in April, he attempted to sidestep the full implications by blaming the principal lobbyist. "Your correspondent voted for the bill," he explained lamely. "He thought it objectionable in many respects; and if in practice it proves a great error, his excuse is the woman did it." The men were skittish. Ohio was only the third state to adopt a relatively comprehensive married women's property act, securing to married women their separate estates in both real and personal property, not under control of a husband or liable for his debts. At the time of the 1860 census, those features were not yet law. A widow who chose not to remarry had a life interest in at least some of her husband's estate, and she had some control over devising the estate to her children or other heirs. If the estate was substantial, and if there were children, remarriage may well have been the least desirable of the available options.[11]

Mary Huntoon Sceva, whose maiden and married names suggest extended family connections in Champaign County, had migrated with her husband from New Hampshire in 1836 when she was twenty-four. Her second child and first son, George, was born in 1840. Sometime subsequently, she was widowed. Choosing to remain with her children on the farm that she and her husband had established, she never remarried. In 1860, George was identified as the farmer in the family but Mary was the head of the household. She remained so for another twenty years, still living on her eighty-acre farm when the Beers history was compiled.[12]

Mary Sceva's independence highlights the constraints of gender. Of the fifteen female heads of household who owned real property in 1860, the youngest was thirty-five and the next youngest was forty-one. With six of the women in their forties, four in their fifties, and four in their sixties, the women in this group were defined by their land wealth more than by their widowhood—if the concession is made that the wealth was maintained at the cost of foregoing remarriage. Discounting the three smallest female head holdings of $100, $200, and $500, the remaining twelve holdings were worth a considerable amount of money. Nevertheless, of these property-owning females, only one claimed the occupation of farmer for herself and one other claimed the occupation of farmer & gardner. The only other occupations claimed by any women in the township were domestic and teacher. The rest claimed no occupation. It simply was not done. Furthermore, and with only one questionable exception, all the property-owning females were in households that included or had direct ties to adult males who carried the designation of farmer or in several instances, farm hand. Settlement patterns could be critically relevant. Rachael Diltz, widow in 1858 of Samuel Diltz, was the head of household and owner of a farm in the immediate neighborhood of the farm of Samuel's brother, Wesley Diltz.[13]

The one woman unambiguously to claim the designation of farmer, Elizabeth Coffenberger, at age sixty owned a sizable portion of land (valued at $5,100). In her household as a farmer was Simon Ropp, Jr., age thirty-four, claiming no land but claiming $10,000 in personal estate, the largest such claim in the township, and presumably including considerable livestock. Her real property and his personal property most probably were complementary business assets. Also in the eleven-member household was Simon's wife, Mary, the mother of five of Elizabeth's grandchildren. Two years earlier, 243 acres of land near the Coffenberger

farm was sold at a sheriff's sale in resolution of a suit brought by the
Farmers' Bank of Urbana against Simon and Mary Ropp. The sale notice
does not indicate whether the bank was recovering its investment in a
mortgage on the land itself or whether the outstanding debt was for other
expenses, but the action does seem to have deprived the Ropps of their
home. That would account for their place in Coffenberger's household.
Elizabeth Coffenberger was herself party to another action at about that
same time when 102 acres of her land were sold by the sheriff to satisfy
action brought against the principal defendant, Rolly M. Coffenberger,
she having been the surety for whatever contractual arrangement the
unsuccessful Rolly had made. Elizabeth Coffenberger was much like
Benjamin Cheney in being an independent farmer because it was possible, notwithstanding the social situation in which even the most independent and assertive of the females voiced their decisions and directions
through their males.[14]

The situations of Mary Sceva and Elizabeth Coffenberger illustrate
how much the positive values of family and land wealth were conflict-
ingly intertwined. Gender simply complicated matters. The death of a
middle-aged adult typically left a spouse, children, and property in a
state of insecurity, most easily addressed by the remarriage of the surviving spouse. Given all the reasons anyone might choose to remarry, the
number of widowed females who were of an age to retain control of their
marriage estate without remarrying and who also had children of an age
to assist in making such independence practical seems to have been few.
Those few suggest a cultural and even legal tension between the principles of security through familiar relationships and security maintained
through genuine financial independence.

A related but partly disguised consequence of the same constraining
cultural values was an ambiguity in the status of tenant farming. Were
tenants, even those with more than average prospects, in the Jeffersonian
tradition of the Yeoman Farmer, or were they something else, their independence having been inexorably compromised? When a middle-aged
or older adult land-owning female preserved land for her children by not
remarrying, her adult male son or son-in-law farmer or farm hand was
in a situation no different from his counterpart working for an aging
land-owning father. Both were tenants in the strict sense of working

someone else's land. Both were locked into a long-term dependency relationship that could only be changed by the death or the largesse of the senior generation.

A measure of that relationship was evident in the occupation of farm hand. Of persons in the township listed with an occupation in 1860, 138 are indicated as farm hand. All were male, spanning the age range of fifteen to fifty-five, but that range is deceptive. Only two of the men were in their fifties. No farm hand was in his forties. The next five in age order were thirty-nine, thirty-seven, and a thirty-five-year-old who claimed personal property valued at $800 and who may well have had some special skill and/or equipment. Only fourteen persons identified as Farm Hand were also head of their respective households; the youngest of those was twenty-nine. Judging from the adjacent census schedule entries, most of this smaller group of farm hand/heads was associated with either all-purpose farm labor or with other laborers involved in some trade or craft such as cooper. The vast majority of the persons identified as farm hand (113) were in the households of farmers, irrespective of whether the farmer owned or rented land. The median age for farm hand was twenty-one, and the occupation was overwhelmingly a young man's.

The occupation designation "laborer" superficially resembles farm hand until age is correlated with origin. Then appears a contrast with farm hand and even more so with farmer. Only twenty-three of the farm hands were born outside Ohio; the remaining 115 (83%) were Ohio-born. By contrast, only 65 (51%) of the 127 Laborers were born in Ohio; all but two of those 65 were under forty, and the two exceptions were aged forty-one and forty-five. The remaining sixty-two laborers were born somewhere else, and twenty of them ranged in age from forty to ninety-five. Although nine laborers claimed real property of a few hundred dollars each, the group of laborers as a whole had far fewer assets and far fewer social and family ties than did either the farm hands or the farmers.

Local boys, that is, the children and grandchildren of the farmers, especially of the farmers who owned land, became farm hands. Outside that group were most of the domestics and laborers, including the twelve relatively recent (under age thirty-six) immigrants from Ireland. Here was a decided social status differential. Almost by definition, laborers were outside the portion of the local population that "had or could expect an economic stake in the community." Farm hands, as a group, did have such a stake but it was only evident when age and stage of life were taken into account. Certain persons conveniently illustrate the resulting life cycle pattern. In 1860, Samuel Allison, age thirty-one, was a farm hand, head of his own household/family, and apparently working for his father Christopher, age sixty-eight, owner of land valued at $2,000. Samuel was second in the birth order among his brothers, but as of 1860, his brothers were not associated with farm work. In 1880, Samuel was described as the farmer of 168 acres, specializing in grain. Similarly, Zenas Jones, age twenty-five in 1860, was a farm hand on the farm of his father John. Following service in the Civil War, Zenas began farming for himself, although whether as a tenant is not clear. John died in 1877, and in 1880, Zenas was identified as a farmer of 140 acres. In both of these instances, it was not the inheritance of a specific piece of land that was the factor but the fact that the senior generation owned land at all. Such land was equity, whether for its production potential, for exchange, for loan collateral, or for cash sale, and as such it was a heritage of advantage to the junior generation. Both of the cited instances also point to the factors of timing and of the existence of multiple siblings. Both factors required multiple strategies for dealing with an inheritance. Those young men who lived through the Civil War and who afterwards attempted to continue a normal farming life sometimes had to explore other options, at least temporarily. William Vanmeter, twenty-six in 1860, spent three years in telegraphing before eventually inheriting the family farm. Samuel McAdams, also twenty-six, had no land in 1860 but he did have $500 in personal property. For about a dozen years in the 1860s and 1870s he operated a threshing machine, during which time he too seems to have inherited a share of the family farm. Regardless of the strategy, there was little question that the status of farm hand in a land-owning household made for qualitatively different options than did the status of farm hand in the households owning no land or the status of laborer in almost any household.[15]

Whether an inheritance was in sight or not, a common practice among farmers and would-be farmers of the middle or junior generation was the combination of small-scale land ownership with some form of tenancy, rent, or shares. The practice was found especially among the later arrivals in the township and/or those whose inheritance was not likely to be a large estate. The Beers history mentions five different farms in Union Township in 1880 that consisted formally of eighty or fewer acres but which in each case was supplemented by the renting of additional nearby farmland. Newspaper notices give further indication of situations throughout the county that provided rental opportunities. This includes an array of special cases, such as the provisional rental terms offered by a financial institution so that assets not remain idle and unproductive through a period of continuing litigation. In a few instances, longer term tenancy/rental arrangements were disguised by the language of partnership "in the Farming business." More commonly, a rental agreement allowed a land-owning farmer to retire by providing a form of old age pension. In Ohio in 1859–1860, the tenancy rate state-wide was approximately 130 farms per thousand. The Union Township data suggest higher figures, particularly if the focus is not on a snapshot picture of a single year. Tenancy, especially in the form of "kin tenancy," could be used to generate or accumulate personal wealth. With a minimal head start in the form of some inherited land and/or an independent source of income and/or social connections, one could turn tenancy into ownership.[16]

The question remains as to whether tenant farming more generally led to farm ownership. However common renting was throughout the country, the cautious answer is that for those in Union Township who were not in line to inherit some land and for those without wealth in some other form, it did not. In the period under review, there were no unambiguous instances of laborers or of children of landless farmers becoming themselves land-owning farmers. Perhaps some did later in the century, but they would have been exceptional, not only in Champaign County. The pattern throughout midcentury America was that few hired farm laborers moved successfully to being farm owners. There were other implications as well. The principal tracks toward farm ownership and/or farm management clearly paralleled two different status tiers within the local society. Leadership in matters agricultural, civil, and military drew from those persons who owned land. Land wealth was a factor throughout the officer ranks on both sides in the Civil War. By the same standard, casualties among the lower ranking enlistees and draftees from Union Township were disproportionately among those who had been laborers, those without land.[17]

As a concluding vignette of antebellum Union Township, therefore, one final family example illustrates how advantageously a family could mutually assist its members over several generations both in spite of and because of hardships. The evidence is incomplete but essentially all of the dynamics described above were expressed in some form.

Jacob Vanmeter and his wife Mary Polly (Johnson) migrated from Virginia to Ohio in about 1803, probably to take advantage of Jacob's eligibility to receive military bounty lands. The couple had seven mostly adult children accompanying them, initially to the portion of the Virginia Military District that became northeastern Clark County. The record is not clear as to whether the family stayed together as it began farming, later moving intact into Champaign County, or whether some parts of the family settled separately in each area from the outset. Neither is it clear whether Jacob acquired the bulk of the family land before he died in 1808 or whether his children were the investors and speculators. Jacob's widow Mary survived him by thirty-five years, eventually dying in 1843 in Union Township, presumably where she had been living with one of her children. Two of Jacob's sons, Henry and Jacob, were active in county affairs from the earliest days. Henry, born in 1780, appears in the 1838 County tax duplicate as claiming 719 acres of real property in Union Township on which he placed a value of $4,045. He was County Sheriff that year. He was also among the five initial managers of the just-formed Agricultural Society. As detailed earlier in this study, Henry sustained serious financial reversal in the 1840s, largely in connection with local railroad and banking investments. In the 1850 census record, Henry, at age seventy-one, claimed no real property. At his death in 1851, he was member of the household of his son John R. Vanmeter, age thirty-seven. Meanwhile, Henry's younger brother Jacob, born in 1791, married Sarah Reynolds in Champaign County in 1812 and seems to have begun his farming in that border-band area shared by Champaign and Clark counties. In about 1825, Jacob removed to Champaign County's Union Township where he and his children remained close to "the home place."[18]

Some pieces of the record are clearer than others. Joseph Reynolds Vanmeter, eldest son of Jacob and Sarah, was born in 1817. The 1838 County tax duplicate lists a Joseph R. Vanmeter as the owner of 454 acres valued at $3,088. That was almost certainly a scribal error in the recording of first names. Jacob was still very much alive, for at age sixty-one in the 1850 census, he claimed real property in Union Township valued at $16,000. Son Joseph, recently married (1847) and head of his own young household, was identified in the 1850 census as a farmer who claimed no real property. He was, however, one of the first five managers of the Champaign County Agricultural Society when it reorganized in 1849. Confusingly for the genealogists, another Jacob Vanmeter, apparently a son of Isaac and nephew to Henry and Jacob, born about 1812 in Virginia, that is, after the first Jacob had already left Virginia, had migrated to Union Township and had begun to farm. In 1838, he had a small real property claim worth $600 that he worked until his death in 1857. The 1860 census is interesting for the stories it only hints. There were only two principal Vanmeter property owners in Champaign County in 1860. John R. Vanmeter, the son of Henry, has disappeared; Henry's two older sons had gone "West" to Illinois, and John may have joined them. Joseph R. Vanmeter was a farmer claiming real property worth $8,000. The other Vanmeter was Joseph's father Jacob, now claiming real property worth $33,800, possibly including at least a portion of the land once owned by his brother Henry. In his household as a farm hand was his youngest child, William, age twenty-six. When Jacob died at age seventy-five in 1867, the family farm was taken over by William. Twenty years later, the brothers Joseph and William were managing neighboring farms of 240 and 340 acres.

15.

Adaptive Diversity

Regardless of the differences in size of their farms, most Champaign County farm operators faced substantially similar challenges and opportunities. How they worked their lands, and particularly why there was effort to increase improved farmland acreage, was related to two significant geographic shifts in the nation's production of small grains, especially wheat, during the 1840s and 1850s. The first was national in scope. In 1850, Ohio ranked second behind Pennsylvania in number of bushels of wheat produced. By 1860, although Ohio's production increased, its relative position declined to fourth. The three leading states—Illinois, Indiana, and Wisconsin in that order—were to the west of Ohio, had been opened to settlement more recently, and were more immediately shaped by the ongoing "revolution" in transportation. Farmers in the more settled eastern portions of the country were finding that their customary practices, especially concerning the choice of which crops they should plant and the total acreage they could profitably cultivate, were no longer as remunerative as they had once been.[1]

For some Americans, therefore, "improvement" meant packing up and moving to take advantage of presumed opportunities in the "West." Some of the migrants found what they were expecting, others did not, and while the actual reasons for such moves were most likely mixed and usually not publicized, what the public learned after the fact could be poignantly incomplete. Benjamin Kenaga of Salem Township was active in the Champaign County Agricultural Society, and in 1841 received the county fair's premium award for best sow. By the standards of his peers he was doing very well, and in the view of one observer, had "the prettiest model farm house in the county." The public record does not indicate why, but in March of 1855, Kenaga held a sale of his personal property consisting of farm utensils and animals. Within six months came the news of Kenaga's death at age forty-eight at his new residence near Janesville, Wisconsin. In other situations, the public record was slightly fuller but without actually being any more explanatory. Lewis H. Clark, "having concluded to change my business," tried unsuccessfully to sell his farm in 1854. Three years later he tried again, this time publicly stating his "view of going to the West." The lapse of time covering Clark's announcements implies honorable intentions. Occasionally the public record could hint at something otherwise. In January of 1861, Robert Jones sued Willis Horr and Julia A. Horr for an unpaid mortgage on property in Mechanicsburg. As stated in the legal notice, the couple was somewhere "in the Territory of Kansas" and was not likely to respond. On the other hand, when letters from Kansas or Iowa brought stories of success, the letters were featured prominently in county newspapers. The occasional death notices also appearing in the newspapers were a strong witness to the demographic fact that regardless of success or failure, those who ventured west frequently left behind extended family ties. Thus, the relevant detail in the brief 1858 paragraph reporting the death of Marshall Kist in Kosciusko County, Indiana, was that the young man was son of Champaign's John Kist. When John Kist himself died in the spring of 1860, his Union Township farm of 147 acres was sold at public auction. The willingness of the executors, also named Kist, to sell the land in two separate parcels of fifty and ninety-seven acres suggests there was no longer anyone in the family interested in taking up the farm.[2]

For the persons who remained to farm, fortunes were shaped by a second significant geographical change, a shift within Ohio. Over the decade from the mid-1840s to the mid-1850s, the state's most concentrated grain-growing moved from the northern east-central backbone counties of the state, the "old wheat belt," west and southwest diagonally toward a "new wheat belt" comprised of the counties parallel to the

Miami Canal. There, in 1848, along with significant increases in commercial output of all commodities, wheat specifically was "the leading
article of export" from Champaign County, more than half of it in the
form of flour produced in the county's twelve flouring mills.[3]

The two geographic shifts—the one broadly Midwestern and the
other more narrowly sub-regional—placed the farmers of Champaign
County in sight of unprecedented potential while simultaneously introducing them to unfamiliar risk and some disturbing consequence. Certainly the railroad was a factor. The same could be said of the many new
machines available to farmers. Efficiencies of production, scale of operation, and demand for product were all up, and one scholar has calculated
that in 1859, the average Midwestern farm produced sufficient surplus
food to feed 8.8 adults, or roughly, two other families. By many standards, the early 1850s were years of agricultural prosperity. More disturb-
ingly, John H. Klippart's analysis of Miami Valley crop statistics at the
very end of the antebellum period documented an average decrease in
yield per acre by about one-third through the decade. Here was a challenge neither as comfortably longstanding nor as American as making
a machine or moving "West," for it exposed a tension in the uses of
"improved," that is, between larger scale and greater efficiency.[4]

For the landowning leadership of Champaign County, the trade-off
between increased acreage and decreased yields was acknowledged and
addressed—conservatively. Thus, almost despite themselves, they slowly
but steadily increased their use of horse-drawn machinery. Stated nega-
tively, profit-oriented farmers could not afford *not* to adopt such machinery. Similarly, some practices simply needed to be followed more intentionally. Lack of crop rotation was recognized as leading to the greater
likelihood of "the growth of chess, cockle and other noxious weeds."
"Rust" was similarly associated with repeated plantings of wheat in the
same soil. Crop rotation was urged as a means of disease control, and for
those who followed the advice, here was a conservative form of adaptation. Other custom was not in itself either good or bad but rather was of
uncertain effect, as in controlling the rapidly destructive wheat "midge."
Agriculture Board President M. L. Sullivant could only report that some
better yields were evident in those fields planted as early as possible, as
well as from using a "sub-soil" plow. Improved plowing technique was

especially persuasive if it could provide multiple benefits, and in 1856, Agricultural Society President Frederick Stokes reported that "Deep plowing is becoming pretty generally practiced among our farmers." Customs could indeed change.[5]

Champaign County grain farmers were thus much like their counterparts throughout the northern United States in facing two interrelated concerns. Mode of tillage was one. Seed choice and planting custom were another. Although the Agricultural Society did not publish any detail of the best high-yield practices, some informal sharing of information can be presumed as neighbors observed and adopted those features that struck them individually as good or useful. Successful farmers with the atypically high yields of brothers James and Wilson Dallas provided models. In 1855, the Dallas brothers took the county prizes for both wheat and corn, Wilson with thirty-six bushels per acre of wheat and James with 135 bushels per acre of corn—using a corn known locally as "Dallas Corn" because the Dallas family had introduced it into the county. Moreso in wheat culture than in corn, hopes for higher-yield seed varieties were interrelated with the immediately practical interest in varietal resistance to disease. In the late 1830s and early 1840s, "Velvet Chaff" displaced "Red Chaff Beardy." Both varieties grew well and produced full heads of plump berries, and both proved extremely vulnerable to "rust," as did varieties called "White Flint" and "Michigan." The reddish "Mediterranean" showed somewhat greater disease resistance, a virtue problematically offset by its consistently lower market price.[6]

The years 1831 for wet and rust, 1832 for cold and wet, 1845 for drought, 1849 for rust, 1854 for midge, 1856 for drought, and 1859 for frost and then drought were notably critical in Champaign County. Because crop years 1850, 1851, and 1853 had been bountiful, a failed bounty in crop year 1854 due to the midge was painful, and drought in 1856 prevented a recovery bounce. The years from 1853 to 1868 were later described as a period "of discouraging, low yields to Ohio wheat farmers." Wheat alone was not sufficiently "remunerative," and farmers were rhetorically asking, "Shall we continue the culture of wheat or shall we abandon it, and if it is abandoned what shall be substituted for it?" Contemporary observers noted that increased attention to livestock always seemed to follow years of serious grain disasters. The financial imperative was diversification.[7]

Already for a decade prior to the Civil War, county reporters had been assembling details of yield and price on oats, rye, and barley. Hay was a special concern because its bulk relative to its cash value and its transportation cost made for varied pricing even within the county. The formal statistical record compiled by the State Board of Agriculture included data on rye, barley, oats, buckwheat and hay only from 1858. The silent witness is that the named crops had become sufficiently important in Ohio's agriculture to merit the additional record keeping. The further implication of silence is that other minor crops and horticultural produce were still relatively unimportant. In the longer term following the Civil War, county record keeping and reports, both narrative and statistical, did include vegetables, tobacco, apples, grapes. In March of 1871, Happersett & Hovey's Grocery in Urbana promoted its "first Lettuce, Onions and Radishes of the season," and two years later a local independent gardener retailed his own early vegetables. Gardening was common enough even in town that the market for such produce must have been small. Fruits were more commercially significant. Farm sale notices always mentioned an orchard if one existed. At the annual county fair, a rich variety of fruit was always on full display. Prizewinning horticulturalists and the more competitive orchards tended to be located in hilly areas near flowing water. Exceptions were strategically located with reference to potential town markets or to mixed farming, and were occasions for mostly small-scale business opportunity such as the local manufacture of the "Buckeye Cider Mill." For whatever reasons of local economy and horticultural taste, orchards became more visible in their extent, their variety, and their quality during and immediately following the Civil War. And, fruits were different from other crops in stimulating an awareness of, and some attention to, bee keeping. "There is a steady advance in horticulture, and we are glad to see it," remarked the reporter for the Agricultural Society in 1868. Prior to that time, the extent of horticultural enterprise largely blurred with the production of fruits and vegetables for home consumption. The best hints of activity were in the irregularly appearing produce prices in the weekly market listing and in the itemizations some merchants published for the kinds of country produce they were willing to exchange, always in addition to the presumed wheat and corn.[8]

Diversity was thus demonstrably a conservative adaptive strategy, constantly tempted by the attractions of concentration. Unambiguously the most tempting distraction was wheat, for it was always a cash crop, even when a portion of the crop was reserved for home use. Urbana, Union, and Salem Townships were always the leading wheat producing areas, exactly where wheat could benefit from economies of scale. Nevertheless, what Champaign County farmers produced in actual greater bulk than anything else was "our other great staple, Indian corn," and the number of acres planted to Indian corn rose steadily, from 27,680 in 1850 to 40,358 in 1860. With Ohio as the lead corn-producing state in 1850, followed in order by Kentucky, Illinois, and Tennessee, total corn production was increasing everywhere in the nation except in New England. Even more notably, and again with the exception of New England, corn production per capita increased. While the bulk of the production was fed to animals, corn also continued to be a food staple for humans throughout antebellum rural America. In the techno-economic scheme of the day, it was consistently dependable.[9]

For both cultural and technical reasons within that scheme, corn culture tended to be more labor intensive than wheat. Corn was usually planted in spacious rows of mounds, in fields cross-hatched by the process of cultivating. It was tradition, and any mechanical aides had to be consistent with the customary manner of cultivation. Aggravatingly restraining was the tendency of the early mechanical corn planters to clog or to fail for reason of some problem in gearing or adjustment. Unlike wheat drills, therefore, the mechanical corn planters of the mid-1850s were likely to be hand operated, not horse-drawn, and the number of hand corn planters exhibited at the 1856 State Fair indicated how viable hand techniques continued to be. Regardless of the planting implements, the plant's growth cycle dictated between-row cultivation multiple times through the season. Innovations in horse-drawn implements provided some labor relief as the traditional shovel plow evolved into a form of cultivator, first with two or three light shovels and then by the 1850s with five or six teeth rather than shovels. Where mechanical assistance of corn culture was most promising was in harvesting and processing. The 1856 State Fair Committee on Agricultural Machines made special note of the large number of shellers and cob mills exhibited, and commercial

interest in these implements was evident in the many newspaper advertisements appearing in Urbana. The county could also boast its own
inventive contributions. In 1852, Sylvanus Miller demonstrated his rotary
corn sheller. At the 1853 State Fair, Seneca Lapham was awarded a
premium for his corn cutting machine.[10]

Again for both cultural and technical reasons, corn was compatible
with a wide variety of growing conditions and scale of farming operations. Apart from their "country produce," therefore, all farmers in the
county planted both wheat and corn. Only the proportions varied. This
was obvious to the farmers themselves. Except for those whose livestock
required a considerable investment in corn culture, the leaders of the
County Agricultural Society were disproportionately invested in wheat
culture. By contrast, the county's many smallholders were likely to be
diversified for reasons of more practical necessity. For all of them, the
uneven evidence is that a steadily increasing quantity of corn was marketed in unprocessed form. In 1850, just two years after the railroad came
to Urbana, Society leadership reported that corn "is fed to hogs or beef
cattle, also sold to distilleries, and at the ware houses in Urbana, and
shipped sometimes North, and sometimes to the distilleries about Cincinnati and along the Miami. Price at this time 31 cents per bushel." The
more important change was not in the price for the grain itself but the
extent to which the railroad was facilitating eastern markets for beef and
especially pork products. Increased numbers of hogs and cattle within
the county correlate directly with the increased corn production. Most
of the county's corn still went to market on the hoof and what really
mattered were the quality and the price of corn-fed livestock.[11]

Cattle raising provoked remarkably little record of contemporary
practice. Significant as much for its absence of detail as its overall assessment was Samuel Keener's compact statement in 1848: "There is a visible
improvement in the breeds of cattle and sheep, going on in this county."
Despite the efforts of Joseph Vance and John Reynolds to introduce the
Hereford breed, "cattle" meant the Shorthorn breed, classified according
to one of three intended uses: work, dairy, or beef. The number of work
cattle, or oxen, was small and declining everywhere in the settled agricultural states of the North because most of the many new agricultural
implements were designed for horse traction. By reputation the Short-

horn breed made strong but rather slow and clumsy draft animals. Nevertheless, a handful of county farmers were known for their preferred use of oxen. Smith Minturn's award-winning yoke of Ben and Joe attained some popular notoriety, while John Weller of Johnson Township was unusual in having four yoke. Countywide in 1860, there were only 276 working oxen.[12]

More numerous than oxen but less consistently identified by census and tax assessor enumerators were dairy cattle. Public sales notices always gave the number of "milch cows" in any given herd, with the proportion strongly indicating that dairy was essentially a household matter. That did include some sale of butter and cheese, and just as with oxen, a very small number of farmers sought to develop quality dairy herds. Otherwise, apart from specific herd sales, the county's milk-producing animals were likely to be silently included in the dominant category of record that accounted for most cattle: beef.[13]

Beef cattle were a presumed constant. Although numbers are soft, essentially all Champaign County farmers had some investment in beef cattle as part of their diversified enterprises. The exceptions were the highly visible breeders and a handful of individuals who might be described variously as drovers or brokers or forwarding merchants, or some combination of those occupations. Unclear is the extent of annual turnover in the county cattle population. Some animals were raised in the county, some were brought in for feeding and finishing, some were sent away from the county for feeding and final sale, some were shipped out live by rail, and some were slaughtered in Urbana. Neighboring Clark County claimed in 1850 to have exported about three thousand head, and probably a similar but smaller figure would fit Champaign County's export. For a few early years of its history, the Mad River & Lake Erie railroad carried both cattle and hogs north to Sandusky where they were transferred to lake steamers for transport to Buffalo and then again by rail eventually to New York and Boston. Later, when the Agricultural Society acquired a secure home site for the annual county fair, the grounds became a convenient venue for professionally managed stock auctions. What a Goshen Township farmer wrote in 1860 described much of the county: "Cattle also are well cared for, and much dealt in—many small capitalists making it their business through the growing season to buy and sell."[14]

Just as proudly, Joseph C. Brand's 1850 summary account covered the relevant issues relating to raising hogs: "Our county raises a large surplus of Pork." Self-consciously unable to provide firm statistics, he noted that "Our packers compete fairly with foreign purchasers and speculators, and are now engaged in packing, and our pork will either be shipped by New Orleans to New York or Boston this winter, or held over till Lake navigation opens in the spring. Some hogs are shipped alive to Boston, via Railroad and Lake, but owing to the rise in the pork market in the West this fall, it does not pay very well, and hence this trade has been light thus far the present season." The report was deceptive for here was an implicit indicator of Urbana's limited regional economic status. In the late 1840s, William Wiley began a seasonal packing operation in Urbana, doing business in the 1850s as Wiley, Mosgrove, & Winslow. Certainly a packing operation at the center of Champaign County near a through railroad connection benefited the local producers. In John H. Klippart's tabular summaries of hog processing in Ohio in 1857–1858 and 1858–1859, however, no Champaign County town was among the fifty-one named places with packing operations. Urbana's absence may have been an oversight. More likely, Urbana had a smaller pack than any of the listed locations. The local newspapers regularly carried notice of current hog prices that, through the 1840s and beyond, were primarily determined in Cincinnati. Thus, while Urbana may well have been a significant factor in local hog processing, issues of scale cannot be so easily ignored. Just as with the Urbana manufacture of Hussey reapers, the very conditions that encouraged processing operations in Urbana and in neighboring towns also made those operations vulnerable to competition from the larger service centers developing around more favorable transportation nodes.[15]

That assessment does not minimize contemporary concern for the quality and the health of the hog population. As a consequence of selective swine breeding and a more intense reliance on corn feeding, hog market weight was steadily rising. County farmers were receptive to arguments about the relative merits of the variously sized breeds, and Joel Funk's "Cuff" was described by one observer as "truly a noble hog." "Every thing in reference to the price of hogs just now is interesting to the farmer," observed Urbana's newspaper editor just before the start of the 1857 packing season. Growth rates, finishing time, lard production, amount of offal and bone, and such essential concerns as the market value of feed corn all were relevant. So also was the fatal hog epidemic that swept through portions of the nation earlier that year. Several times again through the next two decades, "hog cholera" would devastate the herds of Champaign County. Even in a well-diversified agricultural setting, therefore, market prices were only one among the many risk factors that county farmer-producers had to weigh in their individual decisions about whether to invest more or less in wheat or corn or sheep or hogs or cattle. Pragmatically offsetting some of that risk was the fact that most antebellum hog raisers operated on a small scale because that was the most efficient management of typical farm resources.[16]

Risk management through diversification of resources and product was the cultural heritage of the earliest Mad River Valley pioneers. The varied terrain they found invited diverse uses, and their successors continued to see it so, increasingly as a factor in their appreciation of some need for market flexibility. In the first *Annual Report* of the State Board of Agriculture, Samuel Keener reported that "The principal crops of this county are wheat, corn, oats, barley, and hay. Wool, and beef cattle are also important staples." Two years later he could add that the county's "chief articles of export—wheat, wool, corn, and pork" were marketed through Urbana, and "sent to New York and Buffalo, by railroad." Not everyone tried to do everything, but the mention of wool in a railroad context was noteworthy for what it indicated of a commerce-oriented pragmatism. Under pioneer conditions, few families maintained any sheep until after the War of 1812. Sheep then quickly became an essential part of the rural economy as the county sustained a significant eastward pass-through activity in sheep droving, comparable to the droving of cattle and pigs. When the nation's railroads began to displace droving with the shipment of live animals, they also facilitated a favorable regional shift in the nation's wool production. Through the 1840s, Ohio sheep production doubled. Increases in the next decade placed Ohio first in the nation in wool production, a strategically significant position when the Civil War cut off sources of cotton. Through those final two antebellum decades, Champaign County consistently counted more sheep than pigs. Toward the very end of that time, interest in wool production surged.[17]

Nevertheless, while the majority of county farmers raised some sheep, their investment was almost always understated. Especially in the principal grain farming areas, interest in sheep was low-level and usually with a hint of ambivalence. When John Evans of Salem Township announced a public sale in 1851, his printed list included the simple designation, "Sheep." The contrast was to be found in the corner townships, notably Rush and Goshen. A Goshen Township farmer remarked in an 1860 newspaper letter that "There is scarcely a landholder in the township that does not own sheep, or in some way have something to do with the 'wooly breed.'" Regardless of setting, all of the interest and most of the market was in wool. County agriculturists were like other Ohio farmers in implicitly acknowledging that some folks in America valued sheep as a food source. Disinterest in mutton was explicitly evident in Joseph C. Brand's report for 1849 when he remarked that a Mr. Flint, of New York "is slaughtering a large quantity of sheep at West Liberty, his profit being principally in the tallow and pelts." A gratuitous note added that the carcass was fed to hogs. More quantitatively revealing of attitude were the printed reports on the principal Urbana firm engaged in slaughtering sheep for the 1855–1856 season. J. W. Hitt & Co. processed "some six thousand sheep," rendering the carcass after separating the pelt and the hams. With the hams selling at four cents per pound, and presuming similarly low prices for the tallow and pelts, the newspaper editor allowed himself a bit of skeptical prejudice: "At least we suppose they find the business profitable, or they would not continue it from year to year as they do."[18]

Such public attitudes disguise the extent of county agricultural leadership in supporting efforts to improve the wool-producing breeds of sheep, principally the Merino and the various French and Spanish cross breeds. The first US importation of Spanish Merino had been at the very beginning of the century, and the breeding of Merino sheep became something of a fad in south-central Ohio in the 1820s. The speculative mania broke when the supply of animals increased, but the purity of the flocks was never consistently high. Whenever the Merino pedigree of an animal could be asserted with any confidence, it was always mentioned. Pedigree mattered. When Mechanicsburg physician and agricultural entrepreneur Obed Hor announced a public sale of the animals he owned in partnership with F. W. Morris, his phrasing ranged from generic ("a lot of hogs") to loosely descriptive (an "entire herd of Short Horn Cattle") to specific ("Together with 111 head pure blood Spanish Merino Sheep, original stock, imported by Mr. Rockwell, from Vermont").[19]

Dating from the earliest commercial activity within the county was a lively competition in serving the local needs for wool carding and fulling. Parallel enterprises promoted the sale of implements such as shears, and of spinning and weaving machines for home use, some made in Urbana as late as 1834. The commercial provision of those services centered at many mill sites and at facilities in Urbana and in North Lewisburg. Wool growers would bring their fleece to a mill for sale, for exchange, or for direct custom carding, a drawing out or combing of the fibers to clean and align them so they could be spun into thread or yarn. The carded wool was then taken back home where it was spun and either knitted or woven into fabric serving primarily domestic needs. The woven fabric was again taken to the mill for mechanical fulling. This entailed treating the fabric with fuller's earth, any of several clay compounds that removed the natural grease and bleached the fiber, and washing and beating the fabric to shrink and thicken it. Where possible, water or steam power drove the fulling machine paddles and probably also the carding machine combs, while smaller operations away from falling water used horse power. Urbana's "woolen factory" had been established soon after 1814 as a carding and fulling operation. Steam power to drive the machinery was introduced in the 1830s, and human-powered spinning and weaving may have taken place on the premises. More likely, even the weaving of cloth for commercial sale was done off-site through a putting-out system comprised of artisans in town and/or members of farm households. The 1849 County report to the State Board of Agriculture claimed "three woolen manufactures," but because those three were distinguished from "a number" of fulling mills, the nature of the actual enterprises is not clear. The 1860 Census of Manufactures counted three manufactories of woolen goods in the county, employing thirteen workers. No fulling mills were separately indicated. Power spinning jacks and power looms were rare except in the nation's eastern establishments, and probably all of the county's woolen mills remained primarily carding and fulling operations until after the Civil War. In the

1850s, meanwhile, the Urbana newspapers aggressively advertised sewing machines for use in the home, and dry goods retailers promoted all kinds of "imported" fabrics. Clothing could be purchased "ready-made," especially for men, or homemade from purchased fabric. An unmeasurable but decreasing portion of county farm families wore garments made from fibers actually produced on their own farms.[20]

Wool production was a business, not a necessity. The highly pragmatic determining factor seems to have been terrain, in a negative sense. If the land could not be used to raise wheat or corn profitably, particularly during times of depressed grain prices, it could at least be turned to some profit through the pasturing of sheep. Even then there were costs and hidden expenses such as fencing and surveillance, largely because of the depredations of dogs. Markets both east and west were fickle, and profit was not a guarantee. Railroad transportation allowed buyers to draw on an increased geographic area of supply, and the increased volume introduced new producer concerns about fair grading. Because the effect of lowered transportation costs and access to better markets was a period of rising prices for farm products other than wool, Champaign County's overall investment in sheep increased only modestly until the brief and artificial market stimulation of the Civil War. Until then, the typical individual farmer's investment in sheep production was low.[21]

16.

The Relevance of Horses

Cattle, swine, and sheep were the characteristic livestock of the Mad River Valley's diversified farming. Horses held a special status. At the nexus of all matters agricultural and economic, horses carried mixed and sometimes conflicted social values. Some individual horses, such as Joseph Vance's prized "Joe Gales," were known by sight and by name throughout the county. Such horses had end value simply because other people wanted them and would pay for them. Horses could therefore be raised and sold as a commodity, and horses certainly had cash value. During the financial crises of the early 1840s and again in the late 1850s, horses were liable to be taken by the sheriff in execution of debts. At the same time, horses could be raised and retained for any variety of uses, principally as draft animals, providing the motive power for an increasing variety of agricultural machines. In 1849, Joseph C. Brand put the emphasis on the commodity value of horses, reporting that about one thousand horses and mules had been sold that year at an average price of $60. Four years later William Vance reported a less confidently stated higher average sales figure of $100. All values were captured in the sentiment of a Goshen Township farmer: "The horse is a favorite animal and receives much attention at our hands."[1]

Sometimes subtle, sometimes not, therefore, was the measurable and audible configuration emerging in connection with horse-drawn implements. Across America, the sound of agriculture was changing. New was the regularity of machine clatter from horse-drawn implements in the fields. New also, therefore, was an escalation in the noises from the creak and jangle of harness and from the bodies of draft animals under strain. Different in kind were the human calls, commands, and cries necessary to keep horse-drawn implements under control and to keep farm steam engines steady, fueled, and safe. Occasionally present on grain farms by the outbreak of the Civil War, "portable" steam engines were smaller than their counterparts on rails. They were not light, they were not cheap, and they were not easily transported. Their mobility depended upon the harnessing of real horses, and the measure of their motive power was similarly framed: horse power.[2]

In its several literal meanings in the 1840s and 1850s, the mechanical measure of "horse power" in agriculture was most clear in the complex of processes loosely called threshing. The earliest threshing machines were designed for stationary use only. Just as traditional threshing involved bringing bundles of grain to the threshing floor, so now the bundles were carried to the implement. The make named most often in Champaign County was the Pitts machine, manufactured in Springfield and Massillon and elsewhere. What the customers later recollected was the sound. Because of its posture on the ground and because it seemed to growl as grain passed through it, the popular Pitts machine of the mid-1840s was commonly called the "groundhog." Prior to the development of practical portable steam engines, the "groundhog" and most other threshing machines were powered by a "Horse Power."[3]

"Horse powers" were generally of two types. A *sweep*, which in some configurations was called a *whim*, involved harnessing one or more animals to the outer end of a boom that was pinned or pivoted at the other end to a capstan and gears and some kind of drive wheel. The boom was a radius arm and the animals walked continuously in a circle. By extending the boom of a sweep, more animals could be harnessed and greater mechanical force could be applied. Although a larger machine meant a more cumbersome and typically more expensive implement, the trade-off was in threshing volume. An enlarged Pitts thresher of the late 1840s, powered by a sweep with six or eight or sometimes ten horses attached, could thresh three hundred or more bushels of wheat a day.

Despite the ready availability of such high-volume threshers and sweeps for purchase, most Champaign County farmers did not own them. Instead, they hired the work from enterprising owner-operators who took on the new role and risk of being "custom threshermen."[4]

The other type of horse power was tread power, not yet commonly called a treadmill. One or two animals walked continuously up the incline of an "endless chain" as gearing beneath or beside the revolving belt transferred the motion to attached machinery. Treadmills generated less power than did sweeps but were more portable and less expensive, costing perhaps half the price of a sweep. Tread powers were also well suited for use in discrete tasks, such as cleaning grain with a fanning mill, or wherever space was limited, such as in woolen factories. Not efficient for more than two animals, some were lightweight enough to be powered even by sheep or single dogs. In Mechanicsburg at an unclear early date, "Colonel Jesse S. Bates had a carding machine run by tread power, using an ox for the purpose." In Urbana as early as 1822, the machine carding of wool was carried on at Thomas F. M'Clanahan's "horse factory." A year later, new machinery powered by a "30 foot Horse Wheel" was installed. The mention of the sweep implied higher volume and perhaps more uniform quality.[5]

Treadmills and smaller sweeps were attractive to those mid- to large-size grain farmers who wanted to control their own equipment. That was the appeal of "Clark & Stark's Patent Thrashing Machine," designed to be powered by two horses. Likewise, the four-horse grain separator made by John R. Moffitt of Piqua was "designed for the Farmer's own use." By the 1850s, farmers could choose from among several designs of horse power manufactured in the Miami Valley, among them "Taplin's Patent Portable Horse Power" made in Dayton. Widely used in Ohio and elsewhere was the Wheeler Horse Power and Thresher, a treadmill driven by two horses in combination with a machine that threshed about 150 bushels a day. No one disputed the potential usefulness of steam power on the farm, but potential was not the same as practical. In threshing, use of portable steam engines was not yet practical enough to be widespread. Instead, the more practical combination included a separable horse power useful in powering an array of other farm implements, variously grinders and shellers and cutters.[6]

Through the decade from 1850 to 1860, the county's reported horse population increased from 7,063 to 8,167 in 1856, and to 9,463 in 1860, a rate of increase of 34% for the decade and slightly below the statewide rate of 38%. The "horse" was quite literally the favored animal, for Champaign County did not parallel the statewide increased use of mules. While the county's mule population did rise 50%, from a reported 95 animals to a reported 144, the mule population statewide increased by 250%. Mules were most commonly used in drayage and in cultivation, especially in corn, and were found more generally in the southern parts of Ohio. Rather than using mules, Champaign County farmers selected horses for multi-use efficiency, opting increasingly for heavier work-horses, and/or they continued to cultivate their expanded corn acreage by hand hoe. At the same time, and just as with attitudes about sheep and oxen, the small number of mules in the county may simply have represented personal preferences.[7]

Breed names rarely mattered. What did matter were the reputed features of individual stallions, such as speed. When the 1858 State Fair was held at Sandusky City, five of the twenty entries competing in the category of thoroughbreds were from Champaign County. Indicative of increased attention to specialty breeding, however, were the two catego-ries with largest numbers of entries, "All Work" and "Roadsters." There, too, Champaign County entries showed well. The breed named as par-ticularly attractive for road work ("roadsters") was the Morgan. Consid-ered by some farmers not strong enough for normal farm work, the Morgan was the favorite for general versatility. The greater significance of the 1858 fair was its serious focus on the working breeds, especially several recently imported horses. Variously denominated "French" or "Norman" draft horses, these were larger animals able to sustain the heavy work that Morgans could not. In 1851, Rush Township farmers Erastus Martin and Pearl Howard, together with James Fullington of Milford Center in adjacent Union County, were in England and France, purportedly seeking Merino sheep for breeding when they realized the potential advantages of the large horses they were encountering in Nor-mandy. Martin bought a three-year-old Percheron colt named "Louis Napoleon" and brought the horse back to the Darby Plains area. The horse stood for service for two seasons in the vicinity of Woodstock and one season in the Dayton area before being sold and taken to Illinois. The venture was not an initial success in Champaign County, and the offspring of the stallion were slow to mature into the points proving their worth as draft animals. By 1856, that value was apparent enough to encourage Martin and another Woodstock-area farmer, John Gordon, to repeat an importation. Known in local newspaper notices as "The imported Norman horse Rollin," the horse stood for service until 1859 when it too was sold and taken to Illinois. In 1857, meanwhile, the Darby Plains Importing Company—which included several other Woodstock and Mechanicsburg investors—arranged for the purchase of three stallions, again in Rouen, and their subsequent shipment to Ohio. At least one of those stallions would sire a significant number of offspring in Champaign County over the next decade or so.[8]

Proper care of work horses required the services of skilled specialists. Speed and efficiency were the familiar measures when the managers of the Agricultural Society introduced a new challenge into fair competitions, specifically for "the Blacksmith who will forge and finish the greatest number of Horse Shoes in a given time, to be done in a good, workmanlike manner." Beyond the friendly competitions, the horse/implement configuration implicated all decisions about land use and labor allocation and especially whether to purchase and maintain any specialty-bred draft horses. Horses make more efficient food use of oats than of the other fodder grains. To maintain an increased number of horses required an increased investment in oats and hay. The nature of the oat plant and its seed is such that refinements in mechanical reapers introduced a greater efficiency in oat harvesting than was the case for the other small grains. The result was a nearly closed circle. Those producers with enough acreage to specialize in wheat sufficient to justify investment in a mechanical reaper gained the cost advantages also of being able to grow their own oats to feed their draft horses.[9]

Biased toward the speed, efficiency, and scale integral to a concentrated commercial market-oriented approach to agriculture, the evolving horse/implement configuration had a down side as well. It was beginning to strain the balance of resources characteristic of a diversified family-centered approach to farming. This was especially evident when periods of fiscal constriction exposed new degrees of interconnectedness

and risk. In the Panic of 1857, several Champaign County entrepreneurial farmers who had tried too much, too fast, discovered that their neighbors were themselves sufficiently overextended not to be able to help.
The ripple of effects spread through the entire community, as did also
some convenient panic-related language used to describe the poor
harvest in 1858 actually due to insects and weather.[10]

Genuine and quite general financial panic-related strains on all
resources, social as well as financial, contributed to an extended horse-
related controversy within the Agricultural Society. Integral with the
reorganization of the County Agricultural Society at the end of the 1840s
were plans for an eventual permanent setting for society uses, always
with horse competitions in the plans. When "permanently" located on
grounds just south of Urbana, the annual fair immediately became a
setting for horse-related display and brag. In contemporary opinion, this
exposed both the best and the worst of rural life and values. Any negative exposure may not have been anticipated because the site acquisition
itself was almost serendipitous, a process in which the widespread desire
for horse competitions was surprisingly influential.

In November 1853, a number of "enterprising gentlemen" purchased
part of a farm located a mile south of Urbana "at the forks of the Valley
Turnpike and Springfield Road." Officially the purchase was entirely
private, undertaken by a dozen men, eight of whom happened to be officers or managers of the Agricultural Society. The group further invested
in the property, building exhibit-related fencing. Then, following successful use of the site for the 1854 fair, the group requested purchase-reim-
bursement by the society. A year passed without realization of the necessary $2,000. Some of the original investors became impatient and
threatened to find another buyer. The news provoked "A Farmer" to write
an impassioned appeal to the self-interest of all county farmers, insisting
that every farmer gained benefit from the exhibitions of "a more prolific
kind of corn, an earlier and hardier wheat, a breed of hogs, that will
mature and fatten on a third less feed." A significant portion of the county
agreed and bought share certificates at $5.00 each. When the March 1856,
deadline arrived, the property was transferred to the society.[11]

The public record does not indicate what debt-holding device was
created but the society did not fully meet the purchase obligation. Several

hundred dollars remained outstanding through the next two annual fairs. In that interval, the nation entered a period of credit constriction. One or more of the original dozen investors experienced some kind of financial strain, making the situation of the grounds an "emergency." Rescue came when the County Commissioners agreed to pay for a half interest in the grounds, provided that those persons holding stock in the property give up their certificates to the society.[12]

The unanticipated financial issue revealed an uncomfortable social division. For two segments of the population, sacrificing for the benefit of a County Agricultural Society was simply not a priority. One segment was comprised of the less affluent smallholders and cash-poor agricultural laborers in the county whose families and livelihoods had not allowed risking investment in even a single $5.00 certificate. A second segment was more problematic because it was actually competitive with the Urbana-oriented Society. The agricultural and business communities centering on Mechanicsburg had taken initiative in the spring of 1855 to form their own Goshen Township Farmer's Club. Although the club's leaders participated in the county fairs variously as exhibitors and judges, they tended to keep their political and social identities very separate from Urbana. Whether the club had any more aggressive organizational intentions was not yet clear, perhaps even to the members themselves, but the potential was a threat to the ideal of a single inclusive countywide agricultural society and its annual exhibition.[13]

The leadership of the Agricultural Society read the Goshen club as a message and responded by reorganizing its board of managers. By custom as well as by encouragement from the State Board of Agriculture, county societies were to have four executive officers and five managers. At the annual meeting and election on 1 December 1855, the Champaign County Agricultural Society selected the usual executive officers, this time entirely from Urbana, but expanded the board of managers to include a representative from each of the twelve townships. The new intentional inclusiveness was immediately evident in all exhibits in the next annual fair, spread out over a longer period of three days and then beginning in 1857, of four days. Each year for the next three years, the county fair seemed bigger and better than each previous year's fair. Measured in total number of exhibits, attendance estimates, and fiscal solvency, the fair in its new location was a stunning success. A threat from the Mechanicsburg area was forestalled for several years.[14]

The interim success was disturbing for very different reasons. The fair was providing something for everyone, especially "shows," regardless of farm relevance. "The Grand feature" of the 1858 Fair, for example, was "the Balloon ascension" of a "daring young Aeronaut," immediately preceded by a grand procession led by a Brass Band. Such shows were a manageable distraction. Not so wherever horses were the prideful focus. Management proved surprisingly contentious. The new field and track in 1854 allowed an exhibition of "horsewomanship" in "the equestrian exercises of the ladies." At issue was the display of customarily unarticulated expectations relating to age and gender and decorum, and the newspaper language was pre-emptive. At the next fair, again, "the ladies acquitted themselves handsomely," and in 1856, the Friday evening finale event was the Ladies Equestrianism, conducted "with great propriety." Following the 1855 fair and its very muddy and very undisciplined riding competition among the young men, "Mingo" had written his objections: "In our humble opinion, these equestrian exhibitions are decidedly dangerous, and not at all profitable, being no evidence of superior horsemanship whatever...and the sooner they are abolished the better." The editor's response was amorally populist: "The masses approve of them, as is abundantly evidenced by the large crowd of men, women and children who assemble to witness the performance. And until better satisfied that it is productive of evil, we shall not feel at liberty to condemn it."[15]

The editor knew that division of opinion about horseracing extended precisely to include the "best citizens," but "Mingo" also had allies. When a Columbus firm gave notice that it was bringing its Morgan trotter to compete for the sweepstake prize, one county citizen was provoked to ask rhetorically, "Do the managers really propose to outrage the moral sense of the religious public by such arrangements?" Racing compromised the fundamental purposes of the county fair, calling into question the integrity of the sponsoring society. Making their own counterargument were attendance numbers. Although the State Board of Agriculture in 1858 adopted a resolution objecting to premiums being offered for horse racing at state or county fairs, a local correspondent in 1859 humorously derided the hypocrisy of "men of acknowledged piety and prominence in the churches" who "attend the races, and go into fits almost, that would scorn the idea of going and judging a race out in the highway." The controversy was hardly unique to Champaign County, nor was it soon resolved.[16]

The national economy, meanwhile, was returning to its pre-panic optimism. For almost two years, few newspaper ads of any kind had promoted the sale of large and capital-intensive implements. Attention and space instead went to items such as mechanical corn shellers. A year into the economic crisis, Newton H. Harr found vehicle for a droll sense of humor when he broke his own lengthy advertising silence with a one-line appeal to "Farmers!!! Don't forget that N. H. Harr is still agent for the Manny Reaper and Mower the best combined machine in existence." His investment was in a longer period than any expressed in words such as panic, and his perspective was exactly the primary local strategy for dealing with most matters agricultural. The success of that strategy was evident at fair time in 1859. "The show of horses was very fine, especially in horses of all-work and draught, and the competition very spirited," reported the *Citizen*. Weather was equally fine as a Salem Township correspondent rhapsodized the beautiful foliage in the King's Creek Valley. The annual fair was proclaimed the best ever. Certainly the best of rural life was on display for the benefit of the best relevant audience: friends and neighbors. It was all a very welcome change.[17]

As if to underscore the change, new good feeling mixed easily with new opportunities for commercial transaction. The "Grounds of the Society," which had already provided a convenient venue for the showing of cattle and some commercial horse shows, had hosted a horse fair the previous year. Regional interest in horses was rising, attested in August of 1859 when Piqua hosted a competition grandiosely "open to the world." Union Township organizers chose to understand that a more meaningful competition was always closer to home. They restricted their own 1859 horse fair to persons actually residing in their Township. The Township may have had a privileged claim. An unsigned contribution to the *Citizen* asserted as "a well known fact that the majority of the horses exhibited at our County Fairs are sent in from Union township."[18]

Union Township's inaugural horse fair was successful enough to warrant a repeat in 1860. With it came also a reprise of the same issues controversial at the county fair, such as the questionable liberality of premiums. Promotions rhetorically anticipated the propriety of "whether the ladies were to attend the Fair or not." Answer: "Certainly." The ladies were to be assured that "the managers are mostly single gentlemen, and will not neglect your comfort." The one-day event, held at the edge of Texas (the village later named Mutual), was deemed "a grand triumph." Exhibitor surnames in the list of awards represented the rising genera-tion of successful farmers from both well-established and more recently arrived families. Equally familiar and quite natural in a hotly contested presidential election year, brief speeches followed the races. The finale was "three prolonged, loud and thundering shouts...for good 'Honest Old Abe.'"[19]

In horses, the community had common focus. For now. Discord was distant, elsewhere. The near sound asserted clear identities and social harmony, even as rural life was changing. Some of its most "remarkable" changes had occurred in barely half a lifetime. More change would follow but it would have a different feel and a different sound. Some would find that new soundscape frenetic. Others would hear it as calm, for in the interim were the sounds of war.

17.

Making Sense of Civil War

The Civil War caught everyone and no one by surprise. Because Champaign County's political heritage included both the Northwest Ordinance ban on slavery north of the Ohio River as well as a high proportion of immigrants and ancestors from south of that river, county residents had long felt the national slavery debate with some passion. Mechanicsburg and portions of Goshen Township and neighboring Rush Township were "Yankee." In 1853, "J. H. W." was proud to celebrate Mechanicsburg as "a grand Depot of the Under-ground Railroad." At the opposite both politically and geographically, Mad River Township was sympathetically Southern and "Butternut." The narrowly successful 1857 re-election bid by Ohio's abolitionist Republican Governor Salmon P. Chase was thus a portentous indicator. With a few exceptions, most of the local antagonism was expressed through nonviolent political assemblies and sometimes virulent newspaper diatribes. Partisan following of the news, rumor, misinformation, confusion, and concern about the 1859 raid of "Old Brown" at Harpers Ferry was intense. With the election of Abraham Lincoln, Urbana's Republicans celebrated "the dawn of a new era in the progress of civilization," despite the uneven distribution of Lincoln's 2,325 votes. Goshen voted lopsidedly four-to-one in favor of Lincoln, while the 1,810 Douglas votes represented majorities in Adams, Jackson, Johnson, and Mad River Townships, the latter two at a ratio of three-to-one over Lincoln. The aging Colonel John H. James was among the public figures who perhaps most embodied the conflicted ambivalence felt by many. Slavery was abominable but constitutionally legal, and by the same standard, insurrection and secession were illegal and needed to be suppressed but only "within the law." A real war among the states was unthinkable.[1]

The remarkable—precisely because it was not unusual—Champaign County response to "the rebellion" was fourfold. First, and initially testing everyone's political integrity, were the public meetings and rallies with speeches and resolutions that collectively groped toward social consensus. Many of the rallies were announced as "Union" meetings, partisan gatherings that served to channel expressions of patriotism and concern—as happened in several locations on 16, 18, and 20 April 1861 with the news about Fort Sumter. A parallel, rather special exception for Democratic partisans was the "Citizen's Meeting" held at the Urbana Court House on 4 June 1861 in "Tribute to the Memory of Hon. Stephen A. Douglas." Agricultural Society leaders were among the principal speakers at all similar events.[2]

Secondly, just as throughout most of the North and certainly throughout most of Ohio, President Lincoln's call for ninety-day volunteers was met with local patriotic rallies, with much foolish optimism and confusion, and with quite personal and political machinations for rank and office. A "Volunteer" en route from Washington toward Baltimore by train reported in a letter dated 29 May 1861 that "The boys were in high glee."[3]

Then, and thirdly, when the war extended beyond everyone's early expectations, conflict was a constant topic, always as near as the soldiers' letters printed in the newspapers and the more painfully near presence of furloughed, discharged, and sometimes AWOL wounded men. Occasionally families would make public the letters they had received. By the second year, locally prominent officers such as Edward Fyffe were also providing written descriptions and analysis. As the conflict itself continued, "Union" rhetoric in the *Citizen* righteously excoriated the slaveholder rebellion and the cowardly Copperheads who allegedly sympathized with it, especially the "neutral" *Free Press* and the Democrat-oriented *Union*.[4]

Meanwhile, and fourthly, since no part of any fighting took place within the county, life had the appearance of being quite normal. On 1 June 1861 a "Colt Show" at Woodstock was held as planned. The issue of the *Citizen* carrying the first of its soldier's letters also carried very familiar ads for Gill's Patent Plows, for Dorsey's Self-Raking Reaper & Mower, and for the Massillon Threshing Machine. So it was that seeds were planted and crops were harvested, but soon with a difference. For its duration, war was the defining setting for all aspects of farm life and agriculture. Fewer familiar hands worked the fields. Market changes and machine usage already under way intensified. War-specific production invited opportunism. Contrasting political and economic identities stressed all social relations. Caution and weariness pervaded. For the duration.[5]

It is not just commonplace to observe that no one expected a prolonged conflict. Even less did anyone anticipate the first "modern" war. Within the early weeks, county residents organized several volunteer companies, some as Riflemen intended for action and others as Home Guards while the first groups were away. A lawyer named William Baldwin led one company. Attached to the 2nd Ohio Infantry, it saw little action other than in the digging of trenches. Among the county's early volunteers was John Henry James, son of Colonel John H. James. The younger James, while serving as Adjutant to Urbana's Colonel Edward Fyffe and nearly dying from the lack of hygiene and medicine in army camp life, was personal witness to the noncombat debilitations of ineptitude in the Union army's initial command structure.[6]

However boring and demeaning military experience was for the volunteers, their families back home cautiously followed through the agricultural cycle with essentially no difference in routine. Acreage planted to all the usual cereal grains was down slightly in 1861, a statistic that indicated little other than a pause in the expansions of the previous decade. "A Farmer," writing in May, saw no pressing farm labor scarcity "at present." Oddly incongruous only retrospectively were the regular weekly notices in the *Citizen* for land available in Iowa and Missouri. Notices of farm land for sale closer to home showed ownership transitions in Concord and Johnson Townships, but this also seemed unrelated to the war. Other expectation that the conflict would be brief and the outcome certain was in the July newspaper notice that a certain Captain Smith was purchasing horses for the Army. "Those having horses to dispose of for the cash" were advised to act immediately, "as the capture of so many of the rebel horses in Virginia during the past week, may soon render the purchase of animals for our army unnecessary." Although Ohio farmers—so it was reported at the time—evinced complacency about the significance of the war for agriculture, a sympathetic assessment might note that the farmers were doing precisely what they needed to do. The greatest agricultural worry in 1861 was the unusually cold spring.[7]

Among the earliest farm-related repercussions of the war was an issue of propriety. Should custom be followed and should an annual fair be held during this time of rebellion and war? The agricultural press urged farmers and their counties: "do not give up the fairs." The Ohio State Board of Agriculture and Champaign County's Agricultural Society did not "give up." In September of 1861, the State Fair was held in Dayton, and once again, Champaign County horse entries took several premiums. During the first four days of October, Champaign's own annual fair was held as usual. Inducement to attend and exhibit was the business-as-usual railroad announcement that "The C., P. & Ia. Railroad will carry passengers, at half fare from all stations between Milford and Conover, to Urbana, and return during Champaign County Fair." While the always capricious factor of weather was favorable, "The attendance was not so large as the year previous, but much better than was anticipated." Following the fair, the Society and the County Commissioners made equal financial contributions to fit the grounds as a training facility for the 66th Ohio Volunteer Infantry.[8]

As 1861 became 1862, and as neither the North nor the South crumbled, the nature of the national conflict changed, evident in recruiting and organizing military personnel. Institution of township enlistment/ draft quota expectations gave new intensity to the ever-present competitive spirit within the county. Volunteers could choose from among a variety of units, and a handful of men chose to leave Ohio and serve the Confederacy. Overall, the 66th Ohio Volunteer Infantry became the county's "own" unit and may have accounted for the majority of county participants in the war. Just as in other volunteer units formed during the early years of the war, the organizing officers tended disproportionately to be propertied and professional men from the towns while the soldier volunteers were younger and mostly unmarried laborers.[9]

The agricultural consequence seemed so obvious to so many. An editorial from *Farmer and Gardener*, reprinted in the *Citizen* in November of 1862, surmised that "under the draft which has been ordered by the President, it will be more than ordinary difficult to procure hands to cultivate as much land as usual." Therefore, "Let those who have hitherto relied on hand labor now look to machinery." The national data seemed to show that overall farm productivity was up, as was the manufacture, sale, and use of many new farm implements, while the farm labor force was down. Blurring two quite different issues, the connections seemed natural, even causal. A look at wartime Champaign County reveals a much more ambiguous situation.[10]

Was Champaign County's overall labor pool constrained by the war? The answer is unavoidably affirmative. As of September 1862, Champaign County reportedly had a total of 4,112 men of military age. There is no clear record of how many county residents served, or tried to serve, or served several times under different names, or served not at all. There is some greater certainty that the county lost 578 men over the course of the war, a death casualty rate slightly higher than the rate of about 10% for the North overall. Because of the pattern of vesting farm ownership and decision-making in males who tended to be at the upper end of, if not over, the optimum military age of service, farm management probably sustained less direct impact than did farm morale. The greater impact only became apparent when death or age-related retirement within the property-owning generation occasioned a transition of responsibilities. Adhering to custom was not always possible during war. Long-time Agricultural Society activist S. G. Brecount was elected President of the Society for 1862, only to resign after two months "on account of ill health." A year later, Brecount gave newspaper notice that he wanted to "hire a good, sober, industrious hand, to whom good wages and constant employment will be given." Such public notice was atypical, suggesting a smaller and/or more stressed pool of labor than prior to the war.[11]

The Brecount notice hinted a further demographic condition. While certainly there were normal intergenerational changes in farm ownership and management, probably very few persons took up independent farming during the war years. The imprecise record of transitions represented in farm sale notices published in the *Citizen* suggests four patterns. One, the number of farms offered for sale at any given time was not much smaller during the war years than during the prewar decade. Estate, probate, guardian and sheriff's sales were constrained by court-ordered timeliness, and settlements appear to have been transacted accordingly. By contrast, the majority of the sales notices for unencumbered farms were posted by agents, usually without naming the titular owners. Repeated publication of such notices over several months implied that sales were slow.

Two, over the period of war years, more than a handful of well-established farms were offered for sale by estate administrators who carried the same surnames as the deceased farm owners. The legal notices sometimes specified dower or claims to proportionate shares by sibling heirs but context and phrasing also suggest that some of those well-established farms were passing out of family ownership. In such instances, the presumption must include the death or disability or disinterest of the maturing generation, due at least in part to war conditions.[12]

Three, private land sales seem to have been most active in two extremes of size and value. More evident than in the 1850s, small farms—those with fewer than a couple of dozen acres under cultivation—were available in the corners of the county as well as in the immediate vicinity of Urbana. The corner sites were marginal in their profit potential while being attractive for their relative independence. The near-town sites could support specialty enterprises in fruit, vegetables, and dairy, and were speculative investments in the future expansion of the town. At the other end of operating scale were midsize and larger farms with roughly two hundred or more cultivated acres and which sold at newsworthy prices. In 1863, Urbana's David Barnett purchased William Clarke's Salem Township farm of 270 acres for $60 per acre, land that Clarke had purchased a dozen years earlier for $25 per acre. As noted in the *Citizen*, however, the most attention-getting transactions involved noncounty investors. Thus, barely a year after purchasing the Clarke farm, Barnett sold it to a Cincinnati investor for a reported $90 per acre. Just as elsewhere in the nation, premium productive farm land was appreciating in value, probably both because of and in spite of the war, and was attractive locally and beyond.[13]

New nonresident investors would have had to employ resident managers/renters and to hire most of their farm labor. How did they manage? The silence in the public record suggests the fourth pattern, that virtually all management/employment arrangements were handled privately through established personal networks and that, just as in the recent past, the bulk of county farms were operated by their owners or by persons related to the owners by descent or marriage or by very long-term arrangement. Late in 1863, when farm tenant William M. Swimley decided to retire, his extensive public sale demonstrated that considerable investment in work animals and harvest implements was possible and practical within a matured relationship between tenant and owner. The strength of such personal networks, and probably also their very closed nature, is implied in a contrasting and atypical anonymous 1864 newspaper notice stating that "A practical farmer wishes to rent a farm of 150 acres, or thereabouts, for a term of one or more years, either on a cash or grain rent." Only slightly more frequent during the war years were the few notices to appear in the *Citizen* seeking to hire a "Farm Hand," or in a single instance, a boy aged twelve to sixteen to do chores on a farm.[14]

Was there a war-related farm labor shortage in Champaign County? Probably. One scholar has estimated that at any given time during the war, about one-fifth of Ohio's farm workers were in military service. Labor meant adult males. The consequence was implied by a correspondent from Salem Township who suspected in 1863 that while "there will be a fair average crop of wheat," there seemed not "so great a breadth of land sown as usual." In 1864, a correspondent from Concord Township reported more definitely that the scarcity of labor resulting from "the call of our Independent companies" had indeed "reduced the number of acres of corn." However, "in some instances, where every hand was taken from the farm, our patriotic women have come forth, and assumed the garb of farmers." Mostly unacknowledged, women and children did what they could to offset the absence of young adult males.[15]

Was the county's farm labor shortage offset by increased use of "labor-saving" machinery? Probably somewhat. Was the wartime-increased use of machinery different either in degree or in kind from the trends already established in the 1850s? Probably not. According to State Board Secretary Klippart in 1862, Ohio's farmers were buying all varieties of horse-drawn implements. Allegedly most in demand were mowing and reaping machines and horse-drawn hay-rakes. Threshing machines also seemed to be selling very well. Supporting evidence specifically from Champaign County is meager and contrary. Inventory lists accompanying farm estate sale notices showed slight difference from similar notices in the 1850s. Plows and harrows were more apparent, as was the occasional hay rake, while grain drills, mowers, and reapers were no more frequently listed than they were before the war. A more suggestive measure of implement sales was the commercial advertising content in the *Citizen*. During the prewar years, harvesting and threshing machines made in the Miami Valley and elsewhere were competitively displayed with two- and three-column illustrations nearly every week. Beginning about mid-1861, that display dropped away to almost nothing. The most prominently featured agricultural advertisements in the *Citizen* in 1863 were for steel plows made by rival Urbana blacksmiths. The one new horse-drawn implement promoted with illustration was "The Empire Horse Pitch Fork," manufactured in Urbana under the auspices of L. D. Cook. For other needs, Champaign County farmers, as in the past, had ready access to multiple suppliers but the relevant information was understated. The ads of hardware and dry goods merchants merely mentioned agricultural tools. Such advertising presumed familiarity and was less about an agent or an implement's usefulness than about the war condition of fiscal uncertainty. Major capital investment, such as in new steam engines to power threshing machines, was out of reach for the average farmer. Used equipment, such as "a five horse power engine in good running order," could be managed, and other implements, such as a not-too-expensive grain drill, were widely adopted.[16]

If the question is the extent to which Champaign County farmers intensified their use of "labor-saving machinery" during the war years, the direct evidence from the annual county fair would also seem to be negative. The summary account of the 1862 event was "Weather favorable; attendance large, though not equal to the previous year. The exhibition, in most of the departments, compared favorably with former years; deficiencies were noticeable in the show of implements, mechanical products, vegetables, and fine arts." Much the same diminished interest in new machinery carried through the fairs of 1863 and 1864. The parallel limited record of exhibits and awards at the 1862 State Fair suggests considerable risk aversion on the part of Ohio's farmers. What mattered were innovations designed to improve existing practice with minimal disruption rather than to invite venture into new technique.[17]

It was in a minor noteworthy manner, therefore, that Champaign County was specifically included in the State Board of Agriculture's 1862 *Annual Report* in the observation that "all the [Ohio] establishments engaged in the manufacture of agricultural implements" were working to full capacity and still not meeting customer demand. Listed among the manufacturers located variously in Hamilton, Dayton, Springfield, Piqua, Columbus, Zanesville, Mt. Vernon, Canton, "and others," was "an establishment in Urbana." Unnamed, the establishment may have been Minturn & Co., still insisting that "A Reaper or Mower can be had of us for less money, and on better terms than any other manufacturer." The Minturn claim probably reflected an inventory of previously made machines. If not Minturn & Co., the unnamed establishment may have been the Mechanics' Union Manufacturing Co., formed in July of 1861 by former employees of the Urbana Machine Manufacturing Company, and disappearing from public record almost immediately. Despite the imprecision, the inclusion of Urbana in the 1862 listing was significant for what it indicated of Champaign County's location at the edge of the Miami Valley and the recent expansion of manufacturing throughout the Miami Valley. Hamilton, Dayton, and Springfield in 1860 accounted for 45% of Ohio's total industrial production, and that capacity was now serving both agriculture and the war effort. In 1863, Benjamin H. Warder of Springfield's Lagonda Agricultural Works announced in several Urbana newspaper notices that he wanted to hire mechanics as well as others "to work on government wagons." Overtly war-related, Springfield's implement manufacturing was minimally related to the demands of Champaign farmers in the present. In the near future that would change decisively.[18]

Through the uncertainty of a wartime economy, longer-term transitions in agriculture continued. The strong display of horses in all county fair categories, for example, demonstrated agricultural dependence on horses in multiple ways, both old and new. The rising county horse population of the previous decade peaked at a reported 9,720 horses in 1861 and then dropped back to an unsteady average of about 9,000 through the conflict years. While the war intensified the market for horses and mules, farmers could not sell animals they needed for their work. What developed was a temporary new attention to mules and to the distinction between animals retained for work and animals as commodity. The official high count of 413 mules in 1863, up from 211 two years earlier, dropped again to 236 in 1865 and suggests strongly that the mules were raised specifically for the military market. For all serious tasks at home, whether work or pleasure, mules could not substitute for horses. At each of the regular war-time fairs, breeder pride was evident in draft and work horses, just as each fair's ending show of roadsters confirmed an equally prideful interest in fast horses. Patriotism and practicality could intermix. Six weeks before the 1862 county fair, the grounds were the scene of a horse fair. All of the agricultural and commercial aspects of horse culture were on display, as was also the gesture that net proceeds were contributed to the Soldier's Relief Fund. When the war did end and when the Quartermaster offered for sale twelve thousand horses and fourteen thousand mules, county farmers made no change in their wartime horse stewardship, and the county horse population changed little.[19]

Just as the county's near-steady horse population was consistent with a temporary pause in acquiring/displaying new or additional horse-drawn machinery, so did it fit with crop statistics. Acreage in hay dropped slightly, from just under fourteen thousand acres in 1861 to just over thirteen thousand acres in 1865. Some market for hay was to be found with the military, the only plausible war-time interpretation of the Mosgrove & Wiley effort to purchase five hundred tons of hay in late 1863 and again in 1864. Acreage in oats during the same period was more volatile, dropping from 7,376 acres in 1861 to a low of 5,693 acres the next year, after which the acreage increased again to 8,452 in 1865. In 1862 for the second year in a row, this time "in consequence of a wet spring and dry summer," all cereal grains except wheat produced below-average yields.[20]

While total acreage under cultivation increased in the Northern states, agricultural productivity increased at a lower rate. The reason seems to have been market uncertainties. Loss of Southern markets as well as of some Northern domestic markets was unevenly compensated by increased military demands. The effect of new or expanded markets in Europe was even less consistent. Within Champaign County, market prices for grains and flour dropped from their 1859 and 1860 levels, and through both 1861 and 1862 did not yet show the increases evident later in the war. In July of 1862 the *Citizen* noted that "Our farmers will be glad to learn that Breadstuffs are advancing, in consequence of favorable advices from Europe. We hope it may be permanent," though it turned out not to be. In October of 1862, wheat was holding fairly steady in Urbana, but other grains, especially corn, were selling for sometimes half the price they commanded before the war. Overall, some efficiencies were accomplished in the re-allocation of agricultural resources, offset by some shortsighted and wasteful speculations. The wool interest was one, to be discussed below. As the war dragged beyond its second year, the financial outlook was not likely to have been very clear. Among the few constants were the regular and prominent weekly advertisements placed by Urbana's rival carriage makers.[21]

War-related uncertainty may be the best explanation for a very different kind of agricultural concern, again involving the Agricultural Society. Rancor expressed in the newspaper about the appearance of partiality in the award of fair premiums stimulated an 1862 plan to revise the society's constitution. Then, barely a week before the meeting announced to consider the new constitution, the society board endangered the prospect of new social accord by making an *ad hoc* appointment to fill an unexpected vacancy in the role of president. The procedures rankled some members. Surfacing uncomfortably were the financial repercussions. For whatever reason, the society was short of operating funds and had to borrow $600 to prepare for the 1862 Fair. At the end of the year the managers were satisfied to report that "Notwithstanding the excited state of the country," the interest of those in attendance had allayed any doubts about the "usefulness" of the fair. Nevertheless, the numbers were disturbing. Enhanced by the inclusion of a militia drill competition, participation in the 1863 fair was satisfactory enough, but the total of 1,347 entries was down 15% from two years earlier. More seriously disturbing was the drop in society membership, down at the end of the year by over a third from the membership of two years earlier. The society was in trouble.[22]

Society leadership was fluctuating considerably and may have been difficult to recruit. Through at least one of the war years, no Adams

Township representative sat on the board. In both the 1862 and 1863 elections, the managers turned over by 75%, and in each of the next two years by 50%. Newton Harr retained the presidential position by re-election through the remainder of the war years, but the positions of vice president and of treasurer were occupied by different persons each year. The only persons common to the leadership rosters of 1861 and 1865 were John T. Zombro and John Russell, who traded with each other the secretary position and the position representing the town of Urbana. Zombro's role as the county auditor probably enhanced his service in either capacity.

The worst year financially was 1864, true for both the Ohio State Fair and the Champaign County Fair. Champaign County's special contributing problem was the wet weather that diminished attendance. The opinion of one observer was that receipts would pay the premium list and all expenses, if handled "judiciously." That was exactly the difficulty. A year later, the tone of the society's annual retrospective was decidedly blunt: "When the present Board was elected and came into office [in January 1865], they found not only the treasury empty, but the Society [still] in debt about $600." The board therefore initiated a vigorous campaign "to elevate the interests of agriculture, and stimulate the people to take an active interest in the Fair." One action was an uncharacteristic full-column advertisement in the *Citizen*, promoting the 1865 fair's location and accommodations, the quality of the trotting horse competitions on a daily schedule, and the occasion for reunion in peace. All understood that the "reunion" was to be different from any in the past, as the term itself took on an emotional potency peculiar to that year. All also understood the county's social structure as defined elsewhere in the same promotional column: "Any white person 21 years of age, and a resident of the county, may become a member of the Society by paying One Dollar into the Treasury, and will be privileged to enter as many articles for premiums, as he or the minor members of the family may own." This was not the generation to take on the racial and gender implications of practical agriculture. That would come later. For now, the board's campaign resulted in "a grand success." Even the weather cooperated. About thirteen hundred paid memberships were accompanied by about fifteen hundred fair entries. All current expenses and award premiums were paid, and some progress was made in addressing the society's debt. A longer than usual annual report was self-congratulatory in concluding that "at present Champaign is, without a doubt, awake to the interests of agriculture."[23]

Had there been malfeasance, incompetence, poor judgment, bad luck, lethargy, insensitivity, lack of transparency, inadequate communication, shortsighted optimism, or just war weariness and any combination of the other possibilities? The 1865 leadership gave remarkably little credit to the obvious, that the war was over. Perhaps it still felt very close, for in the month following the fair, the grounds once again became a military encampment, this time for the 4th Regiment, Ohio National Guards. The public record only indicates that Champaign County was among the scant majority of Ohio counties to sustain an annual agricultural fair through the duration of the war. It survived (barely) and it rebounded (not completely in the short term), as did the State Fair the same year.[24]

Through those same fiscally and emotionally volatile years, the county also experienced a special war-related caprice in its livestock interest. Pride notwithstanding, livestock numbers paralleled those of the entire state of Ohio. All either declined or, as in the case of horses and mules, varied around a steady average—all, that is, except sheep. The sheep population of both Champaign County and the State of Ohio nearly doubled between 1861 and 1865, from 35,000 to 65,000 animals in the county and from nearly 4 million to 6.3 million statewide. Commercial interest in wool was up. Even mutton had become a factor in making sheep "a source of sure, profitable income," for mutton prices rose faster than did wool prices and averaged somewhat higher than did either beef or pork for the duration of the war.[25]

The numbers actually tell two different stories. The specific need for military uniforms and blankets created a demand for the coarser wools typically produced west of the Alleghenies. Most of the increased sheep numbers in Ohio were in those counties already having some wool expertise and some wool market connections, and within those areas, there was a war-related sheep "craze." Sheep seemed a sure thing. Not only was the price of wool higher than it had ever been. Satisfying the military demand for wool was a form of patriotism.[26]

Not considered in this thinking was the generous world supply of wool. The gold price for wool was not rising as rapidly as the domestic currency price for wool, and further inflating domestic prices was a US suspension of specie payments at the end of 1861. The real wool market was precarious. Nevertheless, because wool prices were rising faster than prices for other commodities, farmers may have felt little choice. Comprehensive figures do not exist. Clearly some producers were heavily invested. Wartime auctions and retirement or estate sale notices rarely announced a "few" sheep to complement the few cattle or hogs being sold. If sheep were included at all, they were likely to be the principal or most numerous item of the sale. E. M. Bennett's 1866 sale of six hundred sheep was at the high end. The itemization of the animals offered for sale by Samuel Barnett, Jr., in October of 1864 is more representative: six head of horses, two milk cows, seven head of young cattle, three breeding sows, thirteen pigs, and eighty-four head of sheep. Otherwise, sheep were absent from the common public sales.[27]

When peace returned, the market adjustment was brief and severe. In expectation of an ending of the Southern cotton "famine," and anticipating a protective tariff to take effect in 1867, domestic distributors imported large quantities of woolen goods. In addition, the Army released for sale its no-longer-needed inventory of woolens. Wool prices dropped from a high of ninety to ninety-five cents per pound in 1864 to forty-five to fifty-five cents the next year. Wool production actually peaked in 1868, lagging one season behind another significant price drop. While the Champaign County Fair in 1868 included a "very large" show of "fine wooled Sheep," the county's reports to the State Board of Agriculture noted "a tendency to breed large, coarse-wooled or longwooled sheep." Such sheep were "better adapted for feeding and shipping, while there is but a slight difference in the price of wool, at least not enough to justify the breeding of fine wools for that alone." The following year, the sheep pens at the county fair "were very poorly patronized." With prices for beef and pork rising and prices for mutton falling, sheep raisers throughout Ohio again had few options. The county's 1869 Tax Assessor report moved the *Citizen*'s editor to observe, "The slaughter of Sheep last year must have been enormous."[28]

Apart from the war-related woolen craze, most Champaign County farmers, like most other Ohio farmers, continued to engage in general farming. It was the life they knew. With few surprises, the annual summary descriptions submitted to the State Board of Agriculture during the war years echoed the reports of Samuel Keener of fifteen years earlier and together make a litany on behalf of diversified farming: "The principal crops raised in this county are wheat, corn, rye, oats, barley, buckwheat, and potatoes." "The principal crops raised in the county are wheat, corn, rye, oats and potatoes." "The principal crops raised in this county are wheat, corn, rye, oats, barley, buckwheat, and potatoes." "The principal crops raised in the county the last year were wheat, corn, barley, rye, oats, buckwheat, potatoes, and Chinese sugar cane." Only the last item mentioned was at all exceptional. Sorghum, or sorgo as it was more commonly called when introduced in 1855, was a faddish attempt to find a source for sugar and molasses not dependent on foreign importation or Southern cane. State conventions offered information and some encouragement in the form of premium awards; local hardware and implement dealers offered a diversity of processing mills and juice evaporators; and farmers competed with their successes at the county fair. Despite the attempts to exploit the war-related high prices for all sugars, the enterprise proved not cost-effective. No more successful, war-related or not, was a small effort to grow flax for its fibers. What did develop was a new awareness of possible uses for, and the commercial potential for, the oil in flax seed.[29]

In short, the crops grown in Champaign County through the war years were as typically diversified as they were familiar. Corn and wheat dominated although not at their previously high levels. The corn acreage sustained the greater decrease—from forty thousand acres in 1860 to thirty-one thousand acres in 1865—which some contemporaries attributed to loss of Southern markets. Average wheat acreage was much steadier even in decline, for unlike some of the other wheat growing regions in Ohio, Champaign County did not greatly increase its wheat acreage in the early years of the war and neither did it experience a sharp decline immediately following the war. Corn eventually returned to its prewar status in the rural economy but wheat did not. Instead, wheat in the fields served much as did horses at the various fairs; it was a visual assurant of well-being. The feel of handling bushels of grain at harvest and the weather that enhanced or hindered the same mattered almost as much as eventual prices. More numerically apparent was a shifting of some wheat acreage into oats, another indicator of the importance of horses. Directly taking the market place of some wheat was the county's small acreage in barley, which climbed to an acreage figure of fourteen hundred in 1865. This was not a large portion of the county's grain acreage but in the way it paralleled barley acreage statewide, it does indicate market sensitivities. Beer consumption within the state increased sixteen-fold between 1860 and 1865. Immediately following the war, barley acreage peaked both locally and statewide and then dropped back considerably—by about a third.[30]

The overview evidence suggests that the people of Champaign County experienced the final war year as filled with cumulating small stresses and much war-weariness. Attention to many routine matters was distracted, and long-range planning was difficult. Then, with peace in sight at the beginning of 1865, a new world could once again be imagined. It was a different world, in part because two event clusters of the Civil War years had ambiguous short-term effects but decidedly significant long-term consequences. One was the series of Congressional actions changing the relationship between the Federal government and the nation's farmers. The other was the continuing development of the railroads and the ways they related to each other and to the nation they purportedly all served. Both of these event clusters are mentioned here only briefly.[31]

The year 1862 saw four major agriculture-related actions in Congress. Their combined effect made the central war years retrospectively pivotal. Most popularly known, the Homestead Act provided for the disposal of public lands to the presumed advantage of deserving yeoman farmers but was without much direct relevance to the landed shape of Champaign County. What it did provide was a convenient and culturally consonant explanation for the late-nineteenth-century decline in county population, regardless of the extent anyone went "West" to "homestead." More measurably consequential was the railroad legislation, particularly the first Pacific Railroad Act with its generous (or otherwise described) largesse of public lands as encouragement for the building of rail lines to the Pacific. Longer-distance through-traffic was proving profitable, and the next generations of Champaign County agriculturalists farmed in a context in which the nation's farm lands most aggressively served by the railroads were to the west of Ohio. Similarly drawing on the public lands for its financing, the Morrill Act had a central motivation simultaneously to nurture and to reform America's farmers by teaching them better agricultural science. Powerfully protean of possibilities and risk, the goal was not in itself new. Government, however, was inaugurating a new kind of role in relation to agriculture, most portentously true with the fourth Congressional action, the establishment of a US Department of Agriculture.[32]

Experienced as near as a township road crossing, meanwhile, railroads were continuing to expand. So it was that the railroad became the image through which so many Champaign County residents saw the end of the Civil War. News of General Lee's surrender (9 April 1865) was celebrated on 14 April with jubilance. The climactic "Burial Procession of the Confederacy" then became instantly and sadly ironic the following day with news of the assassination of President Lincoln. The special funeral train bearing the president's body left Washington on 21 April and slowly made its way through the heartland to Springfield, Illinois, on a truly national system. Fleetingly brief stops in Woodstock, Cable, and St. Paris were exceeded only slightly by the fifteen-minute pause in Urbana during the night of 22 April. The late hour was no deterrent to homage, nor was the symbolic import lost on anyone. The railroad had come into its majority, and with the violent death of this president, life for everyone in the nation was going to be different from what it had been.[33]

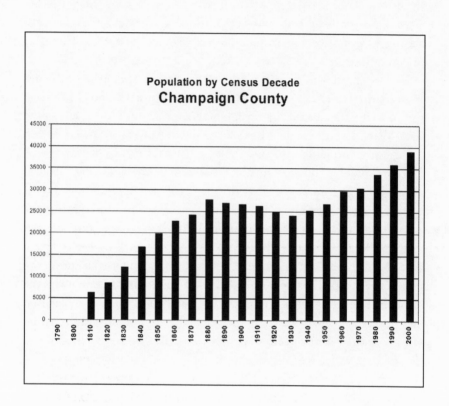

Population by Census Decade
Champaign County

18.

Distant Fields

The decades immediately following the Civil War proved to be a time of transition for agriculture along the Mad River, although what changed was less within Champaign County than within the nation at large and even beyond. Farmers and their advocates knew that the nation's agriculture was related to the expansion of railroad networks in both Europe and North America, completion of the Suez Canal, and escalating use of the steamship worldwide. At ground level in midcontinent America, in places such as rural Ohio where oceans and steamships existed only in newspapers and schoolbooks, however, the new world demanding accommodation was most simply perceived in terms of the nation's railroads. That remained a truth through the end of the century. Brief accounts of the themes considered in this study give witness.[1]

In the nation's centennial year of 1876, total railroad track mileage in Ohio was 4,461, a dramatic increase by one-third from the 3,331 track miles in the state only ten years earlier, but hardly as dramatic as the more than doubling or tripling in Illinois and Minnesota and other western states during the same period. While distant consolidation movements were being watched "with more than ordinary interest," the *Citizen*'s editor gave no hint that the outcomes would be anything but favorable for Urbana. Whether similar benefits would accrue throughout the entire county was less presumptively obvious. Contemporary logic was that with the railroad as anchor and occasion, a hamlet or village would develop as an agricultural service center.[2]

As one instance among several, an attempt to link Urbana through Mutual and Mechanicsburg to Columbus involved a narrow-gauge railroad named The Columbus & Northwestern Railway Company. Here was explicit promise of local economic development, clearly evident in disagreements regarding the proposed route through Concord Township. Here, too, could be a little fun as "Specs, Jr." gently lampooned the citizens of Millerstown for "putting on airs" in anticipation of the railroad passing through their hamlet. Here, so it seemed, was a community in control of its own future, even if enthusiasm for stock subscription was lacking. After three years of public meetings, subscription promotions, and survey work, one of the parties to the construction contract defaulted. Rumors and hopes blurred the facts as to whether there was still viable investor backing for the Chicago-based management. Only the timing was a surprise in the July 1882 announcement that the uncompleted railway had been placed in receivership. The words of a *Citizen* editor captured more than sentiment: "In these latter days as soon as the people build a railroad, it passes out of their hands and control." The hindsight inference is compelling that for the residents of the county's smallest villages, the railroads of post-Civil War America turned out mostly to be a failed promise.[3]

That may miss another truth. For the farmers who lived away from the hamlets and villages, connections to trunk-line rail service were steadily improving. Only as an enhanced national perspective evolved was it evident that the railroad had placed those same farmer-producers in increasingly specialized agricultural regions. In that new setting, realizing the promise of success required adaptation. To the extent that contemporaries saw it that way, usually they saw it positively. By tradition, their farming was diversified. As they neared the twentieth century, the choices were different, and some were quite new. Still they managed mostly to affirm their tradition.[4]

As in the past, the interests and sentiments of Champaign County's diversified farming were most consistently and publicly expressed in the displays at the annual county fair, especially in the exhibits of livestock. Invariably first within the First Department were the several categories of horses. While possibly "disproportionate," the attention given to horses was widely supported. It was certainly central to the scheme of values urged by "Scioto": "a Fair without Horses would simply be no Fair at all.— Horses are as essential to the success of a Fair, as the Ladies. We could not dispense with either class and have a respectable Fair." By all the same standards, cattle were more staid, holding a steady second place both in fair category listings and in fair visitor appeal. Just as with horses, quality and breeding of cattle were of discussable interest, and just as similarly, centered on multipurpose animals. In ways different from the county's multidimensioned horse dependency, however, cattle more narrowly reflected changes in the economy. That was also true of sheep and swine.[5]

The county cattle population peaked just before the Civil War and then dropped during the war by a third, twice the decline documented for the rest of Ohio. For the next decade and a half, just as in previous decades, the presumed and favored breed was the versatile Shorthorn. Apart from a few Alderney, county fair cattle competition during the 1860s and 1870s was among the good and the better Shorthorn. Away from the fairs, dealings in cattle did not specify breed unless the breed was other than Shorthorn, and the exceptions emphasized purity distinctions. The highly visible county advocates of the Alderney, Ayrshire, or Jersey breeds were hardly typical general farmers. Banker, real estate promoter, and agricultural innovator J. B. Armstrong was among the few who made a significant investment in Alderney. Equally atypical was A. C. Jennings and his Nutwood Farm with its locally famous round brick barn located just west of the State Road leading north out of Urbana. Jennings had built the barn originally to house his thoroughbred trotters; its idiosyncratically efficient use now was to house Jersey dairy cattle.[6]

With improvements in transportation and refrigeration over several decades, commercial dairy would become a principal reason for increasing breed diversity in the county's cattle stock. Until that happened, the typical general farmer's herd included two or three and rarely more than four "milch" cows, serving household needs and providing some income from sale of cheese and butter. This was women's work. Production expectations were modest, and the producing animals were not usually noteworthy. Similarly on every farm, the mundane management of poultry and eggs, like that of butter, was women's work, and where it was not the principal farm enterprise, men treated it dismissively. That attitude was a mistake, wrote Salem's S. E. Morgan, because the butter and egg account was "an important one." The evidence was straightforward and newsworthy. In 1873, O. H. Barber, an Urbana grocer, paid out "to farmers' wives" about $11,000 for butter. The scale of butter transactions was rising. Innovations in refrigerated rail transport were creating a new industry.[7]

Through the severe market adjustments of the late 1860s, meanwhile, the typical general farmer stopped raising sheep. In 1870, Ohio still held first place in wool production but as the industry recovered from the war, it resumed its shift into the western half of the country. A minority of county farmers stayed in the business, monitoring the international wool market for trend information, and showing their better animals and their wool products at Fair time. A portion of the annual clip continued to be processed within the county, and both the woolen factory of Henry Fox & Co. of Urbana and the Mechanicsburg facility of Ephraim Stuart were rebuilt and competitively remodeled. In 1877, the *Citizen*'s Fair reporter could allege strong renewed interest in sheep for both wool and feeding. Also renewed was the impulse for competitive braggadocio about weight of fleece, and always more important than any intracounty processing was the purchase of wool for shipment to the "east."[8]

Despite a pervasive "higher standard" in the display of longwools, the numbers suggest a difference between profit and pride. In the official inventory of stock reported for 1873, the County's reported hog number was smaller than the number for sheep. Even so, at the county fair for that year, three pigs were entered for every one sheep (ninety-five and thirty-two entries respectively). Within three more years, and in parallel with increased hog numbers throughout Ohio, the number of county hogs exceeded the number of county sheep by one thousand. No one would have said about sheep even humorously what a newspaper reporter wrote about E. M. Morgan's Poland-China pigs in 1872: "They are worth looking at, as they show how handsome even pigs may become." This was tradition and more, for hogs were often both reason and excuse for competition. Most clearly in demand were Poland-China and the slightly smaller Berkshire breeds. The purity advocates were partial to Berkshire, but it was hard to argue with the numbers thrown out in challenge by those raising "fat hogs."[9]

Within that male commercial world of pork and beef, the post-war railroad presence initially took the form of stockyards. Ambitiously in Urbana, where the three principal rail lines serving the county met and intersected each other on the western edges of town, Ross & Bennett—soon Bennett & Blose—constructed yards which by mid-spring of 1869 were in regular use. A Champaign County Live Stock Association was formed and began to hold monthly auctions. The venue was new but the transactions were familiar. Some stock was shipped out of the county. Other stock may have merely changed ownership within the county. With competing facilities in Mechanicsburg, St. Paris, West Liberty, North Lewisburg, and Mingo, Urbana was not necessarily the most convenient exchange site. The Urbana Stockyards maintained a fitful existence for only a couple of decades.[10]

Nevertheless, railroad-related stockyards were evidence of a profound change in the nation's management and marketing of livestock. Cattle previously driven to market on the hoof were carried in railroad cattle cars. Overland droving essentially ceased. The principal exception was the droving of large horses. Over the next two decades, the railroad displaced that custom as well. "Droves" of cattle still arrived by rail into southwestern Ohio. Portions of Union and Goshen Townships continued to be used for grazing, and the monthly cattle sales in Madison County continued to be significant for the trends in prices they evinced. Different from their previous reliance on open-range grazing, most Champaign County farmers now combined pasturage with the cultivation of corn for supplemental feed. A resulting pattern of land use is implied in the Beers observation that as of 1880, the three largest acreages in Union Township were heavily invested in raising stock, while all of the smaller acreages were under "cultivation." A midsize operation, such as the 167 acres of Samuel Barnett, mixed both pasture and cultivation.[11]

Across the Mississippi, the railroad was just beginning to make possible the fabled era of the cowboy and the long cattle drives north from Texas. The new transportation facilities were also reducing the need for all-purpose breeds such as the Shorthorn, but the effect in Champaign County was neither immediate nor direct. Decidedly outsized in significance instead was the gradual solution of technical problems in mobile refrigeration. Rail transport of dressed beef steadily increased.

Somewhere in the middle of the 1870s, usage and meaning of the term *packing* changed. No longer did it refer primarily to the curing of pork provisions in barrels. The relevant phrase became *meat packers* and connoted cattle as well as pigs. A time-capsule view of the many industry-wide changes was in the weekly newspaper market listings. In the late 1850s, both *The Urbana Free Press* and the *Urbana Citizen and Gazette* (probably drawing on a common source) gave hog prices in two forms. One was the price for the live animal. The other was for processed and packed pork, either as *prime* or as *mess*. The beef market quoted prices only for live animals. Through the 1860s, beef cattle were priced according to grade: best, extra, prime, fair to good, poor. Live hogs were similarly graded as prime, fair, common. Pigs were further price discriminated according to whether still-fed or corn-fed, and occasionally by car lots, meaning live shipment by rail. Usually the designated market was New York. If Chicago was mentioned, it was in relation to grain. The term *dressed* began to appear in regard to hogs, while pre-Civil War terms such as *provisions* and *mess* disappeared. Not directly related to either hog or cattle production but parallel in pointing toward the underlying commercial changes after 1870 was the rapid disappearance of whisky in the market reports. By the late 1870s, changes in terminology indicated refinements in grading and greater orientation toward consumer appeal. Cattle were fancy, premium, choice, and good. Some were designated "slaughterers for the English market." Absent from the listings was a restrictive cold weather season.[12]

Through this period—clearly recognized at the time as one of adjustment, experiment, and quiet innovation—overall grain production increased. Crop reports, both narrative and statistical, documented conservative innovations in the familiar while the familiar itself appeared as though printed in boldface. A well-established social rhythm anticipated completion of winter wheat planting by the end of September, and township schools opened for fall and winter on the first of October, closing in time for spring plowing and corn planting. Wheat harvest usually occurred during the first two weeks of July. Hopefully the corn by then was beyond the crucial early cultivating stage, and the timothy grass had come up enough to allow a cutting of hay. Everything was weather-dependent. Wheat acreage fluctuated with the commercial market but on average held nearly constant. Corn acreage gradually increased by about one-third. No longer did Champaign County farmers rely solely on farming practices described in this study as *extensive*. Neither were they very rigorous in practicing *intensive* agriculture, one aspect of which was systematic crop rotation. Perspective mattered. While nationally the price for wheat was unsteadily dropping, the most ready explanations for harvest losses were always bad weather and parasites.[13]

Perspective really did matter. At distances measured in railroad-paced travel, a new "Wheat Belt" was emerging on the northern Great Plains, and the physical geography was only part of the story. The long-familiar culture-complex of winter wheat could not be sustained through the harsher winters and the lower annual precipitation of the unforested plains. What could be sustained were select varieties of spring wheat, prized for their high-quality gluten. They were also harder, with a more brittle shell, and in the milling practice of the day, required higher grinding speeds and more careful bolting to remove small specks of bran that discolored the flour. The challenge was to find better ways to mill spring wheat. Thus developed the "New Process" in 1870 and 1871, soon enhanced by the introduction of the roller-mill and an industry hegemony by Minneapolis. Once the milling technology was in place, a search for better quality hard wheats followed. A further consequence was the significance of scale. Prior to about 1880, smaller commercial mills maintained some price and labor advantages in regional markets. After that date, they were at a decided disadvantage in both price and quality.[14]

Specialized function became a feature in all grain handling, and the Mad River Valley's multi-purposed gristmills and grain warehouses could not compete. For the gristmills serving their very local clientele, two additional factors intensified the problem. One was the increased competition made possible by steadily improved surface roads. The other was a decline of dependability in their motive power. "Improvement" in farming practice had entailed clearing the land's forest cover and draining the seasonal standing water in wetlands areas. Deep plowing, ditching, and tiling further contributed to an unintended decrease of the efficiency of the land as a natural reservoir. In the drier months, the creeks and springs were no longer "never-failing," and farmers were compelled to pump water from wells. S. E. Morgan recorded the visual evidence: "The wind-mill is now

a feature in every landscape in Salem." Still significant in the Beers history
written in 1880, waterpower is described in the present tense. In the Middleton history of 1917, the perspective is past tense. With the decline of
waterpower for gristmills, most of the mills disappeared.[15]

For the common two-story, multipurpose grain warehouses, the
future was competitively presented by the Urbana Steam Elevator. A
wooden structure much like the many rural elevators beginning to rise
above the North American heartland, it combined multiple recently
developed features for operation on a larger scale than any previous
county facility had attempted. Constructed during the late fall and winter
of 1868 on the west side of Urbana at the single most opportune rail connection site in the county, the visible innovation was the shape and height
of the main building, seventy feet at its highest point, and designed exclusively for the storage and transfer of grain and for such closely related tasks
as shelling. Bins for separating grains by variety and quality received grain
from rail cars or farm wagons by a combination of gravity chute and
shovel. From the ground-level bins, the grain moved through troughs on
a rubber belt and then by screw upward into the appropriate storage bin
until transferred by gravity through a chute directed into a rail car or a
farm wagon. Storage capacity was estimated at sixty-eight thousand
bushels. Parallel to the rail track siding along one side of the building was
the wagon access on the opposite side, with appropriate scales on each
side. An engine and boiler house at one end of the structure provided the
steam power to drive all the relevant machinery. Within a few years, three
more "elevators" were operating in Urbana, and others like them were
changing the skyline of the county's rural "stations" as well.[16]

The Urbana Stock Yards and the Urbana Steam Elevator were
unmistakable expressions of far-reaching transformations. Town-centered and inextricably tied to the railroads, the business side of agriculture was redefining the ideological world within which agriculture was
practiced. Most fundamental was the development of forward markets
and the commercial trade in commodities futures. For the farmers, the
implications were enormous. And yet, nothing *they* did had brought on
any of this. The question was in how to respond. They were practical
more than they were political, but they also faced fundamental identity
issues. Among their options were to stay on the farm to plant their corn

in the spring and wheat in the fall. Or, they could emigrate to better farming opportunities elsewhere. Or, they could get out of farming.[17]

For those who stayed to farm, adaptation took the form of ever greater use of horse-drawn riding implements. Dating from the mid-1860s and widely adopted by the end of the 1870s, for example, the traditional walking plow gained two or three wheels. The addition of a seat allowed an operator to ride "sulky style"; it also allowed removal of the plow's landside, decreasing the plow's draft resistance and increasing productivity still further. The exaggerated ideal was that if an implement could be pulled by horses, the operator should be riding on it. The advertising appeal was especially direct at harvest time. Practice itself is harder to gauge. Farmers rode their plows and harrows of all kinds, seed drills for virtually all the grains, cultivators, reapers and mowers, hay rakes, and farm wagons of all sizes. Farmers also continued to use nonriding implements for specific efficiencies, and walking plows and cradle reapers were made within the county through the end of the century. Not ridden except when moved from one field to another, were the largest of the implements, the steam-powered threshing machines and their engines.[18]

Tangible and visible, farm machines of all kinds were more numerous, more diverse, and more available than ever previously. They were better, and each in succession was essential. Such was the self-binding harvester. Used on a few farms in Champaign County in 1878, the binder was quickly and widely adopted. Despite the aggressive and wearying commercial advertising, observers affirmed its laborsaving and money-saving features. As T. S. McFarland saw matters in Concord Township, peer pressure and social standing could also underlie decisions. "The crop was generally cut with self-binders," he wrote in 1883, "and the man that raises wheat and has no binder is looked upon as an old fogy." For "Index" in the southwestern corner of the county, the wage-labor effect was direct and obvious: "A few years ago farmers were in town hunting harvest hands, offering high wages, and were often disappointed in getting them. The laborers now go to the farmers and are glad to get work at ordinary wages." Here was a new normal. So also was the sound that A. J. Broyles of Westville was hearing: "the click of the binder."[19]

A cluster of interrelated customs was coalescing into an adjustment in the entire configuration of grain production. For many years, machine threshing of grain had not been newsworthy. Apart from sensational accounts of boiler explosions or cinder-induced fires, usually only the start of threshing season was noted, as were exceptional yields or unusual working conditions such as extreme heat. That changed with the adoption of platform harvesters and then especially with the development of self-binding harvesters. In the fields was a uniform product, sheaves ready to be stacked or shocked and nearly ready to be threshed. Threshing machines and their portable steam engines could be moved into the fields—no longer the farmyard—as soon as the grain was fully ripe and dry, and that is what was happening with new efficiencies and another new familiar sound, "the whistle of the busy thresher."[20]

In some ways it was all very familiar. Only in hindsight, and only with the help of demographers and statisticians did the farmers realize the extent of the changes they were trying to manage, although one dimension began to feel uncomfortably personal. The nation and the state were growing. Champaign County was not. The trend line— upward curves in the population charts for nation and state—was unmistakably different in shape for the county. In very rounded numbers, the population of Champaign County had doubled from just over six thousand in 1810 to about twelve thousand in 1830, and reached nearly twenty thousand by 1850. The early rates of dramatic growth slowed almost as dramatically. The 1860 population of just under twenty-three thousand increased over the next decade by only fifteen hundred. The slowing came finally to a complete stop, recorded as part of the 1880 census when the population officially peaked at 27,817. Then began a population decline that continued until the 1930s.[21]

Which was cause and which was effect? Were new machine efficiencies driving people off the farm, or were the new machines needed to compensate the losses? Or both? Looking back over a lifetime that began in the 1860s, W. J. Knight contended that the self-binder displaced four or more laborers, "some of whom eventually found their way to the towns and factories where the machinery was made." Nearby Springfield was the destination for some of them. Employment in Ohio's other manufacturing towns would not have required removing much farther. The census data show all of Ohio's principal cities growing in size, diversity, and industrial importance. The same census data also show that many Ohioans did leave the state, some to take up agricultural work in nearby Indiana and Illinois, and then in the newer trans-Mississippi states. Less commonly, pass-through migration could still be observed, such as the wagons that rolled through Kingston in 1878. A small portion of the traffic paused, disconcertingly for T. S. McFarland. In-migration from Pennsylvania and Virginia "still continues to flow into Concord," he wrote, "and judging from their appearance, will add materially to the Democratic party." These two dominant patterns—rural-to-urban and state-to-state migrations—were complemented by an equally significant third pattern with special implications for rural identities. Through the entirety of the 1800s, the fertility rate declined among white rural females.[22]

Picking up to join the traffic in its exit from the county was nothing new, and the reasons were almost never articulated in print. In some instances, a sales notice carried a resoluteness inviting speculation. In 1867, William Whisler was determined to sell his Union Township farm "at a sacrifice," stating his intention of "going West so soon as it is disposed of." A Salem Township correspondent in 1870 was more typical in noting merely that "Some [of] our farmers continue to sell out and move, some west and others south." Encouraged by land agents and by enticing railroad "inspection" fares, neighbors were migrating in quite diverse directions, and at varied distances. Wes Eichelberger sold his Salem Township farm to move only as far west as Darke County, Ohio; Joseph Detwiler left the Kennard area in 1870 to go to Tennessee; Thomas Kiger left Adams Township in 1879 to go to the northwest corner of Michigan; and Kirk Taylor and family left the Mechanicsburg area in 1882 for a new home in central Kansas. Even Santa Rosa, California, had its county emigrants and their descendants. Popularly the most virulent and explanatory strain of the migration syndrome was "Kansas fever."[23]

Most of the migration was outward. The settling realization was uncomfortable. Emigration of young farmers in their prime working years, of older farmers with substantial wealth and experience, of extended families or communities with their common history and shared values—all this was felt as loss. Variously expressed, the statements appearing in print combined sadness, resignation, and always generous confidence in the future fortunes of the émigrés. Absent was the sense of finality characteristic of earlier migrations. Ties remained, and could

on occasion be renewed through the convenience of the railroad. Occasionally a young male made good on his promise to come back to wed
and to take his wife to a new home across the Mississippi. Poignant were
the telegram summons to attend to a burial of family members. More
pained were the recognitions that some young adults were leaving the
county out of discouragement with farming or disaffection with the
farming way of life. Every township had its stories.[24]

By circumstance, by opportunity, by choice, those who remained to
farm used more of the land in steadily larger farm sizes. In the brief span
of the census decade 1870–1880, the county's improved acreage increased
by forty thousand acres. Approximately half of the increased acreage was
land not even counted in the 1870 census, indicating a significant degree
of draining and other improvement. T. S. McFarland noted that T. J. B.
Hough had placed "a large amount of drain tile" on his Concord Township farm, "and the old pond which used to produce so many turtles, frogs
and skunk cabbage, is now covered with corn." Nine tile factories in the
county were running at full capacity, selling everything they could make,
with three fourths of the output used within the county. The *Citizen*'s
Addison correspondent expressed puzzlement that more farmers did not
see the obvious cost benefit of ditching relative to the cost of repeated
plowing and reseeding. That did not prevent his neighbors from quarrel-
ling about ditches. Less litigiously, local opinion was also divided on clearing woodlands. One observer in 1883 was seriously disturbed at the pace
of denuding the timbered ridge along the State Road in Salem Township.
The pattern was statewide. More acreage was being improved and more
of that acreage was being tilled, and the costs were variously calculated.[25]

Regardless of farm size, farm residents were all increasingly more
alike than they were different from each other. An increased proportion
of the county population was "native," in two senses. In 1880, 95% of the
county's population had been born in the United States, up one percentage point since the beginning of the Civil War. The bigger change was
in reported state of nativity. In 1870, just over 73% had been born somewhere in Ohio. Ten years later the Ohio-born percentage was just over
78%. That five-point increase, when placed alongside the simultaneous
decrease in number of county residents born in Virginia and Pennsylvania, marks the passing of a generation. Even the second generation of

migrants from the source states was thinning, again by a combination of death and further migration. The result was clear. A declining percentage of the population had experienced life in any environment other than one very much like that of the county, if not always the county itself.[26]

That does not mean a frictionless social interaction. Within the world of late nineteenth-century agriculture, measures of community showed evidence of strain. In view of the many transformations of the sort presented in this study as better machines and fewer farmers, social common ground could be elusive. The very traditional value, that what mattered most was close to home, was hard to maintain when seemingly all the newest dimensions of agriculture pulled the farmers into intellectually distant fields. Custom was challenged by experts, homegrown and other kinds. Personality was a factor. So was political heritage, so was religion, and so most certainly was the economy. Unsurprisingly, farmer interactions with each other briefly found institutional expression in the ideals of the nation's Granger movement.

Throughout the agricultural regions of the United States, the social movement known popularly as the Grange was nearly unmatched in the focus it gave to farm and farmer identity. It was diversely economic, social, political, and moral in its organization and aims, and was as diversely uneven in its successes as in its failures. From little more than a spark of high-minded beginnings in the nation's capital in 1867, the movement found its Ohio tinder in 1872 and then spread like a prairie fire. Champaign County was not spared. A "Farmers' Convention" met near North Lewisburg on a Saturday in August 1873, "for the purpose of forming a Grange, or Club, or some other political organization." A county Grange structure began to take shape. In October, a correspondent to the *Citizen* noted that "a large number of ladies and gentlemen" were initiated into the Grange that month, and the news three weeks later was that Ohio had 150 Granges. When the Harmony Grange was instituted at Kennard in November, the number of Ohio Granges was placed at 220. An unsigned series of promotional articles explaining "The Farmers' Grange" appeared on the front page of the *Citizen* beginning in December, and a flurry of organizational events in December and January resulted in Grange representation in every Champaign Township. Lists of officers of the various (and variously named—Union,

Laurel, Nettle Creek, Fairview, Buckeye, Fern, Pretty Prairie, Terre Haute) Granges are striking for the names of leaders who do not otherwise appear in any public agricultural leadership role. That was especially true of the roles exercised by women. Equally striking in some of the lists was the leadership, if not dominance, of extended families.[27]

Some of the felt need for a new farmer organization arose from disappointment and disagreement with the Agricultural Society. Certainly always in the emotional and economic background was the railroad, the quality and fairness of its services, and the effects of the freight rates it charged for agricultural commodities. Inflammatory newspaper description of those rates as "extortion" made focus on state regulation of railroad activity a serious motivating issue for all Ohio farmers in the planning for Ohio's constitutional convention of 1874. Here was occasion for some critics of the Agricultural Society to fault its lack of political assertiveness. This was hardly a narrowly confined Grange issue, however, and for some of the personalities involved, neither was it recent. For the Republican editor of the Urbana *Citizen*, the state's constitutional convention was conveniently and brashly an opportunity once again to impugn the motives and railroad-compromised integrity of county Democratic leaders, especially General John H. Young. Apart from that convention and the published political rhetoric of a very small number of individual Grangers, no recorded collective political actions of the Grange membership took place within Champaign County. What the newspaper record of Grange activities showed instead was a new confidence in advocating and celebrating the virtues of agricultural life, almost as though the national movement gave permission to express something normally presumed without social notice. A countywide Grange "Pic Nic" in early June 1874 began with farm wagons bearing an estimated five thousand people moving in procession from Urbana's Monument Square to the fairgrounds where a full day of food and speeches impressed all observers for its logistic successes and gracious rural decorum. The day promised much, yet it was probably near the apogee of the movement's rapidly rising curve of expectations within the county. A downward curve was imminent.[28]

By early 1881, the mixed social and educational functions of Granger activities were being pre-empted by the rapid development of Farmers'

Institutes. Under the leadership of State Board Secretary Chamberlain, local committees arranged time and place, county agricultural societies sponsored the events, and faculty from the Ohio State University donated their time to give lectures. Champaign's initial Institute was in May of 1881, promoted jointly by the Agricultural Society and by the Grange. A follow-up meeting organized more enduring arrangements, including a constitution that made every farmer in the county a member. The Institute idea seemed the right combination of features at the right time. The Grange in more limited form did not disappear, but never again did it command the extent or the intensity of the following it briefly rallied. Its importance instead was more nuanced. Arising in response to farmer frustrations with distant changes, the Grange and other farmer movements like it were profoundly conventional in goals and affirmations. However radical in rhetoric and occasional activism, the legacy of the Grange was as witness to shared values closer to home, something that might cautiously be termed common ground.[29]

19.

Common Ground

During the decades following the Civil War, the residents of Champaign County found numerous occasions to pause and to reflect on their states of affairs. Invariably the timing was determined by some event cluster in the larger world beyond the Mad River Valley. The nation's 1876 centennial was one such. Another was a series of Midwestern county histories published by the W. H. Beers company of Chicago. Champaign County's volume was issued in 1881, with much of the preparation completed the previous year under the supervision of John W. Ogden. Essential to the sales potential of the volume was a section of biographical notes developed from contributions by and about county residents who were also the presumptive subscribers. An unsolicited review in the *Citizen* faulted this feature for the seriously imbalanced account that resulted. The overall tone of the volume is positive, bland when not optimistic, restrained in its filiopiety, and unique as a source for much of the information provided. T. S. McFarland was generous in his praise of Ogden's lengthy chapter on the history of the county, finding only one important error in date. The history seemed to document an amazing record of progress without an awareness that "progress" was not even an active term in the lexicon of the county's earliest settlers. Ogden's measures included the Lucifer match, the kerosene lantern, labor-saving farm machinery, a daily newspaper, the palace car, steam and telegraph, and longer life expectancy. The contributors to the Beers volume could not have known how much more life-changing "progress" was still to come within a very short two decades, and the volume stands as a less-than-neutral witness to the state of affairs in 1880.[1]

What the Beers contributors did realize with pain was that memories were passing into the graveyards. The death of highly regarded James Dallas in 1871 at the age of ninety provoked a newspaper tribute with this laconic opening: "Thus another of the old pioneers of the county has passed away." A Pioneer Association gathered up its members' memories, letters, and formal addresses into *The History of Champaign and Logan Counties, from Their First Settlement*, published in 1872. Much of the same material, some verbatim, subsequently appeared in the Beers volume. The sponsoring Association continued to meet with a diminishing membership, surviving by consolidating with other loosely organized Pioneer Clubs from an increasingly wider geography. The gathering in Addison in September 1886 welcomed Champaign, Clark, and Miami counties.[2]

The quarter century following publication of the Beers history brought rural America into what has commonly been described as the Golden Age of Agriculture in the United States. It was, as with all "ages," transitory and yet also peculiarly definitive. The passing of the pioneer generation was complete. All links to the hard times of yesterday were memories shaped by the wonders of modernity. The lives of the ancestors—the pioneers—were the selective measure of a very secure common ground. Certain traits of the pioneers were lauded—their hard work most especially—and at least one trait was totally ignored—their attitudes toward the land.[3]

For the immigrant settlers, land was the reason they came to the Mad River Valley. And, while the land was sometimes lauded, never was it sentimentalized. Toil and sweat were not the stuff of sentiment. The early record is replete with sales and exchanges, consolidations, relocations. The land was a commodity which could even be left behind if something better were available, whether new lands in the "West" or new employment in the cities. Then came a gradual change. The persons who remained on the land began explicitly to associate particular plots with particular ancestors and particular institutions. A later generation would carry this forward with bronze marker plaques for all kinds of

"firsts." Families counted the number of generations they had been resident on their farms. And there was another difference, really a measure
of distance from actually working the land. The *Urbana Daily Citizen*,
from its first issues in 1883, continued to rely on township correspondents,
but their very local details were mostly demographic minutiae. Absent
was news of plowing and planting, of seed choice and yield, of monstrous
hogs. That sort of news was no longer the defining public idiom of the
people who lived in Ohio's Mad River Valley.

Or so it seems, unless one happens to visit the annual County Fair.
There one also finds a measure of social common ground, one very different from the tributes in books of county history. The events comprising
the successes of each annual County Fair have depended on an actively
renewed inclusive social consensus. The worrisome question in the 1860s
and 1870s was whether the inclusively named Champaign County Agricultural Society had outlived its time. The founding generation had been
motivated by the reform-minded goal of "improvement" in all matters
agricultural. Integral to the accomplishment of that goal was an annual
exhibition or fair. The postwar generation of leadership was burdened
almost exclusively by operating such an annual fair and maintaining the
grounds. Newer institutions such as the Farmers' Institutes had displaced
some of the Society's other original intended functions. Consequently,
the organization was still the Champaign County Agricultural Society,
but in reality, it was "The Champaign Fair Board," recognized in print as
such for the first time in 1883. Could a renewal of countywide social consensus still be accomplished through the Society and its Fair? This study
concludes with a brief narrative answering that question.[4]

County, district, and state fairs were widely popular in the late 1800s
and equally so they were contentious for the social issues they exposed.
For the Urbana-based Agricultural Society, a special challenge was the
intracounty rival Central Ohio Fair held at Mechanicsburg since 1869,
and briefly beginning in 1881 also the Tri-County Agricultural Society
Fair, held at North Lewisburg. While exhibitors, competitors, and fair-
loving patrons participated in all three venues, the fact of multiple
opportunities was an unwelcome reality check on the presumptive role
of the county's official Fair. The region's fair patronage resources were
not unlimited. Rarely did any two of the county's fairs do well in the

same year, suggesting something of a zero-sum contest for patron loyalty and attendant identity.

The problems began in the recovery years following the Civil War. In Urbana, the newly challenged Agricultural Society paid all of its bills and premiums in 1870. It could not do so in 1871 except by borrowing, and it ended the year in debt. By contrast, the Central Ohio Fair held at Mechanicsburg was acclaimed "a success, not only financially, but in the extent and variety of the exhibition in all its departments." Amid early and fervid preparations for the 1872 Champaign County Fair, therefore, the *Citizen* was candidly desperate in its phrasing: "In truth, the Champaign County Fair is a Champaign county necessity. We need a Fair, we must have a Fair, we will have a Fair, and we will have the best County Fair this season that will be held in the State." Participation numbers did not fulfill the hopes. Undisputed was the *Citizen*'s assessment that "The greatest show of animals was, as is always the case, in horses." More precisely, "The races drew the crowds." And, as if the races were not making enough contrast with neighboring fairs, there was "the Beer Question." Ohioans in 1874 defeated a revised state constitution that included provision for regulating the liquor traffic within the state, ostensibly on grounds that regulating liquor was somehow approving of liquor. Propriety and public image, morality and social control all combined. The board answered the beer question firmly by not allowing "any intoxicating liquors to be sold on the grounds of the Society." Discretion had to come on other issues as the Managers tried to find a socially satisfying solution to popular interest in horse racing and its covert gambling. Newspaper appeals redundantly urged farmers and other "citizens" to remember the main purposes of the Fair. The language was familiar. So was the result. Through the 1870s, "the attendance was not what it should have been," and the exhibitions were "pecuniarily" a failure. The Managers were discouraged that the society would ever be free of debt.[5]

Matters came to focus in 1881: "The question of fair or no fair must be met." When the 1881 board met for its regular meetings in January and February, the Managers made a decision and held firm: no fair in 1881 but also no diminution of board activities. Groping toward a new consensus, the Managers were holding out for something more significant than a few days of agricultural exhibitions. Committees made plans

with the Grange for a Farmers' Institute, and met with County Commissioners about repairs of the fairgrounds. When the annual exhibition
resumed in 1882, success was gratifyingly surprising for what it hinted of
prospects. Success again the next year brought an unsolicited proposal
to change the location of the fairgrounds. A committee of Managers
recommended against the proffered land deal but not against the principle of improvement by expansion of activities and facilities. The con-
versation was open. Fair enthusiasm was generally high. The time seemed
right, and the board petitioned for a tax levy on the ballot of the next
regular April election to purchase and improve new grounds. Register-
ing very longstanding county political fault lines, the levy failed by
several hundred votes. Undeterred, the Managers opted to make do for
another year. Their rigid concern "to banish liquors and gambling devices
from the grounds" was not compromised. New features such as a bicycle
race and a Children's Day were promoted. Premiums were generally
revised upward. This time the overall effect was exactly as the Managers
hoped. Not only was the 1887 Fair itself successful on all the usual measures. The talk about it was direct. "There was never such a universal
sentiment for new Fair Grounds," wrote the *Citizen*'s editor.[6]

Sentiment was very different about the Central Ohio Fair in
Mechanicsburg, and it was faltering. Its horse races were extremely
popular but it had been inconsistent on "The beer question." As a privately held joint stock enterprise, it faced creditor issues which attendance deficiencies intensified, and in 1888 it suspended for one year as
did also the Tri-County Fair. Although annual exhibitions did resume
in Mechanicsburg, the privately owned Association was too financially
precarious to survive a time of national fiscal uncertainty. In January of
1896, the proudly published "Souvenir Edition" of *The Mechanicsburg
News* enthusiastically endorsed the year's announced fair, not knowing
that it would be the last one before the Association liquidated its assets
and ceased to exist.[7]

By contrast, everything in Urbana seemed to cooperate, including
the weather. A Concord correspondent was surprised at the 1888 consequence: "the Champaign county Fair has assumed gigantic proportions,
and to attempt to confine it to its present small limits is ridiculous." To
the editor of the *St. Paris Era-Dispatch*, the need for new fairgrounds was

"plainly and forcibly demonstrated." Over six hundred other persons agreed, signing a petition requesting the County Commissioners to resubmit a levy proposition to the voters. At election time, a simple but clear majority of the voters also agreed. Equally clear in the vote tallies by township was proof that the voters of Champaign County were hardly of one mind.[8]

Despite the abundance of social and political ambiguity, the Managers elected in January of 1889 believed they had a mandate, and they acted quickly, setting the date for the next Fair in full expectation that it would be held on new grounds. Within the week, four sites had been visited. At a special meeting early in March, the Board reviewed the options and agreed to a purchase proposal. The practical worry was the intense and rapid effort required to prepare the new grounds sufficiently enough to be ready for opening day, 20 August. To much general acclaim, they succeeded. *The West Liberty Banner* pronounced the 1889 event as "The greatest Fair ever held in our neighboring county of Champaign." The county's own 1889 annual report to the State Board of Agriculture opened with phrasing sounding suspiciously like a sigh of relief: "The Champaign County Agricultural Society dedicated a long and much needed new fair grounds." It was, of course, "the most successful fair ever held in the county under the auspices of the society."[9]

Of course it was. Precisely in embracing even those who opposed it, it had become the new common ground. And, because what matters most is close to home and to the land, it still is. The future would have its new challenges and its own narratives recounting renewal of the social consensus. For Champaign County and its Mad River Valley, the agriculture of the past has become almost unrecognizable in the agribusiness of today. Except at Fair time. Then the whole county, it seems, finds occasion to visit the fair site first used in 1889, still maintained by the "Champaign County Agricultural Society." There, with relief and satisfaction each year, patrons laud "the most successful fair ever held in the county under the auspices of the society."

Notes

The brief-form references in the notes are keyed to full citations in the bibliography. Because of their frequency, three references are further abbreviated. *AR* together with a named year and page numbers refers to an *Annual Report* of the Ohio State Board of Agriculture. Beers is the *History of Champaign County, Ohio* issued by the Beers Company in 1881. *Citizen* is the weekly *Urbana Citizen and Gazette* for the years 1849–1889. The newspaper did not number its four pages and was inconsistent in ascribing authorship. The presumption is that all unsigned articles, reports, and opinions were those of the "proprietor" who through most of its history was Joshua Saxton.

1. THE LAND

1. Quinn, "The Late Glacial History of the Cedar Bog Area"; Quinn and Goldthwait, "Glacial Geology of Champaign County."

2. Thorne, in Lloyd, Falconer, and Thorne, *The Agriculture of Ohio*, 270.

3. Cutler, *A Topographical Description*, 43. Temperature and rainfall figures are as reported from Urbana for 1854–1870; see *AR* for 1876: 544. In 1876, nearly a century after clearing the land of its forest cover had begun, the ten most abundant timber trees in the county were reported as oak, beech, hickory, black walnut, ash, poplar, cherry, sugar maple, elm, and linn; see *AR* for 1876: 520–21; Bidwell and Falconer, *History of Agriculture*, Chapter 11.

4. Bluntly illustrative of the cultural tradition underlying this understanding in the Mad River Valley are the first sentences of the Publishers' Preface in the 1881 Beers *History of Champaign County*: "Prior to the advent of the white man,

the woodlands and prairies of Champaign County had been the camping-ground of the red warriors, who had full sway over this, one of the finest counties in these United States. Nature's hand had been too lavish in the distribution of natural advantages, to let it remain longer in possession of those who refused, even in the slightest degree, to develop any of her great resources; and, early in the present century, the westward tread of the sturdy pioneer was heard and the might of his arm was felt by the savage" (iii). In the same volume, John W. Ogden conveyed a similar attitude: "Of the history of Champaign County, as associated with the Indian tribes, little need be said" (230). Native American burning of surface vegetation in Champaign County remains poignantly under-documented. On 22 March 2005, in the Q&A following his presentation in the Champaign County Bicentennial Lecture Series, longtime Cedar Bog Nature Preserve Manager Terry Jaworski remarked that he was aware of evidence of burning throughout much of the county. The occasion was not conducive to much specific detail. Whatever Jaworski knew, he did not put in writing, and barely a week following his lecture, he sustained a fatal heart attack.

5. Relevant studies include Hinderaker, *Elusive Empires*; Hinderaker and Mancall, *At the Edge of Empire*; McConnell, *A Country Between*; Richard White, *The Middle Ground*; and the contributions by Callender, Griffin, and Hunter in Trigger, *Handbook*.

6. See especially Hurt, *The Ohio Frontier*, chapter 1.

7. Patrick, "Urbana of Lang Syne," in *Citizen* for 12 May 1881; *AR* for 1876: 504; Henry Howe, *Historical Collections of Ohio*, 81. The myth of "the sturdy pioneer" bringing civilization to tame the wilderness simply did not allow any recognition of Native American horticultural practice as legitimate agriculture. Scholarly documentation otherwise has been steadily increasing. A useful starting point for general inquiry is the set of volumes making up the *Handbook of North American Indians*; see also the first chapter of Hurt, *American Agriculture*. For Ohio's Miami Valley in particular, Hudson, *Making the Corn Belt*, chapters 1 and 2, notes repeatedly how the Native Americans consistently selected the best lands and carefully prepared them for their own culturally appropriate uses.

2. THE PEOPLE AND THEIR CULTURE

1. Owens' place as "first" is not secure. Pierre Dugan's uncertain residential tenure in what became Salem Township may have preceded Owens. The principal source of information is a newspaper article under the title "Dugan Prairie—How It Got Its Name," written by "Jake" and describing the land at

the time—without giving dates—when he "first came to this country"; see *Citizen* for 1 June 1860; and Antrim, *The History of Champaign and Logan Counties*, 6. For the general history, see Chaddock, *Ohio Before 1850*; Downes, *Frontier Ohio*, chapter 3; Goodwin, "The Development of the Miami Country"; Hurt, *The Ohio Frontier*, chapter 6; Perkins, *Border Life*; Rohrbough, "Diversity and Unity"; Swierenga, "The Settlement of the Old Northwest"; and Wilhelm, *The Origin and Distribution*, part 2.

2. Brief death notice for Silas Johnson, in *Citizen* for 3 August 1865; "Moses B. Corwin" tribute, in *Citizen* for 18 April 1872; Beers, 431–32, 441; Ogden, in Beers, 380–81.

3. Flagg, *Pioneer Letters*, 10; "The Fiftieth Anniversary of the First Meeting of the Council of Urbana," in *Citizen* for 22 March 1866; Middleton, *History of Champaign County* 950, 961. "The History of Mt. Pisgah Neighborhood: II," in *Citizen* for 30 December 1880, documents the multigenerational interconnected families who migrated to Union Township. For more on migration patterns, see Atack and Bateman, *To Their Own Soil*, chapter 5; Chaddock, *Ohio Before 1850*, chapter 2; Lang, "Ohioans in Northern Indiana before 1850"; Lemon, *The Best Poor Man's Country*, chapter 3; McClelland and Zeckhauser, *Demographic Dimensions*, chapter 1; Owsley, *Plain Folk*, especially chapter 2; Perkins, *Border Life*; and Swierenga, "The Settlement of the Old Northwest."

4. Drake, *Natural and Statistical View*, 30; Bidwell and Falconer, *History of Agriculture*, 147. See also Atack and Bateman, "Land and the Development of Mid-Nineteenth Century American Agriculture"; Atack, Bateman, and Parker, "Northern Agriculture"; Friedenberg, *Life, Liberty, and the Pursuit of Land*, part two; Hinderaker, *Elusive Empires*, especially chapters 5 and 6; Kulikoff, *The Agrarian Origins*; Opie, *The Law of the Land*, chapters 2 and 3; Post, "Agrarian Class Structure"; Robbins, *Our Landed Heritage*, chapters 1–2; Alan Taylor, "Land and Liberty"; and George Rogers Taylor, "American Economic Growth." The soil fertility argument and the safety valve theory have carried little scholarly weight since the middle of the twentieth century; see Danhof, "Farm-Making Costs"; Owsley, *Plain Folk*; Parker, "From Northwest to Midwest"; Schlebecker, *Whereby We Thrive*; and Steckel, "The Economic Foundations."

5. Gates, *The Farmer's Age*, 2; Etcheson, *The Emerging Midwest*; Hudson, *Making the Corn Belt*, chapter 5; Tamara Gaskell Miller, "'My Whole Enjoyment'"; Wilhelm, in *The Origin and Distribution*, 13–17.

6. *Western Citizen & Urbana Gazette* for 22 March 1842. See Middleton, *History of Champaign County*, 173, for a partial listing of the original Military District

surveys, ranging from fifty acres to two thousand acres; and for assessment see Hutchinson, "The Bounty Lands"; Soltow, "Inequity Amidst Abundance"; and Soltow, "Land Fragmentation." Neighboring Union County had similar characteristic extremes but also some tendency over time for farms in the Congress and the Military Bounty lands to approach similar sizes; see Thrower, *Original Survey and Land Subdivision*, especially chapters 3 and 4. The hope of financial gain from an anticipated rise in value of western lands was general throughout the antebellum period, and "speculation" by resident land-claimants was probably not different from speculation by absentee landowners except perhaps in degree. Urbana's *Ways of the World* for 1821–1822 gives hint of a pattern. The lead feature of several successive issues was a listing of landowners who were delinquent in their taxes. The notices distinguished between Congress Lands and Military Lands, and for the latter gave the names of both the original land proprietor and the current delinquent, if different. In several instances, both named persons were listed as non-resident, clearly signaling troubled if not failed investments.

7. Bidwell and Falconer, *History of Agriculture*, 266, 81, 119; Craig, *To Sow One Acre More*, 47–48; Danhof, *Change in Agriculture* 118, 120; Frank P. Goodwin, "The Development of the Miami Country"; Jones, *History of Agriculture*, 28; Knight, "A History of Pretty Prairie," 8; Lloyd, in Lloyd, Falconer, and Thorne, *The Agriculture of Ohio*, 44; Primack, "Land Clearing." Lebergott, in *The Americans*, 15, calculates that within the farming technology of the late Colonial/early National period, approximately two acres were necessary to provide adequate food for one person. A pioneer family/household of five to seven persons thus required somewhat fewer than fifteen acres. For an overview of the range of soil types, drainage conditions, and vegetative diversity once present in Ohio's barrens, see Gordon, "The Natural Vegetation," 54–63.

8. Antrim, *The History of Champaign and Logan Counties*, 13, 294–95; Edwards, "American Agriculture,"178; Hutslar, *Log Construction*, 75–76; Jones, "The Horse and Mule Industry," 64; Lloyd, in Lloyd, Falconer, and Thorne, *The Agriculture of Ohio*, 54; Rogin, *The Introduction of Farm Machinery*, 4, 16.

9. "History of Mt. Pisgah. IV," in *Citizen* for 20 January 1881; Arrowsmith, in Antrim, *The History of Champaign and Logan Counties,* 136; Beers, 220, 432; Hart, *The Look of the Land* 6–8; Hutslar, "Ohio Water Powered Sawmills," 7; Jones, *History of Agriculture*, 24; Owsley, *Plain Folk*, 56. Hudson, in *Making the Corn Belt*, argues that the richly fertile bottom lands required the least initial preparation because those lands had already been worked by generations of Native Americans.

10. Beers, 216; Flynn and Flynn, "The Natural Features"; Garber, *Waterwheels*.

11. "Reminiscences," in *Citizen* for 8 February 1883; *The Mechanicsburg News*, 23 January 1896; Aley, "Grist, Grit, and Rural Society"; Beers, 216, 218, 468, 592; Hunter, "Studies in the Economic History of the Ohio Valley"; Hunter, *Water-power*, 8–13 and throughout; C. Wayne Smith, *Crop Production*, 21; Ware, *History of Mechanicsburg*. Little evidence exists to indicate typical diet among the earliest Champaign County settlers. The writer of "History of Mt. Pisgah Neighborhood: IV," in *Citizen* for 20 January 1881, reports corn mush and milk, "Hominy, johnny-cakes, corn-pone and venison," and in the fall, wild turkey. Grinding corn for animal feed was necessary only for the hardest types of flint corn brought by farmers from New England. Farmers from Virginia and Kentucky tended to favor the high yielding and softer gourdseed, a common variety of Southern Dent corn. Ogden, in Beers, 221, later claimed that "The kind usually planted was an eight-rowed variety, called the Harness corn; but the 'Hackberry,' a rough-capped dent-corn, and the 'calico,' a spotted or various-colored species, were planted" with very little effort "to prevent the corn 'mixing,' and the result was a 'mixed multitude.'" See also Baker, "Indian Corn"; Brown and Anderson, "The Northern Flint Corns"; and Hudson, *Making the Corn Belt*, 3, 6, and chapter 4.

12. This is deliberate hyperbole. While a variety of forest and farm products had cash value locally or regionally, wheat had cash or exchange value everywhere in the country. Always relative to the local exchange rate/unit sale price, the farmer-settler could ask rhetorically, "How much wheat (or its equivalent) must I plant to meet my financial obligations? How much (additional) wheat can I plant without jeopardizing the minimally essential time/labor investment I must make in other tasks such as cultivating corn or repairing my housing?" The answers entailed finding a balance among risk assessments, each carrying built-in priority limits. Within such a scheme, the assessing and balancing was inherently rational. See Appleby, "Commercial Farming"; Atack and Bateman, *To Their Own Soil*, 11, and 248ff.; Bidwell and Falconer, *History of Agriculture*, chapters 7 and 10; Clemens, *The Atlantic Economy*; Craven, *Soil Exhaustion*, 66ff.; Gates, *The Farmer's Age*, 166; Klingaman, "The Significance of Grain"; Kuhlmann, *The Development of the Flour-Milling Industry*, chapter 1; LeDuc, "Public Policy," 8–9; Lemon, *The Best Poor Man's Country*, chapter 6; Rothenberg, "The Market"; Rothenberg, "Markets"; Rothstein, *The American West*, 382–83; Schmidt, "The Westward Movement"; Schumacher, *The Northern Farmer*, chapter 2; and Sharp and Weisdorf, "Globalization Revisited." The argument for ambivalence is found in Cayton and Onuf, *The Midwest*, 25; as

well as in Bushman, "Family Security." Danhof, in *Change in Agriculture*, 22, had earlier contended that "the concept of agriculture as a market-focused, profit-making business was by no means universally accepted even in 1850." Little information survives to indicate what varieties of wheat were commonly grown by the earliest North American wheat farmers; see Salmon, Mathews, and Leukel, "A Half Century of Wheat Improvement," 20. Ogden, in Beers, 221, states that the variety sown in Champaign County by the earliest farmers "was a red wheat, and went by the name of red chaff."

3. CLAIMING THE LAND, AND SETTLING IN

1. For the early history of Ohio, see Cayton, *The Frontier Republic*; and Hurt, *The Ohio Frontier*; and for a European perspective, see Furstenberg, "The Significance of the Trans-Appalachian Frontier." For overview histories of the early Republic and of antebellum national expansion, see Wood, *Empire of Liberty*; and Daniel Howe, *What Hath God Wrought*. For the standard but differing accounts of the British agricultural revolution, see Chambers and Mingay, *The Agricultural Revolution*; and Kerridge, *The Agricultural Revolution*; and for criticism of both, see Duncan, "Legal Protection for the Soil of England." As the phrase is used in North America, the *agricultural revolution* connotes the change from human to animal and then mechanical sources of energy. For a schematic outline, see Edwards, "American Agriculture"; and for a slightly differing time scheme, see Danhof, *Change in Agriculture*. McClelland, in *Sowing Modernity*, and Rasmussen, in "The Impact of Technological Change," focus on changing machine usage. For an overview of agricultural economic issues, see Aley, "Bringing About the Dawn"; and Earle, "Regional Economic Development"; and for macro-level economic views which avoid "revolution" language, see Parker, "The Magic of Property"; and Atack, Bateman, and Parker, "The Farm, The Farmer, and The Market."

2. The trough metaphor is as used by Ogden, in Beers, 212. In the recollections of W. H. Fyffe, Colonel William Ward, the putative founder of Urbana, had no more than a preemption claim on the land around town; see *Citizen* for 5 October 1855.

3. "History of Mt. Pisgah Neighborhood: IV," in *Citizen* for 20 January 1881; Burke, *Ohio Lands*, 18–22; Freund, "Military Bounty Lands"; Friedenberg, *Life, Liberty and the Pursuit of Land*; Gates, "Research in the History of American Land Tenure"; Jonathan Hughes, "The Great Land Ordinances"; J. F. Laning, "The Evolution of Ohio Counties"; Lebergott, *The Americans*, chapter 8; Opie,

The Law of the Land, chapter 4; Peters, *Ohio Lands*; Robbins, *Our Landed Heritage*, chapter 2; Timothy J. Shannon, "'This Unpleasant Business'"; Treat, *The National Land System*, chapter 4; Treat, "Origin of the National Land System."

4. Sherman, *Original Ohio Land Subdivisions*, 69, 77; see also Peters, *Ohio Lands*; and Treat, *The National Land System*, chapter 3.

5. William T. Hutchinson, "The Bounty Lands"; Treat, *The National Land System*, 335–36.

6. Berry and Berry, *Early Ohio Settlers*; Stickley and Moore, *Champaign County, Ohio Patent Deeds*. In a study of land speculation in Ohio in the period 1820–1840, Rastatter, in "Nineteenth Century Public Land Policy," finds a lag of approximately two years between time of sale and evidence of productive use of land sold at public auction, and infers that the role of land speculator was not distortive of the process of sale and settlement of government land. The implication here is that temporal patterns of "interest" loosely do reflect patterns of settlement.

7. Petty, *Ohio 1810 Tax Duplicate*.

8. Paraphrased excerpts from county commissioners' journal in newspaper article headed "1809: Champaign County in Olden Times," in *Citizen* for 17 September 1852.

9. Scheerer, "'For Ten Years Past'."

10. Ogden, in Beers, 212; Cowgill, in Beers, 501. As an adult, Zane served under General Anthony Wayne in the campaign of 1794 and hence was eligible for the military bounty. The fear of Tecumseh and his brother, and their efforts to unite the Native Americans in resisting white settlers, was specifically identified by the writer of "History of Mt. Pisgah Neighborhood: IV," in *Citizen* for 20 January 1881.

11. Johnson death notice in *Citizen* for 31 March 1870; Haines, "The Political Career of Joseph Vance," chapter 1. Rawlings' farm of 380 acres, located three and one half miles south of Urbana, was atypically large when sold in 1852; sale notice in *Citizen* for 9 July 1852. See also Atwater, *A History of the State of Ohio* 242; Chaddock, *Ohio Before 1850*; Hurt, *The Ohio Frontier*, chapter 11; Ratcliffe, *Party Spirit*, 167–73; Alan Taylor, *The Civil War of 1812*; and von Ende and Weiss, "Consumption of Farm Output."

12. *Ways of the World*, 15 May, 22 May, 25 June 1822; *Mad-River Courant* for 9 November, 16 November 1826; Beers, 438; Calomiris and Gorton, "The Origin

of Banking Panics," 113–14; Cayton, *The Frontier Republic*, 111; Cayton and Onuf, *The Midwest*, 74; Dupre, "The Panic of 1819," 272–73; Farrell, "Cincinnati"; Gates, *The Farmer's Age*, 63–64; Frank Goodwin, "Building a Commercial System"; Knodell, "Interregional Financial Integration"; Rezneck, "The Depression of 1819–1822"; Rothbard, *The Panic of 1819*; Sylla, Legler, and Wallis, "Banks"; and Temin, *The Jacksonian Economy*, chapter 2. Regularly and often, the county sheriff held auctions of grain and livestock, on the premises of the various producers and at the suit variously of local merchants, disputing heirs, and disgruntled spouses, and sometimes explicitly for nonpayment of taxes. A certain "William S. Rawlings" suffered such indignities in at least a couple of years.

13. Beers, 484, 473; Danhof, *Change in Agriculture*, 105–6; Edwards, "American Agriculture," 196; Robbins, *Our Landed Heritage*, 38–39; Treat, *The National Land System*, 140–41.

14. Downes, "Evolution of Ohio County Boundaries," 371, 398–400, 402–3; see also *Mad-River Courant* for 18 January 1828; Ogden, in Beers, 317. Champaign County formally came into existence on 1 March 1805 by action of the General Assembly on 20 February 1805. The subsequent division into Clark, Champaign, and Logan took effect 1 March 1818 following action by the General Assembly on 26 December 1817. A further adjustment of the boundary between Champaign and Madison Counties was made 16 January 1818, also taking effect 1 March 1818.

15. *Citizen* for 1 January 1863; Aaron, *Cincinnati*; Beers, 429; Farrell, "Cincinnati"; Frank Goodwin, "Building a Commercial System"; Frank Goodwin, "The Rise of Manufactures"; Aaron Miller, "Diary"; Wilhelm, *The Origin and Distribution*, 46, as well as the charts throughout. Contemporary spelling was inconsistent, with a general trend from a single word early in the century, "Madriver," to two separate words, "Mad River," later in the century.

16. Fertility patterns were changing; see Craig, "Farm Output"; Craig, "The Value of Household Labor"; Easterlin, Alter, and Condran, "Farms and Farm Families"; Leet, "The Determinants," particularly 363–64 and 377; and McClelland and Zeckhauser, *Demographic Dimensions*, 13.

17. Beers, 412; Ogden, in Beers, 229; Bidwell and Falconer, *History of Agriculture*, 162; Jones, "Ohio Agriculture," 233. The waves of migration into Champaign County coincide with the periods of rural outmigration from Virginia in the 1820s and 1830s; see Craven, *Soil Exhaustion*, chapter 4.

18. Beers, 421; *Census for 1820*; *Mad-River Courant* for 5 October 1826 and numerous succeeding issues; Jones, "Ohio Agriculture."

19. Scholarly documentation is widespread for the appropriateness of the image that the path followed first is the path most easily followed later, and the concept of "path dependency" is a useful if limited explanatory scheme; see David, "Path Dependence."

4. TRADITIONS AND REVISIONS

1. Drake and Mansfield, *Cincinnati in 1826*, 78; Scheiber, *Ohio Canal Era*, 11; Turner, "The Place of the Ohio Valley."

2. Beers, 412, 488, 220; Bailey, *Farm Tools*; Bidwell and Falconer, *History of Agriculture*, 124; Blandford, *Old Farm Tools*; Cousins, *Hog Plow and Sith*; Craven, *Soil Exhaustion*, 19–20; Hurt, *American Farm Tools*, chapter 2; Jordan and Kaups, *The American Backwoods Frontier*, 119; McClelland, *Sowing Modernity*, chapter 3; Percy, "Ax or Plow?," 72–74.

3. *The Eighth Census. Agriculture*, xvi-xix; Bidwell and Falconer, *History of Agriculture*, chapter 16; Craven, *Soil Exhaustion*, 89–92, 152; Danhof, "Agricultural Technology," 118–22; Danhof, *Change in Agriculture*, 183–94; Gates, *The Farmer's Age*, 280; Gould, and others, *Report of the Trial of Plows*, chapter 4; McClelland, *Sowing Modernity*, chapter 3; Rogin, *The Introduction of Farm Machinery*, 22, 24–25.

4. Antrim, *The History of Champaign and Logan Counties*, 236, 296; *Mad-River Courant* for 17 March 1825; 10 May 1828; *Country Collustrator and Mad-River Courant* for 7 June 1832; 13 September 1834.

5. Ogden, in Beers, 220; see also Burkett, *History of Ohio Agriculture*, chapter 11; Danhof, *Change in Agriculture*, 192; Middleton, *History of Champaign County*, 335; and Rogin, *The Introduction of Farm Machinery*, 26–35.

6. *Mad-River Courant* for 22 August 1829; *Western Citizen & Urbana Gazette* for 23 April 1839; 2 September 1845; *Citizen and Gazette* for 10 June, 8 July 1848; Rogin, *The Introduction of Farm Machinery*, 34–35.

7. Gutridge, in Antrim, *The History of Champaign and Logan Counties*, 235; Danhof, "Agricultural Technology," 127; Danhof, "The Tools and Implements of Agriculture," 85; Edwards, "American Agriculture," 178; Hurt, *American Farm Tools*, chapter 5; McClelland, *Sowing Modernity*, chapter 7, especially 150–51; Rogin, *The Introduction of Farm Machinery*, 69–72, 125; Storck and Teague, *Flour for Man's Bread*, 182.

8. Ogden, in Beers, 222; *Citizen* for 22 October 1852; 7 October 1853; *AR* for 1853: 51; Knight, "A History of Pretty Prairie," 8; Schlebecker, *Whereby We Thrive*,

113–14; Townshend, "History of Agriculture in Ohio," 363. The historical record contains no distinguishing feature or name for the particular style of cradle used in Champaign County.

9. Fletcher, *Diary*, 11; Jones, "The Introduction of Farm Machinery," 4; Rogin, *The Introduction of Farm Machinery*, 126–30; Hutchinson, *Seed-time*, 69–72. As numerous scholars have emphasized, a *farmer* was a male. Kulikoff, in *The Agrarian Origins*, 40, and throughout, describes the ideology as *yeomanry*, even as the term yeoman itself was being displaced by the preferred term, *farmer*. At the core of the ideology was ownership of land with an important implication: "Men who knew they could farm their own land married at youthful ages, in their early to mid-twenties, rather than work on their parents' farms." Consequently, "Northern farmers relied upon exchanges of labor with neighbors, an occasional hired hand, and particularly upon their own families, especially the large numbers of children their wives bore." For comment on gender expectations within antebellum agriculture, a sampling of studies would include Faragher, *Women and Men on the Overland Trail*; Kirby, "Rural Culture"; and McMurry, *Transforming Rural Life*. For a critical perspective on the family as the labor and production unit, see Post, "Agrarian Class Structure."

10. *Country Collustrator and Mad-River Courant* for 23 June 1831, and subsequent issues. Ogden, in Beers, 225, asserts that "Laborers were abundant." The unspecified time context seems to have been the 1830s or early 1840s. In the villages scattered throughout the county, shopkeepers and tradesmen such as blacksmiths and their families whose own livelihoods were intimately tied to the agricultural cycle could be presumed for availability at harvest time. In 1840, however, the total nonfarm portion of Champaign County's population was only about 15%. As stated, Ogden's recollection must be regarded only as "possibly so." See the chapter on "Harvesting," in Schob, *Hired Hands*, 67ff.

11. See Danhof, *Change in Agriculture*, 214.

5. THE TRANSPORTATION PROBLEM

1. Klippart, in *AR* for 1876: 577; Burnet, *Notes on the Early Settlement*, 399; Atwater, *A History of the State of Ohio*, 245. See also Berry, *Western Prices*, chapter 1; Gephart, "Transportation," 42; Scheiber, "Urban Rivalry," 228; Scheiber, *Ohio Canal Era*, 7; and George Rogers Taylor, in Gilchrist and Lewis, *Economic Change in the Civil War Era*, 8.

2. Thomas H. Smith, *The Mapping of Ohio*, 160; Gephart, "Transportation," facing page 56; William Patrick, in *Citizen* for 12 May 1881; Drake, *Natural and*

Statistical View, end piece; Flagg, *Pioneer Letters*, 6; Ogden, in Beers, 230; letter of 18 June 1819, in Fletcher, *Diary*, 14. See also Farrell, "Cincinnati"; and Farrell, "Internal-Improvement."

3. Burnet, *Notes on the Early Settlement*, 397; Earle, "Regional Economic Development"; Larson, *The Market Revolution*; Sellers, *The Market Revolution*; George Rogers Taylor, *The Transportation Revolution*. A useful review of the scholarship on the limits of concepts such as "market" and "commercial" is the postscript in the revised edition of Watson, *Liberty and Power*.

4. Ellis, "The Market Revolution and the Transformation of American Politics, 1801–1837," in *The Market Revolution*; Hulbert, *The Cumberland Road*, 19–25, 54, and throughout; Hulbert, "The Indian Thoroughfares of Ohio"; Kaatz, "The Black Swamp," 7; Lloyd, in Lloyd, Falconer, and Thorne, *The Agriculture of Ohio*, 30; Schneider, "The National Road," 114–18; Wood, "The Idea of a National Road," in Raitz, *The National Road*.

5. Drake, *Natural and Statistical View*, 220–21; Hulbert, "The Old National Road," 415–25, and throughout; Raitz, *The National Road*; Sherman, *Original Ohio Land Subdivisions*, 132–38; Treat, *The National Land System*, 171, 177.

6. Barnhart, *Valley of Democracy*, chapter 2; Victor Clark, *History of Manufactures*, I: chapter 14; Clemen, *American Livestock*, 73–74; Haites, Mak, and Walton, *Western River Transportation*, chapter 1; Hulbert, *The Cumberland Road*; Lippincott, *A History of Manufactures*, 56; Thompson, *A History of Livestock Raising*, chapter 6; Van Metre, "Internal Commerce," chapter 13.

7. Blane journal excerpt, in Ierley, *Traveling the National Road*, 60; see also Berry, *Western Prices*, 21–34; Bruchey, "The Business Economy"; Carson, "Transportation and Traffic on the Ohio and Mississippi"; Farrell, "Cincinnati"; Fishlow, "Antebellum Interregional Trade," 362; Gruenwald, *River of Enterprise*, 30–31; King, "Flat Boating"; Lippincott, *A History of Manufactures*, chapter 3; Meyer, *The Roots of American Industrialization*, part I; Rohrbough, *The Trans-Appalachian Frontier*, 93; Scheiber, "The Ohio-Mississippi Flatboat Trade"; Schmidt, "Internal Commerce," 816–22. The use of flatboats to move agricultural products to market was an efficient transportation system. It was not an efficient marketing system; see Beaver, "Joseph Hough"; John G. Clark, *The Grain Trade*, 37; and Jones, *History of Agriculture*, 30, 31.

6. MAKING DO, WITH ROADS AND WITHOUT

1. By common understanding, a subsistence economy is presumed to be agrarian. Also by common understanding, such an economy produces little more

than life-sustaining essentials, necessarily intended for consumption rather than for exchange beyond the local community. Subsistence and self-sufficiency are frequently blurred, if not confused. They tend to co-occur, but the key distinction is that subsistence implies limitations, and its practitioners do not participate in a larger exchange because they cannot. In practice, sufficiency may be as sparse as subsistence but it carries elements of choice, style, and quality. Here the descriptive use of "subsistence" connotes a matter of degree, not the absence, of market participation. For brief reviews of the literature relating to self-sufficiency and subsistence in antebellum agriculture, see Atack and Bateman, "Marketable Farm Surpluses"; Atack, Bateman, and Parker, "The Farm, the Farmer, and the Market"; Kulikoff, "The Transition to Capitalism"; Merrill, "Putting 'Capitalism' in Its Place"; and Rothenberg, "The Market."

2. *The Mad-River Courant* for 29 April 1824; *Mad-River Courant* for 19 September 1829; 23 April 1831; *Ways of the World* for 15 May 1822.

3. "Uala," in *Citizen* for 21 February 1884.

4. Beers, 225–26, 469; *Mad-River Courant* for 9 February 1828.

5. John G. Clark, *The Grain Trade*, 38, 40; Danhof, *Change in Agriculture*, 2, 27; Lippincott, *A History of Manufactures*, 63; Lloyd, in Lloyd, Falconer, and Thorne, *The Agriculture of Ohio*, 45.

6. *Mad-River Courant* for 23 November 1826; 9 February 1827; Danhof, *Change in Agriculture*, 28; Downes, "Trade in Frontier Ohio"; Gates, *The Farmer's Age*, 157–58; Gruenwald, *River of Enterprise*; Rothstein, "Antebellum Wheat," 94. The merchants who took country produce were providing a linkage between two, sometimes adversarial, marketing mechanisms. Evidence of their recognition of the role was in their cajoling pleas that patrons settle overdue accounts, and on the other side, in the threat and sometimes execution of civil suit for recovery of damages. See, for example, the conflicted messages in the combined advertisement and plea to the "Customers of Vance's Mill," in *Mad-River Courant* for 30 May 1829; see also John G. Clark, *The Grain Trade*, 12; Gruenwald, *River of Enterprise*, 106–13; Kulikoff, *The Agrarian Origins*, 17, 20–21 and throughout; Larson, *The Market Revolution*, 39–45; Lippincott, *A History of Manufactures*, 63, 50; McMurry, *Transforming Rural Life*; Rugh, *Our Common Country*; and Taylor, *The Transportation Revolution*, 337.

7. See the editorial on "The Prospects of Champaign," in *Country Collustrator and Mad-River Courant* for 17 November 1831; Ogden, in Beers, 225; John G. Clark, *The Grain Trade*, 32, 17, 29; Goodwin, "Building a Commercial System," 326; Goodwin, "The Rise of Manufactures," 772; Hurt, *The Ohio Frontier*, 371ff.;

Scheiber, *Ohio Canal Era*, 201; and Smith and Smith, *A Buckeye Titan*, 151, 395. Champaign County's barley production and use is not clear. For a number of years in the late 1820s and early 1830s, John Shryack maintained a brewery in Urbana, buying his barley from local growers, and encouraging other growers with proffered sale of seed. The business was seasonally dependent on a precarious supply of barley. Shryack sold his brewery after the 1832 season, and Urbana's brewing industry was taken over by Isaac Harper and William Best. See *Mad-River Courant* for 19 September 1829, 10 September 1831; *Country Collustrator and Mad-River Courant* for 7 June 1832; 30 August 1834.

8. *Mad-River Courant* for 28 June, 5 December 1828; 22 August, 24 October 1829; *Country Collustrator and Mad-River Courant* for 7 June 1832; 13 September 1834; Garber, *Waterwheels*; Ridder, *An Atlas of Champaign County Landmarks*. Sharrer, in "The Merchant-Millers," 147, provides a typology of three kinds of commercial flour dealers in the period 1783–1860: "general-trade merchants, specialized grain and flour dealers, and the merchant-millers." The special function of the grain dealer as different from general merchant or commercial miller emerged with the expansion of the Miami Canal, and was concentrated in the towns along or near that canal. Such grain dealers seem not to have been specifically present in Champaign County until the development of the railroad in the late 1840s.

9. In the listing of "Prices Current at Urbana," in *The Mad-River Courant* for 8 July 1824, 15 October 1824, and 24 March 1825, corn by the bushel was worth 18 ¾ cents and when ground into meal, again by the bushel, was worth 25 cents. Wheat per bushel was worth 33 cents, wheat flour per hundredweight was worth $1.50, and wheat flour by the barrel was worth $2.50. See also Baxter, in Beers, 595; Cayton, *The Frontier Republic*, 118; John G. Clark, *The Grain Trade*, 13; Gates, *The Farmer's Age*, chapter 8; Hudson, *Making the Corn Belt*, chapters 4, 5, and 9; and Lloyd, in Lloyd, Falconer, and Thorne, *The Agriculture of Ohio*, 49, 52–53.

10. Drake quotation in Goodwin, "Building a Commercial System," 325; Knight, "A History of Pretty Prairie," 9. The timing suggests that Rawlings most likely followed the established trail along the Kanawha and New Rivers into the Appalachian Valley and through the Roanoke Gap where he would have picked up the overland trail to Roanoke and Richmond. See Henlein, "Cattle Driving"; Henlein, "Early Cattle Ranges"; Henlein, "Shifting Range-Feeder Patterns"; Jones, "The Horse and Mule Industry"; MacMaster, "The Cattle Trade"; Plumb, "Felix Renick"; Thompson, *A History of Livestock Raising*; and Wheeler, "The Beef Cattle Industry."

11. *Country Collustrator and Mad-River Courant* for 5 April 1834; Jones, "The Beef Cattle Industry"; King, "The Coming and Going of Ohio Droving," 252.

12. Atwater, *A History of the State of Ohio*, 347; *The Mad-River Courant* for 9 December 1824; Beers, 221; Bidwell and Falconer, *History of Agriculture*, 175; John G. Clark, *The Grain Trade*, 37; Gephart, "Transportation," 96; Goodwin, "Building a Commercial System"; Louis C. Hunter, "Studies in the Economic History of the Ohio Valley"; Mahoney, *River Towns*, 67–68; Rothstein, "Antebellum Wheat," 95.

7. NEW CONNECTIONS, NEW DIRECTIONS

1. Haites, Mak, and Walton, *Western River Transportation*, chapter 3; Hunter, *Steamboats*, 12, 17–18; Van Metre, "Internal Commerce," chapter 14.

2. *Western Citizen & Urbana Gazette* for 1 January, 22 January, 5 February 1839; Mahoney, *River Towns*, 81–84.

3. Berry, *Western Prices*, 22–25; Clemen, *American Livestock*, 4, 48–49; Davis and Duncan, *History of the Poland China*, 1–2; Gephart, "Transportation"; Haites and Mak, "Ohio and Mississippi River Transportation"; Haites and Mak, "Steamboating"; Haites, Mak, and Walton, *Western River Transportation*, chapter 5; Leavitt, "Transportation"; Mak and Walton, "Steamboats"; Scheiber, *Ohio Canal Era*; George Rogers Taylor, *The Transportation Revolution*, 160–61. The extent to which antebellum Southern markets were served by Upper Mississippi and Ohio Valley producers, and the related issue of regional economic interconnection, have long been disputed. Representative studies include John G. Clark, *The Grain Trade*, 46; Fishlow, "Antebellum Interregional Trade"; Gates, *The Farmer's Age*, chapter 1; Kohlmeier, *The Old Northwest*; Lippincott, *A History of Manufactures*, 56–66, 134–44; North, "The United States"; Schmidt, "Internal Commerce"; and the forum in *The American Historical Review*, 85, no. 5 (December 1980): 1095–166.

4. On Vance, see an article from *Supporter and Scioto Gazette*, reprinted in *The Mad-River Courant* for 9 November 1826. On internal improvements, see Clanin, "Internal Improvements"; Etcheson, *The Emerging Midwest*; Farrell, "Internal-Improvement Projects"; Goodrich, "American Development Policy"; Goodrich, "Internal Improvements Reconsidered"; Haines, "The Political Career of Joseph Vance"; Daniel Howe, *What Hath God Wrought*, chapter 7; Hunter, *Steamboats*, 181–92; Larson, *Internal Improvement*; Ratcliffe, *Party Spirit*; Scheiber, *Ohio Canal Era*; Scheiber, "The Transportation Revolution"; and Woods, *Ohio's Grand Canal*.

5. *Ways of the World* for 10 July, 24 July, 7 August 1822; 18 June 1823; *The Mad-River Courant* for 8 July 1824; 31 March 1825. The political repercussions of canal route selection were unavoidable, as evident in *The Ohioan and Mad-River Journal* for 13 October 1825 and *Mad-River Courant* for 26 October 1826.

6. See *Mad-River Courant* for 16 November 1826; 4 May, 1 June, 8 June 1827; and particularly the detailed feature article on "Transportation of Goods," reprinted in the *Mad-River Courant* for 7 September 1826.

7. *Ways of the World* for 15 May 1822; *Urbana Newsletter and Mad-River Courant* for 5 May 1825; *Mad-River Courant* for 4 July 1829; Atwater, *A History of the State of Ohio*, 280; Downes, *Frontier Ohio*, 250; Gephart, "Transportation," 140; Kaatz, "The Settlement of the Black Swamp," 142; Kaatz, "The Black Swamp," 12; Lloyd, in Lloyd, Falconer, and Thorne, *The Agriculture of Ohio*, 71. See also the 1828 "Topographical Map of the State of Ohio," engraved by William Woodruff, and Henry Schenck Tanner's 1823 "Ohio and Indiana," both in Thomas H. Smith, *The Mapping of Ohio*, 174–75, 182.

8. *Mad-River Courant* for 24 May 1828; *Country Collustrator and Mad-River Courant* for 8 November 1834; *Urbana Record* for 21 March 1835; 21 May 1836; *Western Citizen & Urbana Gazette* for 15 May 1838; Beers, 422–23; Smith and Smith, *Buckeye Titan*, 130–31; 145.

9. See, for example, *The Mad-River Courant* for 31 March, 21 April 1825; *Urbana Newsletter and Mad-River Courant* for 19 May 1825; *The Ohioan and Mad-River Journal* for 29 September 1825; *Mad-River Courant* for 14 September, 21 September 1826; 5 January, 12 January, 19 January, 2 February, 20 April, 3 August, 23 November 1827; 13 September 1828. The Canal Commission's complete report in 1827 and again in 1828 received front-page printing, even when that required being spread over several weekly issues.

10. Beers, 465; *Western Citizen & Urbana Gazette* for 28 August, 30 October 1838. See sample summaries of "Canal Commerce" from Dayton to Cincinnati, reprinted in *Mad-River Courant* for 11 April 1829, and in *Country Collustrator* for 29 September 1831; Bernstein, *Wedding of the Waters*; John G. Clark, *The Grain Trade*, chapters 2 and 3; Durand, "The Migration of Cheese Manufacture," 270–71; Fishlow, "Antebellum Interregional Trade," 359; Jones, "Ohio Agriculture," 238; Kuhlman, *The Development of the Flour-Milling Industry*; Odle, "The American Grain Trade"; Scheiber, *Ohio Canal Era*, 191, 200; Schmidt, "The Internal Grain Trade"; and Van Metre, "Internal Commerce."

11. *Ways of the World* for 15 May 1822; *The Mad-River Courant* for 8 July 1824; 17 March 1825; *Mad-River Courant* for 7 September 1826, 26 October 1826;

Country Collustrator for 10 November 1831; *Urbana Record* for 31 January 1835; Beaver, "Joseph Hough"; Gruenwald, *River of Enterprise*, chapter 2; Larson, *Internal Improvement*, 46–61; Woods, *Ohio's Grand Canal*, 18.

12. *Country Collustrator* for 30 June 1831; Earle, "Regional Economic Development," 178. Finn, "The Ohio Canals," 24; Odle, "Entrepreneurial Cooperation," 443–46; Scheiber, *Ohio Canal Era*, 129–30.

13. *Mad-River Courant* for 28 March, 11 April, 6 June, 13 June, 22 August 1829; 30 January 1830; Danhof, *Change in Agriculture*, 29; Garber, *Waterwheels*, chapter 7; Scheiber, *Ohio Canal Era*, 201, 203, 204.

14. The unsigned editorial in *Country Collustrator* for 17 November 1831, if not written by Everett himself, was written by his sometime associate, Robert Barr.

15. *Western Citizen & Urbana Gazette* for 15 January, 26 February, 5 March 1839; 26 January, 2 February 1841; George Jr., "The Miami Canal."

8. URBANA

1. Aley, "Bringing About the Dawn"; Atack, Bateman, and Parker, "Northern Agriculture"; Christopher Clark, *Social Change in America*; Gallman and Howle, "Trends"; Gates, *The Farmer's Age*; Howe, *What Hath God Wrought*, chapters 6 and 7; Hudson, *Making the Corn Belt*; Meinig, *The Shaping of America*, v. 2; Meyer, *The Roots of American Industrialization*; Page and Walker, "From Settlement to Fordism"; Weeks, *Building the Continental Empire*; Woodworth, *Manifest Destinies*. For focus on Vermont, see Barron, *Those Who Stayed Behind*; on Massachusetts, see Christopher Clark, *The Roots of Rural Capitalism*; and Rothenberg, *From Market-Places*; and on New York see Bruegel, *Farm, Shop, Landing*; and McMurry, *Transforming Rural Life*.

2. Ogden, in Beers, 210, 320; Enoch, "A History of Champaign County," 15–16; W. H. Fyffe, in *Citizen* for 5 October 1855; "Specs," in *Citizen* for 24 April 1873; "Urbana of Lang Syne," in *Citizen* for 12 May 1881; Cutler, *A Topographical Description*, 43. Reynolds' business may have been "the oldest Dry Goods house in Central Ohio," so described in an appreciative retrospective on the sequence of owners/partners, in *Citizen* for 28 December 1855, 9 March 1871. The development sequence, which looked to the county form of civic and political administration even before settlement had begun, was characteristic of the northern trans-Appalachian frontier, essentially the Old Northwest; see Rohrbough, *The Trans-Appalachian Frontier*.

3. *The Mad-River Courant* for 25 February 1826; *Mad-River Courant* for 4 December 1830; *Country Collustrator and Mad-River Courant* for 20 September

1832; *Western Citizen & Urbana Gazette* for 4 May 1841. The National Road
reached Springfield in 1832, paused there, and then resumed its extension
westward in 1837. See Hulbert, "The Old National Road," 434–39; Kinnison,
Springfield; and Raitz, *The National Road*.

4. Saxton, in *Citizen* for 12 February 1858; Cayton, *The Frontier Republic*; Wade,
The Urban Frontier. The first newspaper was *The Farmer's Watch Tower*, started
by the newly arrived Moses Corwin in partnership with William Blackburn,
and first issued on 4 July 1812. The Corwin obituary tributes appearing in *Citizen*
for 18 April 1872, imply that population was too small to support the paper,
particularly while Corwin's law practice required his frequent absence from
Urbana as he travelled the court circuit of the day. After about two years, Corwin
sold his interest in the paper to George Fithian and Allen M. Poff, who changed
the name of the paper to *The Spirit of Liberty*, and again later to the *Urbana
Gazette*. Only a few issues from 1812 have survived.

5. *Citizen* for 16 August 1850; Smith and Smith, *Buckeye Titan*, 160–61; see also
Wilhelm, *The Origin and Distribution*, part 4. The *Citizen* for 24 October 1856
claimed that Irishmen "meet in crowds at these hell holes, drink to intoxication,
and fights, riots, and broken heads are the consequence." The "Specs'" column,
in *Citizen* for 10 June 1859, expressed even stronger negative opinion.

6. The loyalties of "place" carried pridefully through adult lives were nurtured
in the county's rural schools. School board actions, maintenance of school
houses, reputations of local teachers, results of annual examinations, commence-
ment events, and memories of school boy pranks and strong friendships are to
be found in the county newspapers with increasing frequency through the 1800s.
At midcentury they were in nearly every issue. For perspective on the nation's
rural Midwestern schools in the second half of the 1800s, see Fuller, "Changing
Concepts of the Country School"; and Fuller, *The Old Country School*.

7. See "History of Mt. Pisgah Neighborhood: II," in *Citizen* for 30 December
1880. See also the same newspaper for 31 August, 14 September 1849; 16 September 1853; 15 November 1866; and 9 November 1876; as well as its predecessor
paper, *Mad-River Courant* for 3 April 1830.

8. See the editor's summary enumeration of business enterprises, all an expression of "the spirit of improvement that was abroad in our town," in *Citizen* for
22 June 1849; see also the issue for 13 July 1860. The quoted phrase is from Barron,
Those Who Stayed Behind.

9. Muller, "Selective Urban Growth"; Rohrbough, *The Trans-Appalachian
Frontier*, 348; *Country Collustrator* for 17 November 1831.

9. THE PROSPECT OF A RAILROAD

1. *Mad-River Courant* for 23 August 1828; Paul F. Laning, "Sandusky and Cleveland"; Smith and Smith, *Buckeye Titan*, 327. In 1826, Cooke was the Huron County Representative in the Ohio House.

2. *Mad-River Courant* for 4 February, 18 February 1832. For the sequence and dating of Ohio's early railroad charters, see Farrell, "Internal-Improvement Projects," 21. See also John G. Clark, *The Grain Trade*, 53–54; Fishlow, *American Railroads*, 262; Larson, *Internal Improvement*, especially chapter 3; Miner, *A Most Magnificent Machine*, Introduction and chapter 1; Porter, "Financing Ohio's Pre-Civil War Railroads"; Rubin, "Canal or Railroad?"; Scheiber, *Ohio Canal Era*, 95, 275, 281; Scheiber, "Urban Rivalry," 236; Smith and Smith, *Buckeye Titan*, 328–30; and Vance, *The North American Railroad*, 13–31.

3. Details appeared in Urbana's *Mad-River Courant* as they became available; see numbers for 7 January, 16 January, 18 February, 3 March 1832; *Country Collustrator and Mad-River Courant* for 19 April, 5 July, 2 August, 9 August 1832; 9 November 1833.

4. *Country Collustrator and Mad-River Courant* for 11 January, 13 September 1834; *Urbana Record* for 24 October 1835; *Western Citizen & Urbana Gazette* for 22 May 1838; Ogden, in Beers, 274; Porter, "Financing Ohio's Pre-Civil War Railroads," 221–22.

5. *Western Citizen & Urbana Gazette* for 19 June, 7 August 1838; 24 September 1839; Smith and Smith, *Buckeye Titan*, chapter 24. Paxson, in "Railroads of the Old Northwest," 247, cautions that something less than certainty should characterize any of the several claims to be "first." Thus, the Erie & Kalamazoo was in operation in 1837 and *may* have operated in 1836; the Mad River & Lake Erie was in operation in 1838 and *may* have operated in 1837.

6. *Western Citizen & Urbana Gazette* for 14 May 1839; 21 January 1840; 26 October, 7 December 1841; 12 September 1843; Calomiris and Gorton, "The Origin of Banking Panics," 113; Fishlow, *American Railroads*, 6, 106–7, 112; Knodell, "The Demise of Central Banking"; Knodell, "Rethinking the Jacksonian Economy"; Larson, *The Market Revolution*, 92–97; Miner, *A Most Magnificent Machine*, chapter 4; George Rogers Taylor, *The Transportation Revolution*, 345–46; Temin, *The Jacksonian Economy*, chapter 5.

7. *Western Citizen & Urbana Gazette* for 15 February, 20 December 1842; 31 January 1843.

8. *Western Citizen & Urbana Gazette* for 7 July 1840; 31 January, 7 February, 14 February, 28 February, 7 March, 21 March, 4 April, 2 May, 9 May, 18 July, 25

July, 1 August, 8 August, 22 August, 5 September, 12 September, 19 September, 10 October, 24 October 1843; Smith and Smith, *Buckeye Titan*, chapter 26.

9. *Western Citizen & Urbana Gazette* for 18 May, 9 November 1841; 14 February 1843; 26 March 1844.

10. *Western Citizen & Urbana Gazette* for 11 February 1845; see also 28 February 1843; 22 January, 12 March 1844; 28 January, 11 February, 4 March, 18 March 1845.

11. *Western Citizen & Urbana Gazette* for 13 May, 20 May, 8 July, 22 July, 26 August 1845; 27 October 1846; *Citizen and Gazette* for 6 May, 2 September 1848; Black, *The Little Miami Railroad*. "Specs, Jr.," in *Citizen* for 21 July 1881, states directly that the account by J. W. Ogden in the Beers History is mistaken "as to the time of the arrival of the first passenger train in Urbana. The published account says 30 June 1848, when it should have been three months earlier, 30 March 1848."

12. Middleton, *History of Champaign County*, 863; *Mad River & Lake Erie Railroad Annual Report*, 1848: 3; Miner, *A Most Magnificent Machine*.

10. CHANGING PROSPECTS

1. *Citizen and Gazette* for 29 April 1848; Smith and Smith, *Buckeye Titan*, 381; Storck and Teague, *Flour for Man's Bread*, 184; Ward, *Railroads*, chapter 5.

2. *Western Citizen & Urbana Gazette* for 19 August 1845; 26 March 1844; 16 November 1841.

3. *Citizen and Gazette* for 6 April, 13 April 1849; *Citizen* for 11 May, 13 July 1849.

4. *Citizen and Gazette* for 30 September 1848; 23 March 1849; *Citizen* for 18 June 1852; John G. Clark, *The Grain Trade*; Cronon, *Nature's Metropolis*; Fishlow, *American Railroads*, 34–35; Louis C. Hunter, "Studies in the Economic History of the Ohio Valley," 21; Laurent, "Trade, Transport and Technology"; Mahoney, *River Towns*, 214ff.; Newcomer, "Construction," 199; Odle, "The American Grain Trade"; Ransom, "Public Canal Investment"; Scheiber, *Ohio Canal Era*; Schmidt, "Internal Commerce," 813–14; Schmidt, "The Internal Grain Trade," 114–16; Leola Stewart, "Sandusky"; George Rogers Taylor, *The Transportation Revolution*, 164–65; Vance, *The North American Railroad*; Gary Walton, "River Transportation," 230–34.

5. *Western Citizen & Urbana Gazette* for 12 February 1839; 18 November 1845; 14 July 1846; *Citizen and Gazette* for 2 February, 9 February, 6 April, 11 May, 17 August 1849; 12 April 1850; Black, *The Little Miami Railroad*; Foner, *Free Soil*;

Sarah Phillips, "Antebellum Agricultural Reform." See also John G. Clark, *The Grain Trade*, 225; Fishlow, *American Railroads*, 112, 195, 268; and Scheiber, *Ohio Canal Era*, 107.

6. See the Report to Stockholders, summarized in *Citizen* for 13 August 1852.

7. *Citizen* for 15 November 1850; 31 January 1851; 28 October 1853; 5 February 1858; Ogden, in Beers, 274; Baxter, in Beers, 602–3; Fishlow, *American Railroads*, 185; Marvin, "The Steubenville and Indiana Railroad," 17.

8. *Urbana Record* for 5 November 1836; *Citizen and Gazette* for 23 February, 23 March, 8 June 1849; *Citizen* for 3 August, 31 August, 14 September, 28 September, 5 October, 19 October, 2 November, 7 December 1849; 8 February, 15 February, 1 March, 8 March , 29 March, 5 April 2 August, 9 August, 1 November, 8 November, 15 November, 20 December 1850; 21 February, 9 May, 30 May, 8 August 1851; 2 July, 27 August, 3 December 1852; 16 September, 9 December 1853; 21 July, 20 October 1854; 10 September 1858; *The Urbana Free Press* for 27 October 1858; 8 April 1859; Ogden, in Beers, 274.

9. *Citizen and Gazette* for 1 December 1848; *Citizen* for 3 January, 21 February 1851; 23 July 1852; 11 February, 18 February, 6 May, 20 May 1853; 22 January, 5 February, 24 September, 29 October 1858; 1 July 1859; Leola Stewart, "Sandusky."

10. See the editorial in *Citizen* for 14 March 1851, and the article extracted from *American Railroad Journal* printed the following week. See also John G. Clark, *The Grain Trade*, 222–23, 226; Scheiber, *Ohio Canal Era*, 230–31, 289, 325; and more generally John F. Stover, *History of the Baltimore and Ohio*, chapter 5; John F. Stover, "Iron Roads"; Taylor and Neu, *The American Railroad Network*; and Vance, *The North American Railroad*.

11. *Citizen* for 3 December, 17 December, 24 December 1852; 28 January, 4 February, 25 February, 18 March, 13 May, 3 June, 1 July, 15 July, 22 July 1853; 20 January, 3 February, 10 February, 10 March 1854; 5 January 1855; 10 September, 1 October, 29 October, 5 November, 3 December 1858; Beers, 1881: 274, 520; Miner, *A Most Magnificent Machine*, 59–64; John F. Stover, *Iron Road to the West*, 49–51.

12. *Citizen* for 19 July 1850; 3 December 1852; John G. Clark, *The Grain Trade*, 282; Scheiber, *Ohio Canal Era*, 321–22; Stewart, "Sandusky," 230; John F. Stover, *Iron Road to the West*, 45–48.

13. *Citizen* for 27 April, 4 May 1849; Marvin, "The Steubenville and Indiana Railroad"; Miner, *A Most Magnificent Machine*, chapter 3; Schotter, *The Growth and Development of The Pennsylvania Railroad*, chapter 1.

14. Railroad development phases are outlined in Vance, *The North American Railroad*, 103–4, 110; see also John G. Clark, *The Grain Trade*, 217; Parker, "From Northwest to Midwest," 27; John Stover, *Iron Road to the West*, 122; Taylor and Neu, *The American Railroad Network*, 5–7 and chapter 4.

15. *Urbana Record* for 17 September 1836; *Citizen and Gazette* for 6 May 1848; *Citizen* for 4 May 1849.

16. *Citizen* for 22 June 1849; *AR* for 1849: 62; *AR* for 1856: 210. See *Citizen and Gazette* for 29 April and 6 May 1848, for representative ads; and for definition and description of the changing role of commission merchants in the 1800s, see Porter and Livesay, *Merchants and Manufacturers*, note 5 on 5, and chapter 2 throughout.

17. The gain was explicitly acknowledged by Samuel Keener, in *AR* for 1848: 161; see also Fishlow, *American Railroads*, 84, 212; Gephart, "Transportation," 171; Louis C. Hunter, *Steam Power*, chapter 7; John H. Klippart, hereafter cited by his initials JHK, in *AR* for 1876: 507; Lebergott, "United States Transport Advance," 444; Mahoney, *River Towns*, 96–97, 210; and Scheiber, *Ohio Canal Era*, chapter 12.

18. *Citizen* for 14 September 1871; Rikoon, *Threshing*, 47, 78; Wik, *Steam Power*, 47. See typical ads for bags, in *Citizen* for 21 June 1866; 30 June 1870; 9 August 1877. An "elevator" is the lift machine, not the building containing the machine, but with the development of single-purpose grain storage facilities, the distinction became moot. The principle of a vertical hollow storage facility using mechanical lift and gravity fall of uniformly graded grain was developed in Buffalo, New York, in 1842, and replicated at other lake ports—Toledo in 1847, and Chicago as well as Sandusky in 1848. See *Citizen and Gazette* for 29 April 1848; Brown, *American Colossus*; Dart, "The Grain Elevators of Buffalo"; Fornari, "Recent Developments in the American Grain Storage Industry"; Lee, "The Historical Significance of the Chicago Grain Elevator System"; and Odle, "The American Grain Trade," Part IV.

19. *AR* for 1863: 60–61, 69, 74–75; *Citizen* for 4 January 1856; 4 January, 13 December 1866; 18 July 1867; 17 January, 14 March 1867; 18 June 1868.

20. *Citizen* for 20 July 1871; White, *The American Railroad Freight Car*, 26, 184.

21. Brand, in *AR* for 1849: 63; *Citizen* for 27 July 1849; 4 November 1853; *The Urbana Free Press* for 8 September 1858.

22. *Western Citizen & Urbana Gazette* for 10 June 1845; *Citizen and Gazette* for 6 May 1848; *Citizen* for 12 February 1858, 3 February 1860; Champaign County

report over the name of William Vance, President, in *AR* for 1851: 250; Bidwell and Falconer, *History of Agriculture*, 399–400; Leavitt, "Transportation," 28, 31.

23. *Citizen* for 11 October 1850; Falconer, in Lloyd, Falconer, and Thorne, *The Agriculture of Ohio*, 202; Gates, *The Farmers' Age*, 402; Jones, "Ohio Agriculture," 243–44.

11. REAPERS

1. Atack and Bateman, *To Their Own Soil*, chapter 10; Atack, Bateman, and Parker, "The Farm, the Farmer, and the Market," 259; Gallman, "The Agricultural Sector," 44; Olmstead and Rhode, "The Red Queen," 929–66; Parker, "Sources of Agricultural Productivity," 1459.

2. *Western Citizen & Urbana Gazette* for 8 July 1845.

3. Danhof, *Change in Agriculture*, 84; Edwards, "American Agriculture," 178; McClelland, *Sowing Modernity*, 165–70; Middleton, *History of Champaign County*, 294. See Rikoon, *Threshing*, chapter 3, for illustration of building shocks and stacks to withstand all weather until the farmer was ready for threshing.

4. *Mad-River Courant* for 17 September, 24 September 1831; Hurt, *American Farm Tools*, chapter 3; Rikoon, *Threshing*, 20; Schlebecker, *Whereby We Thrive*, 192; Wik, *Steam Power*, 16.

5. *Country Collustrator and Mad-River Courant* for 22 March 1834; Ardrey, *American Agricultural Implements*, chapter 6; Edwards, "American Agriculture," 229, and throughout.

6. *The Eighth Census. Agriculture*, xx-xxiii; Deering, *Official Retrospective*, especially 4–45; Greeno, *Obed Hussey*, 65–77, 83–87; McClelland, *Sowing Modernity*, chapter 7, especially 151–64; Quick and Buchele, *The Grain Harvesters*, chapter 3; Steward, *The Reaper*, chapter 1 and 2. By tenacity, legalisms, and a dominance of the marketing media of his day, what McCormick achieved was the survivor's right to tell the story. This is the implicit burden of William T. Hutchinson's definitive two-volume biography, *Cyrus Hall McCormick*. The earlier and more popularly written little books by Herbert N. Casson, *The Romance of the Reaper*, and *Cyrus Hall McCormick*, while offering shameless accounts of McCormick's triumphs, are otherwise honest paeans to the nineteenth-century American myth of entrepreneurial success.

7. See Hutchinson, *Seed-time*.

8. The standard but not very satisfactory source is Greeno, *Obed Hussey*. Much useful information on Hussey is in Hutchinson, *Seed-time*; see also Steward, *The Reaper*, 77–80.

9. Bidwell and Falconer, *History of Agriculture*, 287–88; Danhof, *Change in Agriculture*, 127; Hurt, *American Farm Tools*, 44; Hurt, "Out of the Cradle," 38–51; Hutchinson, *Seed-time*, chapter 3.

10. Bidwell and Falconer, *History of Agriculture*, 287; Rogin, *The Introduction of Farm Machinery*, 73.

11. Hutchinson, *Seed-time*, chapters 8, 11, and 13; Greeno, *Obed Hussey*, 42.

12. *Western Citizen & Urbana Gazette* for 23 April 1844; 18 March 1845.

13. Editor of *Ohio Cultivator* in a feature on Champaign County reprinted in *Western Citizen & Urbana Gazette* for 25 August 1846; *AR* for 1846: 21, 27. Wilson acquired his farm from his father-in-law, Justus Jones, a brother of the sisters who were successively wives of Barton Minturn. Wilson was born in Monongahela County, (West) Virginia in 1799 and migrated as a child when his widowed mother accompanied the senior Jacob Minturn family to Champaign County in 1803. His first name appears in two principle spellings, Rezin and Reason, in various public documents; Rezin is the form in the obituary notice in *Citizen* for 15 February 1877. Taylor immigrated to the county as an adult in about 1830; obituary notice of Mary Taylor, in *Citizen* for 9 November 1871

14. *AR* for 1846: 27; Hutchinson, *Seed-time*, 200; Nader, "The Rise of an Inventive"; Olmstead, "The Mechanization of Reaping"; Quick and Buchele, in *The Grain Harvesters*, 63–65; Sokoloff and Khan, "The Democratization of Invention During Early Industrialization," 364.

15. *Western Citizen & Urbana Gazette* for 1 February 1848; *Citizen* for 8 June, 5 October 1849; 26 September 1851; 20 February, 19 March, 26 March 1852; Hutchinson, *Seed-time*, 200. The alliance of manufacturing firms with merchants in both formal and informal partnerships was the common method of raising capital in the antebellum period; see Porter and Livesay, *Merchants and Manufacturers*, 65 and chapter 4 throughout.

16. *Western Citizen & Urbana Gazette* for 18 August 1846; *Citizen* for 14 June, 22 November, 29 November 1850; 25 August 1854; Keener, in *AR* for 1846: 27; Bateham, in *AR* for 1848: 174; McClelland, *Sowing Modernity*, chapter 4.

17. *Citizen* for 6 September, 13 September, 29 November 1850; 14 February, 6 June, 27 June, 4 July, 1 August, 7 November 1851; 23 July 1852.

18. *AR* for 1850: 728; *Citizen* for 30 September 1853; JHK, in *AR* for 1859: 534–35; Danhof, *Change in Agriculture*, 210–11.

19. Vance, in *AR* for 1853: 93; *Citizen* for 10 October 1851; *AR* for 1850: 116–18, 672–76; JHK, in *AR* for 1861: lix; Danhof, "Agricultural Technology," 125; Falconer, in Lloyd, Falconer, and Thorne, *The Agriculture of Ohio*, 228.

20. *Western Citizen & Urbana Gazette* for 10 June 1845; *Citizen* for 25 June 1852.

21. *Citizen* for 28 June, 18 October 1850; Hurt, *American Farm Tools*, 44.

22. Bateham, in *AR* for 1848: 181–82; *AR* for 1850: 118; *Citizen* for 8 November 1850; 6 June 1851; 4 June, 30 July 1852; 28 January, 25 February, 4 March, 15 April, 2 September 1853; Greeno, *Obed Hussey*, 172–74; Hutchinson, *Seed-time*, 201; Rogin, *The Introduction of Farm Machinery*, 74.

23. *Citizen* for 29 April 1853; *AR* for 1851: 106; *AR* for 1853: 93; *Citizen* for 4 March 1853; 23 February, 7 September 1855; 13 February 1857; 23 July 1858; Hurt, *American Farm Tools*, 44; Rogin, *The Introduction of Farm Machinery*, 75. David, in "The Mechanization of Reaping," page 8, distinguishes between manufacture and actual sale, and determines that up to the time when McCormick began production in Chicago, the known sales of all reapers aggregated to 793. The next three years brought the aggregate total of US-produced and -marketed reapers to 3,373. The dramatic increase in production and sales occurred in the five years following 1853.

24. For examples, see *Citizen* for 17 October and 19 December 1851, and 6 February 1852; and see also the commentary from *Ohio Cultivator* as reprinted in *Citizen* for 19 September 1851. *Citizen* for 23 January, 25 June, 9 July 1852; *AR* for 1852: 121–25.

25. *Citizen* for 22 July 1853; *AR* for 1853: 19; Bidwell and Falconer, *History of Agriculture*, 290; Casson, *The Romance of the Reaper*, 37; Danhof, *Change in Agriculture*, 231–40; Hutchinson, *Seed-time*, chapters 17 and 18; Quick and Buchele, *The Grain Harvesters*, 68; Rogin, *The Introduction of Farm Machinery*, 77. Cornelius Aultman and his co-workers had been making Hussey reapers under license in Canton since about 1849 although the details are neither clear nor consistent; see Philip D. Jordan, *Ohio Comes of Age*, 406.

26. *Citizen* for 11 May, 14 September, 28 September, 12 October, 16 November 1855; 25 April, 19 December 1856; 26 June, 11 December 1857; 20 August 1858; *The Urbana Free Press* for 18 August, 8 December 1858; 6 April, 29 June 1859; *AR* for 1853: 42; *AR* for 1857: 90–91. Ogden, in Beers, 379–80, speculated that Kauffman and Nelson, the silent business partners in the firm, feared the prospect of a costly legal patent entanglement and therefore withdrew their support, but contemporary newspaper evidence does not support the speculation.

27. *Citizen* for 23 January 1857; 6 August 1858; 10 June, 22 July, 29 July 1859; *The Urbana Free Press* for 4 August 1858; 6 April, 18 May, 29 June, 27 July 1859.

28. *Citizen* for 10 June, 22 July, 29 July 1859; *The Urbana Free Press* for 8 June, 13 July 1859.

29. *Citizen* for 16 September 1859; 1 June, 8 June, 22 June 1860.

30. *AR* for 1846: 27; Bidwell and Falconer, *History of Agriculture*, 290; Craig, "Farm Output"; Craig, "The Value of Household Labor"; Danhof, "Agricultural Technology"; Earle, "Regional Economic Development"; Meyer, "Midwestern Industrialization," 933–35; Rogin, *The Introduction of Farm Machinery*, 81, 134–35. The measures vary but the overlapping studies by agricultural and economic historians whose work has appeared since about 1960 concur substantially. A baseline of scholarship was established that year in Gallman, "Commodity Output"; Gates, *The Farmer's Age*; and Towne and Rasmussen, "Farm Gross Product and Gross Investment in the Nineteenth Century." Three important studies appearing six years later were similarly defining: Gallman, "Gross National Product"; Lebergott, "Labor Force"; and Parker and Klein, "Productivity Growth in Grain Production." The literature concerning the interrelated topics of mechanization, innovation, and agricultural productivity is extensive.

31. Keener, in *AR* for 1848: 160; Bidwell and Falconer, *History of Agriculture*, chapter 22; Danhof, *Change in Agriculture*, 233–34; Earle and Hoffman, "The Foundation of the Modern Economy"; Jones, "The Introduction of Farm Machinery"; Schob, *Hired Hands*, 92 and throughout.

32. Ankli, "The Coming of the Reaper," 11ff.; Atack and Bateman, *To Their Own Soil*, 200; Danhof, in *Change in Agriculture*, 244–45.

33. David, "The Mechanization of Reaping"; Olmstead, "The Mechanization of Reaping"; *Citizen* for 10 March 1854.

34. *Citizen* for 1 October, 8 October 1858; Olmstead, "The Mechanization of Reaping," 343.

35. Atack and Bateman, *To Their Own Soil*, 198–99.

36. Atack and Bateman, *To Their Own Soil*, 187–88, 195; Danhof, *Change in Agriculture*, 137–38; David, "The Mechanization of Reaping," 7; Earle, "Regional Economic Development," 190; William T. Hutchinson, "The Reaper," 118.

12. IMPROVING THE LAND

1. *Citizen* for 14 February 1851; *AR* for 1847: 20; Stoll, *Larding the Lean Earth*, especially 19ff.; Storck and Teague, *Flour for Man's Bread*, 232; Towne and Rasmussen, "Farm Gross Product," 257–58. "Management" may carry too much of a later generation's understanding of efficiency, and should be understood as responsible stewardship, with more than a hint of the Biblical idea of dominion.

At the same time, the commercial market was the most culturally endorsed measure of successful improvement, explicitly so by mid-century.

2. Keener, in *AR* for 1846: 26; *Citizen* for 12 February 1858; Danhof, "Farm-making Costs," 334; Gallman, "Gross National Product," 16.

3. *Mad-River Courant* for 4 May 1827; 9 October 1830.

4. *Urbana Record* for 17 January, 24 October 1835; *Citizen* for 9 July 1852; *Western Citizen & Urbana Gazette* for 26 November 1839; 7 November 1843.

5. *Mad-River Courant* for 28 May 1831; *Citizen* for 17 January 1861; Bourcier, "In Excellent Order"; Danhof, "The Fencing Problem in the Eighteen-Fifties," 168-186.

6. *Citizen and Gazette* for 8 December 1848; *Citizen* for 19 March, 26 March 1852.

7. *AR* for 1857: 18–19; *AR* for 1859: 572; *AR* for 1876: 535–36; Gates, *Agriculture and the Civil War*, 222–23, 228, 276.

8. *The Mad-River Courant* for 9 December 1824; "Jake," in *Citizen* for 1 June 1860; Beers, 289; Gordon, "The Natural Vegetation," 26.

9. *Citizen* for 24 December 1858; 13 April, 8 November 1860; *AR* for 1850: 121; *AR* for 1858: xxvi–xxvii; *AR* for 1860: vii; 103–250; *AR* for 1876: 552, 565–68; Beers, 289; Danhof, *Change in Agriculture*, 255–56; Overton, *Agricultural Revolution in England*, 194; Townshend, "History of Agriculture in Ohio," 367.

10. *Western Citizen & Urbana Gazette* for 14 April 1846; *Citizen and Gazette* for 15 December 1848; *Citizen* for 23 August 1850; 27 February 1852; 16 September 1853; 16 March, 30 March 1855; 8 February, 14 March 1856; 25 May, 9 August 1860.

11. Keener, in *AR* for 1848: 34. See the argument in Stoll, *Larding the Lean Earth*, 31–41, under the thematic title, "Laying Waste."

12. Keener, in *AR* for 1848: 34; *Western Citizen & Urbana Gazette* for 27 October, 17 November 1846; *Citizen* for 20 September 1850; 3 October 1851; 5 March 1852; 22 July 1853; 3 February, 17 February 1854; 9 February, 10 August 1855; 16 September 1859; 24 February 1860.

13. *The Eighth Census. Agriculture*, viii, x; Burns, *Pastoral Inventions*; Danhof, *Change in Agriculture*, 251–53, 259–60; Stoll, *Larding the Lean Earth*, Part 3. Expressing a later generation's dismay over this understanding of "improvement" was Walter Brigham Evans, Jr.'s posthumously published essay recounting his adolescent explorations in the 1920s of the fen he called the "Cedar Swamp." Upgrading of the County Line Road defining the border between

Champaign and Clark counties, and dredging to redirect the flow of Cedar Creek, provoked Evans to write, "I have visited the scenes of these 'improvements,' but I found no improvements. With an aching heart I looked for the environments which nourished my love of nature, but they were not there." A portion of the "swamp" survives as Ohio's Cedar Bog State Nature Preserve; see Evans, "Cedar Bog."

13. ORGANIZING FOR IMPROVEMENT

1. See brief discussion of the earliest societies, fairs, and publications in Cheetham, *The Farmers' Centennial History of Ohio*; Flint, "Agriculture," 24–26; Johnstone, "Old Ideals," 114–16; and Rodney H. True, "The Early Development of Agricultural Societies," 293-306.

2. *The Mad-River Courant* for 9 December 1824; 23 November 1826; *Mad-River Courant* for 18 May, 8 June, 15 June, 7 September 1827. For accounts of the early societies, see JHK, in *AR* for 1859: 510; *A Brief History of the State Board of Agriculture*, 3–4; and Jones, *History of Agriculture*, chapter 14. For a summary account that places agricultural societies in the context of changing attitudes toward innovation in farm implements, see McClelland, *Sowing Modernity*, chapter 10. For suggestions about the English heritage and influence on shaping improvements in American agriculture, see Loehr, "The Influence of English Agriculture," 3-15.

3. *Western Citizen & Urbana Gazette* for 28 August, 11 September 1838; Ogden, in Beers, 228; Smith and Smith, *Buckeye Titan*, 150. The profile of leaders is consistent with similar leadership elsewhere in the nation at the time; see Stoll, *Larding the Lean Earth*, 27ff.

4. Keener, in *AR* for 1848: 159. The opinion was that of the editor of *Ohio Cultivator*, in an extract appearing in *Western Citizen & Urbana Gazette* for 25 August 1846. Ogden, in Beers, 310, would have understood his phrase, "higher farming," to mean intensive mixed farming with special attention to crop rotation; see Overton, *Agricultural Revolution in England*, 193.

5. The later 1830s was the second of three antebellum periods of importation of 'higher-quality cattle for breeding stock. In 1833, the Ohio Company for Importing English Cattle formed, and in 1834 its representatives toured the Yorkshire and Durham areas of England, seeking Shorthorn cattle. A front-page two-column article on the importations appeared in Urbana's *Country Collustrator and Mad-River Courant* for 30 August 1834. Sales of the imported Shorthorns took place in Chillicothe at the end of October, 1836; the complete account of

transactions as published in the *Scioto Gazette* was reprinted in *The Urbana Record* for 5 November 1836. The bull purchased in 1837 was "Duke of Norfolk," for which Vance and James reportedly paid $1,445. The heifer was "Blush," and the cow was "Elizabeth," for which the Vance brothers paid $1,555. The figures appear in *Western Citizen & Urbana Gazette* for 7 September 1841; figures in Sanders, *Short-Horn Cattle*, 210–11, are slightly different. The significance of those particular animals and their pedigrees is discussed in Derry, *Bred for Perfection*, chapter 2; see also Smith and Smith, *Buckeye Titan*, 157. The Smiths' reference to a "Durham" bull represents James' recorded phrasing and implied a contemporary distinction not followed by later cattle breeders. The Durham "breed" is considered Shorthorn. See Allen, *American Cattle*, 149ff.; Briggs, *Modern Breeds of Livestock*, chapter 1; Flint, "Agriculture," 47–48; Jones, *History of Agriculture*, 108–9; Leavitt, "Attempts to Improve Cattle," 51–53, 62–63; Malin, *The Evolution of Breeds*, Parts One and Two; Perry, "The Shorthorn Comes of Age"; Plumb, *Types and Breeds of Farm Animals*, 183–84; and Sanders, *Short-Horn Cattle*, chapter 8. The Ward sale may have been an attempt to stay ahead of creditors, apparently unsuccessfully, for a Sheriff's sale was held the following April; see *Western Citizen & Urbana Gazette* for 18 September 1838; 2 April 1839.

6. Ogden, in Beers, 228; *The Mad-River Courant* for 16 March 1827; *Country Collustrator, and Mad-River Courant* for 19 April 1834; *Western Citizen & Urbana Gazette* for 30 October 1838. The date of 28 October 1841 given in Middleton, *History of Champaign County*, 353–56, is wrong. A fair was held on that date but it was not the first Champaign County Fair; see *Western Citizen & Urbana Gazette* for 19 October, 2 November 1841. Kniffen, in "The American Agricultural Fair," 266–68, argues that the American agricultural fair, as it took shape in the period 1810–1830, was peculiarly educational in function, as were the agricultural societies that sponsored them. The example in Champaign County suggests an equally strong pecuniary dimension.

7. *Western Citizen & Urbana Gazette* for 4 December, 18 December 1838; 1 July, 15 July, 18 November 1845; 10 March 1846; *AR* for 1846: 71–74; JHK, in *AR* for 1859: 519–20; L. G. Delano, in *AR* for 1874: 77; *A Brief History of The State Board of Agriculture*, 4–7; Jones, *History of Agriculture*, 287–90; Ross, "The Evolution of the Agricultural Fair," 445–480.

8. *Western Citizen & Urbana Gazette* for 14 May 1839; 3 November 1840.

9. *Western Citizen & Urbana Gazette* for 17 August, 7 September, 14 September 1841. Elected were Joel Funk and Smith Minturn as Vice Presidents, Joseph C. Brand as Secretary, Samuel C. Ward as Treasurer, and seven Managers: Samuel

Keener, J. B. Brown, John Enoch, H. Powell, John W. Hitt, John H. James, and James Long.

10. *Western Citizen & Urbana Gazette* for 5 October, 12 October, 19 October, 2 November 1841

11. *Western Citizen & Urbana Gazette* for 4 October, 11 October, 18 October, 1 November 1, 1842.

12. *Western Citizen & Urbana Gazette* for 30 May 1843; 22 October 1844.

13. *Western Citizen & Urbana Gazette* for 14 April 1846; *Citizen and Gazette* for 13 October 1848.

14. *Citizen and Gazette* for 9 March, 23 March 1849; Jones, *History of Agriculture*, 299. For much of 1849, the *Citizen* detailed the spread of cholera through the country. By July, cholera was documented in Champaign County; see the issue for 27 July 1849. When the "First Annual Fair of the Ohio State Board of Agriculture" was rescheduled for September 1850, again in Cincinnati, and then postponed to the first days of October to reduce apprehension about more cholera, appropriate promotional notices again appeared locally; see, for example, *Citizen* for 9 August, 23 August 1850. For an account of the principal cholera epidemics in the 1800s, see Rosenberg, *The Cholera Years*.

15. *Citizen* for 10 May, 31 May, 5 July 1850.

16. *Citizen* for 12 July, 16 August, 23 August, 27 September, 11 October, 18 October, 22 November 1850. Elba Burnham, Archibald Stewart and James K. Thompson replaced H.M. Black, John W. Hertt, and John Weller. Joel Funk was appointed delegate to the meeting of the State Board of Agriculture to be held in Columbus the following week.

17. *Citizen* for 27 June, 11 July, 15 August, 10 October, 14 November 1851; 16 April, 9 July, 13 August, 17 September 1852; 30 September 1853.

18. Sprague, "Agricultural Associations of Ohio," 37; M. L. Sullivant, in *AR* for 1850: 10; *Citizen* for 30 July, 6 August, 3 September 1858; 10 January 1861.

19. *Citizen* for 3 May, 17 May 1850; 11 June 1858; 9 November 1871; 2 October 1873; 25 November 1875; 15 February 1877; Joseph Schafer, *The Social History of American Agriculture*, 109–10. See also Abbott, "The Agricultural Press"; and Marti, "Agricultural Journalism," 28–31.

20. As two examples among many, see the article reprinted from *Western Farmer* in *Western Citizen & Urbana Gazette* for 17 November 1840; and the un-ascribed extract on "Rural Life" in *Western Citizen & Urbana Gazette* for 7 October 1845.

21. *The Eighth Census. Agriculture*, 222; *Citizen* for 20 January 1860; Atack and Bateman, "The 'Egalitarian Ideal,'" 129; Atack and Bateman, "Yeoman Farming,", 43; Danhof, *Change in Agriculture*, 278–79. See also Atack and Bateman, "Egalitarianism"; Atack and Bateman, *To Their Own Soil*; and Yang, "Notes on the Wealth Distribution," 88-102.

22. Greeno, *Obed Hussey*, 172–74; Klippart, in *AR* for 1859: 565, with tables on 566, 568–71; Keener, in *AR* for 1848: 34, 159; *Western Citizen & Urbana Gazette* for 1 April 1845; *Citizen and Gazette* for 1 December 1848; *Citizen* for 26 March 1852; 25 November 1853; 10 February 1854. See also the Ohio Tax Duplicate for 1838.

14. GEOGRAPHY, GENERATION, AND GENDER

1. See Lindert, "Long-run Trends in American Farmland Values"; Soltow, "Inequality Amidst Abundance"; Soltow, "Land Fragmentation"; and Soltow, *Men and Wealth*.

2. Beers, 396, 398, 402; *Western Citizen & Urbana Gazette* for 25 August 1846. When summaries of the 1850 census data were published locally, Union Township detail was presented as though it was representative of the county; see *Citizen* for 22 November 1850. Of the twelve townships it was fifth in a rank ordering of population. Modest gains through the 1850s brought the township to a population plateau while dropping it to seventh place because of railroad-stimulated growth in both Johnson and Salem Townships. After 1860, Union Township declined in population, reaching a valley figure of 947 in 1930. The trend reversed, and sometime in the 1990s, the township population surpassed its previous plateau high. Starting and ending dates varied but through the same time period, the rural population of each township followed a similar pattern.

3. Microfilm access to manuscript census schedules was provided by the Champaign County and Clark County Public Libraries.

4. In his study of census schedules from neighboring Goshen Township, Schob, in *Hired Hands*, 250, contends that too many persons claimed the occupation of Farmer. That may be true but may also miss the local culture.

5. A sample of northern US township records from the 1860 census studied by Easterlin, Alter, and Condran, in "Farms and Farm Families," 24, revealed that while the full entries often clearly indicated otherwise, "there are actually very few who report themselves as tenants." Atack's study of the same data, in

"Tenants and Yeoman," contends that about 15% of the farmers in Ohio should be understood as tenant, and an unknown percentage of farmers owned some land while also renting additional land.

6. Beers, 904; *Citizen* for 30 April 1858.

7. Sowers, *The Laws of Ohio Relating to Women*, 5–6; *Statutes of the State of Ohio*, 329-32. See also Basch, *Framing American Divorce*; Basch, "Marriage and Domestic Relations," 245-279; Brewer, "The Transformation of Domestic Law," 288-323; Chused, "Late Nineteenth Century Married Women's Property Law," 3–35; Chused, "Married Women's Property Law, 1800-1850"; Grossberg, *Governing the Hearth*; Horwitz, *The Transformation of American Law*; Johnston, "Sex and Property," 1033–92; Konig, "Jurisprudence and Social Policy"; Salmon, *Women and the Law of Property*, chapter 1; Speth, "The Married Women's Property Acts"; Stanley, "Marriage, Property, and Class"; Steinfeld, "Property and Suffrage"; Warbasse, *The Changing Legal Rights*; and Welke, *Law and the Borders of Belonging*.

8. Champaign County Probate Record of Wills, Volume B, pages 142–43; *Western Citizen and Gazette* for 20 November, 4 December 1838. Presumably the sale took place and was executed properly although a detailed examination of the surviving county land records has not turned up any relevant filing associated with either Crain or Vance names. Some positive constraint of custom and propriety may be presumed from the timing, clearly an effort at a rapid legal resolution of the situation because the marriage itself preceded the sale announcement by less than a month.

9. *Citizen* for 24 August 1855; Beers, 914.

10. Beers, 879–80, 904.

11. "Letter from Columbus," in *Citizen* for 14 February, 21 February, 11 April 1861. The personal reference was to Elizabeth Jones of Salem, Columbiana County. Even after 1861, married women did not yet have the unrestricted use of their real estate, nor the power independently to transact business and protect their own property. See Basch, "Equity vs. Equality"; Basch, *Framing American Divorce*; Speth, "The Married Women's Property Acts"; and Warbasse, *The Changing Legal Rights*, chapters 5 and 6.

12. Beers, 912.

13. For a brief introduction to its title topic, see Effland, Rogers, and Grim, "Women as Agricultural Landowners."

14. *Citizen* for 30 April, 7 May 1858.

15. Barron, in Ferleger, *Agriculture and National Development*, 10; Beers, 903, 908, 913. The Union Township data on domestics are consistent with Dudden's analysis, in *Serving Women*. Schob, in *Hired Hands*, 266, finds that "renting or working a farm on shares was considered more respectable by society than working for wages."

16. *Western Citizen & Urbana Gazette* for 16 February 1841; 21 February 1843; *Citizen* for 18 July, 31 October 1851; 24 September 1852; 29 July 1853; 25 August 1854; 14 March 1856; 27 March, 7 August 1857; 25 June 1858; Atack, "The Agricultural Ladder Revisited"; Atack, "Tenants and Yeomen"; Yang, "Farm Tenancy." State Board Secretary John H. Klippart's mistaken assertion, in *AR* for 1858: xxvi, that farm tenancy, in contrast with the situation of twenty-five years earlier, was a "rare" exception was most likely an expression of contemporary ambivalence about farm tenancy.

17. Danhof, *Change in Agriculture*, 88–89; Schob, *Hired Hands*, 271; Thackery, *A Light and Uncertain Hold*. The relevant material from antebellum Union Township suggests that the viability of "the agricultural ladder" as a metaphor for a sequence of stages or steps toward farm ownership was not appropriate. For historiographical perspectives on the issue, see Atack, "The Agricultural Ladder Revisited"; and Winters, "Agricultural Tenancy."

18. Beers, 913; *Western Citizen & Urbana Gazette* for 25 July 1843; *Citizen* for 25 April 1867. See also Cox, *A Van Meter Chapter*; and the manuscript notes on the Vanmeter family filed in the Champaign County Public Library. The account of the family outlined here differs slightly from the biographical notes in Beers.

15. ADAPTIVE DIVERSITY

1. For detail and comment see Edwards, "American Agriculture," 203; and also John G. Clark, *The Grain Trade*, 143, 198, 202, 240; Earle, "Regional Economic Development," 184–86; Fishlow, *American Railroads*, 214, 216; and George Taylor, *The Transportation Revolution*.

2. "Specs," in *Citizen* for 25 June 1852; *Citizen* for 18 August 1854; 23 February, 21 September 1855; 20 February 1857; 1 October 1858; 20 July 1860; 21 February 1861. For the farmer-entrepreneur-settler of this generation, start-up costs were significantly higher than had faced previous pioneers, and were accompanied by an initial period of lowered, not increased, productivity; see Danhof, "Farm-making Costs"; and Easterlin, "Farm Production," 99.

3. Keener, in *AR* for 1848: 158; Keener, in *AR* for 1849: 64. See also John G. Clark, *The Grain Trade*, 132–33, 210; 165; Falconer, in Lloyd, Falconer, and Thorne, *The*

Agriculture of Ohio, 129; Leavitt, "Transportation," 30–31; Mak, "Intraregional Trade"; and Winkle, *The Politics of Community*, chapter 1.

4. Gallman, "Changes in Total US Agricultural Factor Productivity"; Klippart, in *AR* for 1859: 542; see also Bateman and Atack, "The Profitability of Northern Agriculture"; Danhof, *Change in Agriculture*, 44–45; Danhof, "The Farm Enterprise," 169–72.

5. *Citizen* for 15 June 1849; 1 June 1855; Keener, in *AR* for 1848: 158–59; Sullivant, in *AR* for 1849: 8; Stokes, in *AR* for 1856: 210. Graphic illustration of the county's corn acreage, corn yield, and geographic place at the northern edge of Ohio's principal corn-producing region is in the maps in Lloyd, Falconer, and Thorne, *The Agriculture of Ohio*, 116–17; see also Atack and Bateman, *To Their Own Soil*, 11.

6. *Citizen* for 15 July 1853; 14 December 1855; 16 September 1859; 20 July 1860; Smith Minturn, in *Report of the Commissioner of Patents, for the Year 1850*, 397; "Specs," in *Citizen* for 25 June 1852; Olmstead and Rhode, "The Red Queen," 951–54.

7. *Mad-River Courant* for 30 July 1831; *Country Collustrator and Mad-River Courant* for 7 June 1832; *Western Citizen & Urbana Gazette* for 10 June 1845; *Citizen* for 28 March, 27 June 1851; 1 June, 22 June, 29 June, 21 September 1855; 29 July, 5 August 1859; *AR* for 1853: 92; Falconer, in Lloyd, Falconer, and Thorne, *The Agriculture of Ohio*, 131–32.

8. *AR* for 1850: 116–18; *AR* for 1859: 137; *AR* for 1868: 192; *AR* for 1879: 169; JHK, in *AR* for 1860: 12; *Western Citizen & Urbana Gazette* for 15 February 1842; 10 October 1843; 13 February 1844; *Citizen* for 16 October 1862; 8 July, 22 July, 5 August, 21 October 1869; 9 March, 24 August 1871; 14 August 1873; Lyon-Jenness, "Bergamot Balm and Verbenas"; Pauly, *Fruits and Plains*, especially chapter 3.

9. Here as elsewhere in this study the agricultural statistics are primarily drawn from the Annual Reports of the State Board of Agriculture and only secondarily from the US census reports. Seldom do the numbers match exactly. Brand, in *AR* for 1849: 64; Sullivant, in *AR* for 1849: 8; Klippart, in *AR* for 1857: 28; *The Seventh Census. Report*, 60; Edwards, "American Agriculture," 203–4.

10. *Western Citizen & Urbana Gazette* for 8 July 1845; *Citizen* for 6 July 1849; 3 December 1852; 7 October 1853; 8 December 1854; 29 February 1856; *AR* for 1853: 52; *AR* for 1856: 71–72, 144–45, 175–77; *AR* for 1859: 542; Danhof, "Agricultural Technology"; Falconer, in Lloyd, Falconer, and Thorne, *The Agriculture in Ohio*, 226; Hardeman, *Shucks, Shocks, and Hominy Blocks*, chapters 7, 9, 11; McClelland, *Sowing Modernity*, chapter 6.

11. Brand, in *AR* for 1850: 115; *Citizen* for 17 June, 1 July, 22 July, 1859; 27 April, 25 May, 1 June 1860; Bidwell and Falconer, *History of Agriculture*, 440; Hudson, *Making the Corn Belt*, 136; Scheiber, *Ohio Canal Era*, 328–33.

12. Keener, in *AR* for 1848: 34; *Western Citizen & Urbana Gazette* for 2 November 1841; 17 October 1843; *Citizen* for 23 July 1858; Allen, *American Cattle*, 161, and chapter 24.

13. *Western Citizen & Urbana Gazette* for 2 November 1841; *Citizen* for 13 September, 8 November 1850; 3 October 1851.

14. *AR* for 1850: 120; *AR* for 1854: 11; *AR* for 1859: 136; *AR* for 1861: xxi-xxx; *Western Citizen & Urbana Gazette* for 7 September 1841; 29 March, 1 November 1842; *Citizen* for 15 July, 4 November 1853; 10 March 1854; 17 October 1856; 2 March, 15 June 1860; Horowitz, *Putting Meat on the American Table*, chapter 2; Mak, "Intraregional Trade."

15. Brand, in *AR* for 1850: 116–18; Klippart, in *AR* for 1858: 645–46; *Western Citizen & Urbana Gazette* for 16 November, 7 December 1841; 13 June 1843; *Citizen* for 26 October, 23 November 1849; 3 December 1852. Walsh, in *The Rise of the Midwestern Meat Packing Industry*, 98–99, estimates the average output of a packing plant in the 1840s as six thousand hogs, increased to eight thousand in the 1850s. Neither Urbana nor Champaign County appears in her study. In 1856, the *Citizen* gave summary figures for the 1855–1856 hog and sheep packing season in Urbana and added: "These items will show that we do something of the slaughtering line in Urbana, although we are never reported in the statistical tables made up by the Cincinnati papers." See *Citizen* for 29 February 1856.

16. "A Western Farmer," in *Western Citizen & Urbana Gazette* for 11 January 1842; *Citizen* for 21 January 1853; 10 March 1854; 27 November 1857; 10 December 1858; *AR* for 1858: 643; *The Urbana Free Press* for 30 June 1858; Clemen, *American Livestock*; Davis and Duncan, *History of the Poland China*; Murray and Coşgel, "Market, Religion, and Culture."

17. Keener, in *AR* for 1846: 26; Keener, in *AR* for 1848: 34; *AR* for 1860: 8; *Citizen* for 15 June 1860; *The Seventh Census. Report*, 52, 54–55; Bidwell and Falconer, *History of Agriculture*, 414ff.; Connor, "A Brief History of the Sheep Industry"; King, "The Coming and Going of Ohio Droving"; Schumacher, *The Northern Farmer*, chapter 1; Stephen L. Stover, "Early Sheep Husbandry." Klippart, in *AR* for 1865: 350, believed that the hog population of the state was consistently undercounted because the assessors typically made their surveys in April or May, when usually only breeding stock was present. The ratio is still significant even when USDA "animal units" are used, for at an equivalence of seven sheep

to five swine, Champaign County had twice the number of units in sheep to the number of units in hogs.

18. *Citizen* for 14 March 1851; 14 December 1855; 29 February 1856; 15 June 1860; Brand, in *AR* for 1849: 63.

19. *Mad-River Courant* for 9 May 1829; *Citizen* for 19 July 1850; 17 October 1856; 16 July, 17 December, 24 December 1858; Cole, "Agricultural Crazes"; Cole, *American Wool Manufacture*, chapter 5; Connor, "A Brief History of the Sheep Industry," 102ff.; Crockett, *The Woolen Industry*, chapter 3; Thompson, *A History of Livestock Raising*, 95–96; and Wentworth, *America's Sheep Trails*, chapter 6.

20. *Ways of the World* for 15 May, 16 October 1822; *Urbana Newsletter and Mad-River Courant* for 2 June 1825; *The Mad-River Courant* for 11 June 1823; 29 April 1824; 25 February, 29 December 1826; *Mad-River Courant* for 17 May 1827; 27 November 1830; *Western Citizen & Urbana Gazette* for 7 May 1839; 2 May, 9 May 1843; 12 March 1844; *Citizen* for 20 August 1852; 15 April 1853; 8 June 1855; 8 June, 15 June, 2 July, 9 July, 16 July 1858; 22 July 1859; Patrick, in *Citizen* for 22 January 1880; *AR* for 1849: 64; Ogden, in Beers, 219, 380; Cole, *American Wool Manufacture*, especially chapters 6 and 12; Crockett, *The Woolen Industry*, chapters 1 and 2; Frank P. Goodwin, "The Rise of Manufactures"; Jeremy, "The Diffusion of New Woolen Manufacturing Technology," 118-40; Lippincott, *A History of Manufactures in the Ohio Valley*, 166; Wentworth, *America's Sheep Trails*, 46; *The Eighth Census. Manufactures*, xlvi; 443. Particularly as found in census records, the widely-used term "manufactory" was never precise. See Hitz, *A Technical and Business Revolution*, chapter 3, for useful distinctions. In the same volume, chapter 4 documents the mechanization of woolen manufacture in the US in the period 1813–1832, all of it in the coastal band of states from Maine to Maryland. According to Greenberg, in "Reassessing the Power Patterns," 1246, as late as 1850, "both hand spinning of ordinary woolen yarn and hand-loom weaving of cloth dominated manufacturing." Ulrich, in *The Age of Homespun*, 5, documents the long view which sees that "Far from being in opposition to one another, 'store-bought' and 'homemade' fabrics developed together." See also Victor S. Clark, *History of Manufactures*, I: 422–35.

21. *AR* for 1849: 12; *AR* for 1857: 58; *AR* for 1861: lxxvii; *Citizen* for 25 May 1849; 11 October 1850; 4 June 1852; 29 April 1853; 3 February 1854; 25 May 1855; 8 June 1860; *The Urbana Free Press* for 6 June 1860; Connor, "A Brief History of the Sheep Industry," 114–15, 121–24; Crockett, *The Woolen Industry*, 51; Falconer, in Lloyd, Falconer, and Thorne, *The Agriculture of Ohio*, 107; Hurt, "The Sheep Industry in Ohio," 237-54.

16. THE RELEVANCE OF HORSES

1. *Western Citizen & Urbana Gazette* for 16 March 1851; Brand, in *AR* for 1849: 63; Vance, in *AR* for 1853: 92; "H. H. F.," in *Citizen* for 15 June 1860; Jones, "The Horse and Mule Industry," 72–75.

2. Danhof, *Change in Agriculture*; David, "The Mechanization of Reaping." Greenberg, in "Reassessing the Power Patterns," 1237 and throughout, contends that the extension of steam power beyond transportation has been presumed more than it has been documented, and that "the transition to fossil-fueled power supplies for machine technology was uneven and prolonged." The standard historical investigation of steam power in industry is Hunter, *Steam Power*. The same scholar, in *Waterpower*, points out that water power and horse power were essentially non-competing in agricultural work, and that until steam largely displaced water power, the widespread dependence on water power for grist and saw mills was a constant. On the beginnings of efforts to apply steam power to agriculture, see Wik, *Steam Power*, chapter 1. On the measure and metaphor of horse power applied to steam power, see Thomas, *Farm Implements*, 167; and Ward, *Railroads*, chapters 1 and 2.

3. *Citizen* for 23 July 1858; Bidwell and Falconer, *History of Agriculture*, 281; Danhof, "The Tools and Implements of Agriculture," 84; Rikoon, *Threshing*, 22–25; Schlebecker, *Whereby We Thrive*, 119; Wik, *Steam Power*, 16.

4. *Citizen and Gazette* for 8 July 1848; Bidwell and Falconer, *History of Agriculture*, 299; Falconer, in Lloyd, Falconer, and Thorne, *The Agriculture of Ohio*, 231; Rikoon, *Threshing*, 30; Wik, *Steam Power*, 25.

5. *Ways of the World* for 15 May 1822; *The Mad-River Courant* for 11 June 1823; Hurt, *American Farm Tools*, 69–74; Ware, *History of Mechanicsburg*, 15.

6. *Mad-River Courant* for 17 September 1831; *AR* for 1851: 511, 515; *Citizen* for 1 June 1, 1855; *AR* for 1870: 136; Bidwell and Falconer, *History of Agriculture*, 299; Hudson, *Making the Corn Belt*; Hurt, *American Farm Tools*, chapter 6; Rikoon, *Threshing*, 30, 35; Wik, in *Steam Power*, 29.

7. *Citizen* for 2 May 1851; 13 February 1857; *AR* for 1861: xxxviii. As reported in the newspaper, the Assessor's record of valued items in 1857 also included fifty pianos, 1,050 watches, 3,314 carriages, and 23,840 hogs.

8. *Citizen* for 10 October 1851; 10 April 1857; 1 January, 16 April, 21 May 1858; *The Urbana Free Press* for 29 June 1859; *AR* for 1854: 11, 28–37; *AR* for 1858: 59–62, 190–19; *The Seventh Census. Report*, 51; Howard, *The Horse in America*, chapter 12; Jones, "The Horse and Mule Industry"; Sanders and Dinsmore, *A History*

of the Percheron Horse, 118–21, 125–31; Thompson, *A History of Livestock Raising*, chapter 9; Weld, *The Percheron Horse*, 19–20.

9. *Citizen* for 4 October 1860; Danhof, *Change in Agriculture*, 162–63; Gates, *The Farmer's Age*, 166.

10. *Citizen* for 29 January, 9 April 1858; 26 August, 7 October, 28 October 1859; *The Urbana Free Press* for 29 June, 5 October 1859; Cayton and Onuf, *The Midwest*; Danhof, *Change in Agriculture*.

11. *Citizen* for 8 July, 7 October, 14 October, 18 November 1853; 24 November 1854; 21 December 1855; 8 February, 29 February 1856.

12. *Citizen* for 23 October, 13 November, 20 November, 4 December 1857.

13. *Citizen* for 16 March, 6 April 1855.

14. *Citizen* for 3 April 1857; 1 October, 8 October 1858; *The Urbana Free Press* for 29 September, 6 October 1858.

15. *Citizen* for 1 October, 8 October, 15 October 1858; 12 August, 23 September 1859; 20 July, 18 October 1860; *The Urbana Free Press* for 14 September, 28 September, 5 October 1859. See *Citizen* for 24 September 1852, for "excellent hints in regard to the attendance of ladies at fair, from the pen of Mrs. Bateham, who conducts the 'Ladies Department' of the Ohio Cultivator…" *AR* for 1854: 250; *Citizen* for 20 October 1854; 14 September 1855; 17 October 1856; "Mingo," in *Citizen* for 21 September 1855.

16. *Citizen* for 7 September, 14 September, 21 September 1855; 12 September, 19 September, 17 October 1856; 24 December 1858; 2 March 1860; "Rustic," in *Citizen* for 7 October 1859; Betts, "Agricultural Fairs and the Rise of Harness Raising"; Ross, "The Evolution of the Agricultural Fair," 454–59. See also the exchange of letters between "Specs" and "Speculum," in *Citizen* for 6 May, 13 May, 20 May, 10 June 17 June 1859.

17. *Citizen* for 22 January, April 1858; "Uala," in *Citizen* for 11 November 1859.

18. *Citizen* for 28 May 1858; 22 July, 5 August, 12 August, 9 December 1859; 27 July 1860; *The Urbana Free Press* for 9 June, 16 June 1858; 4 July 1860. President of the Union Township Horse Fair Board of Managers was the redoubtable John Earsom, and Secretary was the seemingly tireless W. A. Humes.

19. *Citizen* for 7 July, 13 July 1860; *The Urbana Free Press* for 4 July 1860. "H," in *Citizen* for 20 July 1860; "Reporter," in *Citizen* for 9 August 1860.

17. MAKING SENSE OF CIVIL WAR

1. *Citizen* for 8 November, 27 December 1860; 17 January, 24 January, 31 January, 21 February, 7 March, 14 March 1861; Beers, 605–10; Etcheson, *The Emerging Midwest*, especially chapters 7 and 8; "J. H. W.," in *Citizen* for 25 February 1853; Kevin Phillips, *The Cousins' Wars*, chapters 9 and 10; Smith and Smith, *Buckeye Titan*, 476, 502–3; Thackery, *A Light and Uncertain Hold*, chapter 1. The columns of the *Citizen* carried accounts of the Addison White "rescue" and its various local and legal repercussions through 1857, 1858, and 1859; see especially 22 May, 29 May, 5 June, 12 June 1857. For expression of related issues, see *Citizen* for 21 October, 28 October, 4 November 1859; and *The Urbana Free Press* for 7 March, 4 April, 11 April, 18 April 1860. The four 1860 Douglas majority townships four years later voted majorities for McClellan Democrats over Lincoln Unionists by roughly the same proportions, although Jackson Township voters moved toward an almost even division. Lincoln's 1864 majority in the County overall was 2,519 to McClellan's 1,730, a difference of 789 and an increase over 1860 of 239 votes. Results printed in *Citizen* for 17 November 1864.

2. *Citizen* for 18 April, 25 April, 6 June 1861. See Ogden's recollection, in Beers, 266–67, of the meeting of 17 January 1861 in Urbana, and see *The Urbana Free Press* for 23 January 1861 for contemporary perspective.

3. *Citizen* for 6 June 1861; Thackery, *A Light and Uncertain Hold*, chaps. 2 and 3.

4. *Citizen* for 27 March 1862. Soldier letters appeared as early as 24 April 1861, in *The Urbana Free Press*, and could be found almost weekly in the Urbana papers for the next three years. By 1864, soldier reports had been mostly displaced by tributes to fallen comrades, usually with some detail of final circumstances. For examples of editorial partisanship, see *Citizen* for 23 October 1862; 19 February 1863. Two representative 1862 *Union* editorials as well as an 1863 soldier's letter to the *Union* are included in Dee, *Ohio's War*, 77–78, 81–82, 87–90.

5. *Citizen* for 2 May, 6 June 1861.

6. *Citizen* for 4 April, 18 April, 25 April, 2 May, 9 May, 4 July 1861; *The Urbana Free Press* for 24 April, 1 May 1861; Thackery, *A Light and Uncertain Hold*, 14–15; Smith and Smith, *Buckeye Titan*, 460–63. For an entry into the discussion of the concepts of "modern" war and "total" war, see Engerman and Gallman, "The Civil War Economy"; McPherson, *Battle Cry of Freedom*; McPherson, "From Limited War to Total War"; and Neely, "Was the Civil War a Total War?"

7. "A Farmer," in *The Urbana Free Press* for 22 May 1861; *Citizen* for 14 March, 16 May, 20 June, 18 July 1861; Jones, *Ohio Agriculture During the Civil War*, 5.

8. *Citizen* for 16 May, 23 May, 29 August, 12 September, 19 September, 26 September, 10 October 1861; 24 July 1862; Jones, *Ohio Agriculture During the Civil War*, 17; Ross, "The Evolution of the Agricultural Fair," 459–61. The railroad in the newspaper notice was the Columbus, Piqua, & Indiana.

9. See Thackery, *A Light and Uncertain Hold*.

10. *Citizen* for 20 November 1862. A fairly straightforward exposition of the causal view is the substance of Gilford, "The Agricultural Labor Shortage in the Northwest During the Civil War."

11. *Citizen* for 21 November 1861; 30 January 1862; 22 January, 29 January, 5 February 1863; 18 March 1869. County figures are drawn from Middleton, *History of Champaign County*, 683, and reported in Thackery, *A Light and Uncertain Hold*, 226; the national figure is noted in Engerman and Gallman, "The Civil War Economy," 225. R. Douglas Hurt, in "The Agricultural Power of the Midwest During the Civil War," 81, states that "by the summer of 1864, the agricultural labor problem became severe."

12. Such seemed to be the intimation in the farm sale notice placed by Jacob Selbert on behalf of the heirs of John Selbert and his 212-acre farm on the Pretty Prairie four miles south of Urbana; see *Citizen* for 23 July 1863.

13. *Citizen* for 5 February 1863; 14 July, 15 September, 6 October 1864. During the final year of the war, monthly summary listings of county transactions appeared in the *Citizen*. Within about a year after the ending of the war, the monthly listing stopped and did not resume for several years.

14. *Citizen* for 20 November 1863; 28 July, 13 October 1864.

15. Rasmussen, "The Civil War," 190; *Citizen* for 6 August 1863; "Specs, Jr.," in *Citizen* for 23 June 1864. Gates, in *Agriculture and the Civil War*, 229, has estimated that over the course of the war, about half of all farm families in the North provided men for the army. See Craig and Weiss, "Agricultural Productivity Growth During the Decade of the Civil War"; Glymph, "The Civil War Era"; Jones, *Ohio Agriculture During the Civil War*; and the contributions by Aley, Anderson, and Hurt, in Aley and Anderson, *Union Heartland*.

16. JHK, in *AR* for 1862: xvii, lvi; *Citizen* for 14 August, 23 October 1862; 19 February, 2 July, 30 July, 6 August 1863; 30 March 1865; Gates, *Agriculture and the Civil War*, 237–38; Hurt, "The Agricultural Power of the Midwest," 79–83. As Rasmussen points out, in "The Civil War," machine usage patterns in older settled agricultural states such as Ohio must be distinguished from more recently developing farm regions such as Wisconsin or "frontier" Iowa where machine adoption was both new and newly effective.

17. *AR* for 1862: 66–69, 141–42; *AR* for 1864: 155.

18. *Citizen* for 13 June, 20 June, 4 July 1861; 28 May 1863; Becker, "Entrepreneurial Invention," 6–7, 12–16; Hurt, "The Agricultural Power of the Midwest," 82–83.

19. *Citizen* for 14 August, 28 August 1862; 12 May, 22 September, 29 September 1864; 27 July 1865; JHK, in *AR* for 1861: xvii-xviii; JHK, in *AR* for 1862: lx; Greene, *Horses at Work*, chapter 5; Hurt, "The Agricultural Power of the Midwest," 68–70, 84; Jones, "The Horse and Mule Industry," 80–87.

20. *Citizen* for 27 November 1863; 29 December 1864.

21. *Citizen* for 29 October, 5 November 1858; 8 July, 14 October, 11 November 1859; 12 September 1861; 12 June, 24 July, 23 October 1862; JHK, in *AR* for 1867: xxxviii; Engerman and Gallman, "The Civil War Economy," 227–29; Gates, *Agriculture and the Civil War*, 228–29, 245–46; Jones, *Ohio Agriculture During the Civil War*, 19. For historical views about continuing sales of grains in Great Britain and France, see also Rothstein, "The American West," 391–92; Fred A. Shannon, *The Farmer's Last Frontier*, 127; and Trimble, "Historical Aspects of the Surplus Food Production," 223–24.

22. *Citizen* for 23 January, 13 March 27 March, 4 September 1862; 17 September 1863; *AR* for 1862: 141; *AR* for 1863: 135; *AR* for 1865: 212–13.

23. *Citizen* for 29 September, 6 October 1864; 31 August, 28 September, 5 October 1865; *AR* for 1865: 212.

24. *Citizen* for 21 September, 5 October 1865; Jones, *Ohio Agriculture During the Civil War*, 18–19.

25. Irving F. Willis, in *AR* for 1861: xxxi; JHK, in *AR* for 1865: 247; Connor, "A Brief History of the Sheep Industry," 131; Gates, *Agriculture and the Civil War*, 161–62; Jones, *Ohio Agriculture During the Civil War*, 7.

26. Gates, *Agriculture and the Civil War*, 165, 167.

27. *Citizen* for 2 June, 14 July, 27 October 1864; 22 February 1866; Connor, "A Brief History of the Sheep Industry," 128–29; Craig and Weiss, "Agricultural Productivity Growth"; Gates, *Agriculture and the Civil War*, 161; Jones, *Ohio Agriculture During the Civil War*, 7–8; Kindahl, "Economic Factors in Specie Resumption,"31–32; Stephen L. Stover, "Ohio's Sheep Year," 105–6.

28. *Citizen* for 14 July 1864; 6 July 1865; 13 June 1867; 12 August 1869; *AR* for 1868: 191–92; *AR* for 1869: 242; *AR* for 1871: 260; and *AR* for 1872: 171; Connor, "A Brief History of the Sheep Industry," 133–36; Gates, *Agriculture and the Civil War*, 175; Stephen S. Stover, "Ohio's Sheep Year," 102, 106.

29. *AR* for 1862: 142; *AR* for 1863: 135; *AR* for 1864: 155; *AR* for 1865: 212; *Citizen* for 6 March, 13 March, 20 March 1857; 24 December 1858; 2 March 1860; 17 July, 23 October 1862; 1 January, 22 January, 5 March, 7 May, 8 October 1863; 21 July 1864; JHK, in *AR* for 1862: xxx, xxxvii-xxxviii; Hurt, "The Agricultural Power of the Midwest," 87–88; Jones, *Ohio Agriculture During the Civil War*, 15; Winberry, "The Sorghum Syrup Industry."

30. *Citizen* for 23 May 1861; 10 July 1862; 27 November 1863; 23 June, 7 July 1864; and 6 July 1865; JHK, in *AR* for 1862: xxi, xxvi; Hurt, "The Agricultural Power of the Midwest," 73–79; Jones, *Ohio Agriculture During the Civil War*, 11–13; Rasmussen, "The Civil War," 189.

31. See Gates, *The Farmer's Age*, 244.

32. Duran, "The First US Transcontinental Railroad"; Fite, *The Farmers' Frontier*, 21–24; Gates, *The Farmer's Age*; LeDuc, "Public Policy"; LeDuc, "State Disposal of the Agricultural College Land Scrip"; Rasmussen, "The Civil War," 194 and throughout; Fred A. Shannon, "The Homestead Act."

33. *Citizen* for 13 April, 20 April, 27 April, 4 May 1865; Smith and Smith, *Buckeye Titan*, 518–21.

18. DISTANT FIELDS

1. See Christopher Clark's chapter on "The Agrarian Context of American Capitalist Development," in Zakim and Kornblith, *Capitalism Takes Command*, 13–37; John E. Clark, *Railroads in the Civil War*; Fisher and Temin, "Regional Specialization," especially 147–48; Higgs, *The Transformation of the American Economy*; Klein, *Unfinished Business*; McCalla, "Protectionism"; Martin, *Railroads Triumphant*; Morgan, *Merchants of Grain*, chapters 2 and 3; Rothstein, in Gilchrist and Lewis, *Economic Change in the Civil War Era*, 62–63; Taylor and Neu, *The American Railroad Network*; and Weber, *The Northern Railroads*.

2. *Citizen* for 7 January, 14 January 1869; JHK, in *AR* for 1876: 578–79; *Statistical Abstract of the United States* for 1878, Table 144; Mould, *Dividing Lines*, especially chapter 6.

3. *Citizen* for 5 April, 7 June, 18 October, 25 October, 1 November, 22 November, 29 November 1877; 4 April, 11 April, 2 May 1878; 29 May, 5 June, 19 June, 28 August 1879; 21 July, 17 November 1881; 13 April, 1 June, 15 June, 13 July, 20 July, 27 July, 21 September 1882; 22 March 1883; Editor, in *Citizen* for 9 October 1879; "Specs, Jr.," in *Citizen* for 29 November, 20 December 1877; 8 December 1881; Baxter, in Beers, 603.

4. See remarks by State Board President L. G. Delano, in *AR* for 1874: 76; Schmidt, "The Internal Grain Trade," 80, 106–7; and the editorial from the *American Agriculturist* entitled "The Great Wheat Region," reprinted on the front page of *Citizen* for 26 December 1872.

5. "Agricultural" column, in *Citizen* for 11 October 1877; "Scioto," in *Citizen* for 24 September 1868; see also *Citizen* for 11 October 1866; and *AR* for 1866: 144.

6. *AR* for 1869: 242; *AR* for 1871: 260; *AR* for 1873: 60; *AR* for 1879: 232; *AR* for 1881: 199; *Citizen* for 30 October 1873; 13 July 1876; 5 October 1876; 28 April, 23 June 1881; "Agricultural" column, in *Citizen* for 18 October 1877; "A Visit to Nutwood," in *Citizen* for 27 January 1881; "Prodder," in *Citizen* for 25 January 1883; *Urbana Daily Citizen* for 12 May 1888; Dodge, "Report of the Statistician," 67, 70; Dodge, "Short Horn Cattle," 190–93. The county's cattle population had spiked in the early 1850s, and the post-Civil War figures represented a return to a more balanced and sustainable population; see the Auditor's reports, in *Citizen* for 2 May 1851 and 13 February 1857.

7. *AR* for 1867: 168; *AR* for 1869: 242; *AR* for 1872: 171; *AR* for 1873: 123; *AR* for 1874: 192; *AR* for 1877: 95–96, 239; *AR* for 1878: 123, 259; *Citizen* for 8 August 1872; "Produce Trade," in *Citizen* for 25 December 1873; "Uala," in *Citizen* for 23 June 1881; Anderson, *Refrigeration in America,* 47; Horowitz, *Putting Meat on the American Table,* chapter 5; McCormick, "Butter and Egg Business"; McCormick, *Farm Wife,* 91–98; Rees, *Refrigeration Nation,* chapters 1–3; Weiner, "Rural Women"; White, *The Great Yellow Fleet,* chapters 1 and 2.

8. *Citizen* for 31 May 1866; 2 July 1868; 5 August 1869; 5 June 1873; 11 June 1874; 25 October 1877; 13 February 1879; Falconer, in Lloyd, Falconer, and Thorne. *The Agriculture of Ohio,* 108–9; Gates, *Agriculture and the Civil War,* 158–59, 167; Jones, *Ohio Agriculture During the Civil War,* 8; Stephen L. Stover, "Ohio's Sheep Year," 103–4. A brief item on the clip of E. M. Morgan was headed, "Who Can Beat It?" in *Citizen* for 29 July 1875.

9. Unsigned Fair reports in *Citizen* for 26 September, 3 October 1872; 8 October 1874; 5 October 1876; 4 October 1877; *AR* for 1872: 171; *AR* for 1877: 90–95; *AR* for 1878: 118–22, 144–45. See the challenges and counter-challenges from Wayne, Salem, Concord, and Union Townships, in *Citizen* for 1 December, 8 December, 29 December 1881; 5 January, 19 January 1882. See also Lush and Anderson, "A Genetic History of Poland-China Swine."

10. *Citizen* for 7 September, 12 October, 23 November, 14 December 1865; 1 February 1866; 17 October 1867; 13 February 1868; 14 January, 20 May, 10 June 1869; 27 August, 3 September, 24 September 1874; 20 December 1877; 28 June 1883, 2 July 1885.

11. *AR* for 1846: 28; *AR* for 1887: 267; Renick, in *AR* for 1866: 142–54; *Citizen* for 1 September 1854; 25 May, 28 December 1855; 19 November 1868; 3 February, 4 March, 17 November 1870; 24 February 1876; "Archie," in *Citizen* for 7 June 1877; *The Urbana Free Press* for 4 May 1859; Beers, 378, 397, 903, 907; John G. Clark, *The Grain Trade*, 142; Falconer, in Lloyd, Falconer, and Thorne, *The Agriculture of Ohio*, 234, 241; Fishlow, *American Railroads*, 265; Gates, *Agriculture and the Civil War*, 180–82; Henlein, "Early Cattle Ranges of the Ohio Valley"; Kristin Hoganson, "Meat in the Middle," 1025-51 1042; Hudson, *Making the Corn Belt*, chapter 1; Jones, "The Beef Cattle Industry," 313; Jones, *History of Agriculture*, 7; Terry G. Jordan, *North American Cattle-Ranching Frontiers;* Leavitt, "Attempts to Improve Cattle Breeds," 51-67; Leavitt, "Transportation," 27–28; Skaggs, *Prime Cut,* chapter 3; White, *The American Railroad Freight Car*, 172–76, 255–68.

12. *Citizen* for 2 July 1874; Anderson, *Refrigeration in America*, chapters 2 and 3; Clemen, *American Livestock*, chapters 9 and 10; Goodwin, Grennes, and Craig, "Mechanical Refrigeration"; Harley, "Steers Afloat," 1028-58; Kujovich, "The Refrigerator Car"; Macdonald, *Food from the Far West;* Rees, *Refrigeration Nation*, chapter 4; Skaggs, *Prime Cut;* Walsh, *The Rise of the Midwestern Meat Packing Industry;* White, *The American Railroad Freight Car*, 244–45, 270–84. For representative market listings, see *The Urbana Free Press* for 18 August, 13 October 1858; and *Citizen* for 15 October 1858; 11 June, 6 August 1868; 4 February 1869; 18 October 1877.

13. *AR* for 1866: 145; *AR* for 1878: 193; *AR* for 1882: 207; *Citizen* for 23 July 1868; 29 June 1871; 22 May 1873; "Justice," in *Citizen* for 31 May, 9 August 1866; "Specs," in *Citizen* for 28 March 1851; "Uala," in *Citizen* for 16 September 1859; Cayton, "The Middle West"; Fuller, *The Old Country School;* Jones, "Ohio Agriculture."

14. Ball, "The History of American Wheat Improvement"; Buck, "Improved Minnesota Flour"; Earle, "Regional Economic Development"; Goldstein, *Marketing,* 104–7; Greenberg, "Reassessing the Power Patterns," 1250–251; Hudson, *Making the Corn Belt,* chapters 1 and 9; Kane, *The Falls of St. Anthony;* Kuhlman, *The Development of the Flour-Milling Industry,* 119–20 and throughout; Quisenberry and Reitz, "Turkey Wheat," 98–104; Schmidt, "The Internal Grain Trade"; C. Wayne Smith, *Crop Production,* 61–64, 70, 77; Storck and Teague, *Flour for Man's Bread,* 176, 185, 188.

15. *AR* for 1879: 232; *Citizen* for 12 November 1868; "Uala," in *Citizen* for 31 March 1887; Flynn and Flynn, "The Natural Features," 34–35; Kuhlman, *The Development of the Flour-Milling Industry,* 114; Storck and Teague, *Flour for Man's Bread,* 188, 268; Townshend, "History of Agriculture in Ohio," 367.

16. *Citizen* for 14 January, 28 January, 4 February, 20 May 1869; 20 January, 12 May 1887. The steel-and-concrete structures built at the principal Great Lakes grain ports were much larger, with capacities upward from a quarter million bushels, and were designed for very different functions. For images and some explanation of construction, see Banham, *A Concrete Atlantis*; Becher and Becher, *Grain Elevators*; Brown, *American Colossus*; Lee, "The Historical Significance of the Chicago Grain Elevator System"; Mahar-Keplinger, *Grain Elevators*.

17. *Citizen* for 24 August 1871; Atack, Bateman, and Parker, "The Farm, the Farmer, and the Market," 250–53; Atack, Coclanis, and Grantham, "Creating Abundance"; Brown, *American Colossus*; Fabian, *Card Sharps and Bucket Shops*, chapter 4; Goldstein, *Marketing*, Part II; Harley, "Transportation," 218-50 ; Hoffman, *Future Trading*; Jacks, "Populists Versus Theorists," 342-62; Levy, "Contemplating Delivery"; Lurie, *The Chicago Board of Trade*; Lurie, "Speculation, Risk, and Profits"; Morgan, *Merchants of Grain*, chapter 9; Odle, "Entrepreneurial Cooperation"; Parker and Decanio, "Two Hidden Sources of Productivity Growth"; Paul, "The Past and Future of the Commodities Exchanges"; Price, "Grain Standardization"; Rothstein, "America in the International Rivalry"; Rothstein, in Gilchrist and Lewis, *Economic Change in the Civil War Era*; Schlebecker, *Whereby We Thrive*, 169; Schmidt, "The Internal Grain Trade," 431ff.; Ulen, "The Regulation of Grain Warehousing." Zerbe, "The Origin and Effect of Grain Trade Regulations."

18. Ellis, "A Study of Farm Equipment"; Hurt, *American Farm Tools*, chapter 2; Schlebecker, *Whereby We Thrive*, 175. For representative ads for cradles, see *Citizen* for 30 May 1872; and 31 August 1882.

19. *Citizen* for 15 June 1876; 11 April 1878; 5 June 1879; 29 September 1881; "Index," in *Citizen* for 9 July 1885; "J. W. O.," in *Citizen* for 13 May 1880; "Mack," in *Citizen* for 7 July, 14 July 1881; "Mites from Mingo," in *Citizen* for 8 July 1880; "Specs, Jr.," in *Citizen* for 4 July 1878; 1 July 1880; 26 July 1883; "Top," in *Citizen* for 9 July 1885; "Uala," in *Citizen* for 14 July 1881; Danhof, "Agricultural Technology," 130; Denison, *Harvest Triumphant*; McMurry, *Families and Farmhouses*, 102; Rogin, *The Introduction of Farm Machinery*, 110, 115–19, 139; Schlebecker, *Whereby We Thrive*, 190. The issues of the *Citizen* for 14 February 1884 and the next several weeks carried near-saturation advertising for harvesters and binders, four in one issue alone from Baker Brothers. Significant for its absence from the surviving public record in Champaign County was any account of labor-induced machine-breaking such as did occur elsewhere in Ohio with the introduction of the self-binder; see Argersinger and Argersinger, "The Machine Breakers."

20. *Citizen* for 14 March 1867; 3 July 1873; 20 July 1876; 28 April 1881; "Concord Items," in *Citizen* for 25 July 1878; "Mites from Mingo," in *Citizen* for 14 July 1881; "O.," in *Citizen* for 29 August 1878; "Specs, Jr.," in *Citizen* for 25 July 1878. Putting the wheat "in shock" appears to have been more common than stacking. "Mack" presumes shocks in his "Mites from Mingo" contribution, in *Citizen* for 7 July 1881. Three years earlier, a news item about the theft of threshed sacks of wheat in Salem Township included reference to threshing at a "stack." In 1886, a "Brief Local" item stated simply that "Wheat in the neighborhood of Terre Haute is all cut and shocked, and the work of threshing is now going on." See *Citizen* for 8 August 1878; 15 July 1886.

21. *AR* for 1886: 301; *AR* for 1887: 267.

22. Knight, "A History of Pretty Prairie," 21–22; "Archie," in *Citizen* for 4 April 1878; "Specs, Jr.," in *Citizen* for 18 April 1878; "Uala," in *Citizen* for 14 February 1884; Craig, "Farm Output"; Craig, "The Value of Household Labor"; Craig, *To Sow One Acre More*; Easterlin, "Factors in the Decline of Farm Family Fertility"; Florey and Guest, "Coming of Age Among US Farm Boys"; Shepherd, "Restless Americans."

23. *Citizen* for 26 December 1867; 23 April, 2 July 1874; 13 April 1876; 1 December, 8 December 1881; 12 August, 18 November 1886; "Junius," in *Citizen* for 28 July 1870; "Specs, Jr.," in *Citizen* for 9 October 1879; "Specs," in *Citizen* for 23 November 1882; Gates, "The Promotion of Agriculture"; Shepherd, "Restless Americans."

24. *Citizen* for 16 February 1871; 5 March 1885; 18 March 1886; 27 January 1887; "Uala," in *Citizen* for 22 January, 10 December 1885; "Specs, Jr.," in *Citizen* for 24 September, 17 December 1885; "W. H.," in *Citizen* for 13 April 1876.

25. *Citizen* for 9 July, 16 July 1885; "Specs, Jr.," in *Citizen* for 24 July 1884; "Index," in *Citizen* for 4 September 1884; "Prodder," in *Citizen* for 25 January 1883; *AR* for 1883: 274; Jones, *History of Agriculture*, 28.

26. "Specs, Jr.," in *Citizen* for 26 February 1885.

27. *Citizen* for 27 March, 7 August, 16 October, 6 November, 27 November, 4 December, 11 December, 25 December 1873; 1 January, 29 January 1874; Jones, "Ohio Agriculture"; Marti, "Sisters of the Grange"; Nordin, *Rich Harvest*, chapters 1, 2, and 4; Rothstein, "Farmer Movements."

28. *Citizen* for 8 January, 7 May, 11 June 1874; Aldrich, "A Note on Railroad Rates"; Beers, 250; Mayhew, "A Reappraisal of the Causes of Farm Protest"; Middleton, *History of Champaign County*, 351–52; Nordin, *Rich Harvest*, 105–8

and chapter 6; Rothstein, "Farmer Movements." Granger picnics were faddishly widespread; see Warren J. Gates, "Modernization as a Function of an Agricultural Fair." McGuire, in "Economic Causes," finds a strong correlation between high levels of agricultural price uncertainty and high levels of protest agrarian activity. When compared with other Northern farm states, Ohio ranked near the bottom on both measures. To the extent that Champaign County farmer organizations were largely apolitical is an indicator that economic uncertainty may not have been a principal motivating factor for them.

29. *Citizen* for 23 May 1878; 2 June, 16 June, 30 June 1881; "J. W. O.," in *Citizen* for 3 November 1881; *AR* for 1880: 347ff.; *AR* for 1882: xv; 1883: xiii–xiv; Moss and Lass, "A History of Farmers' Institutes."

19. COMMON GROUND

1. "Incog.," in *Citizen* for 3 March 1881; "Specs, Jr.," in *Citizen* for 21 July 1881; Beers, 323. In 1876, using the nation's Centennial as the occasion for a comprehensive assessment of the "condition of agriculture in Ohio," State Board of Agriculture Secretary John H. Klippart sent out an extensive circular to the state's county and district agricultural societies. Responses were compiled into a 200-page essay that interspersed background information and comment with tabular listings. Champaign County responses generally reflected the detail already noted in this study. A few responses were peculiar to the interests or position of the principal preparer who almost certainly was John W. Ogden, an Urbana attorney who served as Secretary of the Agricultural Society for six years, 1874–1879. See *AR* for 1876. Four years later Ogden was instrumental in the preparation of *The History of Champaign County, Ohio.* The collaborative volume does not name an editor, and is cited extensively throughout this study simply as Beers. The error was the date of arrival of the first railroad in Urbana; see note 11, chapter 9 above.

2. "H. H. T.," in *Citizen* for 9 November 1871; *Citizen* for 2 September 1886.

3. For an argument that a parallel development in a western Illinois county contributed explicitly to rural America's "agrarian myth," see Rugh, *Our Common Country.*

4. *Citizen* for 11 January 1883.

5. *Citizen* for 22 December 1870; 19 January, 13 July, 3 August, 24 August, 21 September, 28 September 1871; 18 April, 3 October 1872; 19 February 1873; 1 October, 8 October 1874; 21 January 1875; 20 January, 28 September, 5 October

1876; 18 January, 16 August, 23 August 1877; 12 September, 3 October 1878; "J. W. O.," in *Citizen* for 9 January, 27 March, 26 June, 18 September, 2 October, 11 December 1879; *AR* for 1871: 259–60; *AR* for 1872: 171.

6. *AR* for 1881: 198; *Citizen* for 13 January, 3 February, 10 November, 1 December 1881; 2 August, 9 August 1883; 10 June, 24 June, 29 July, 5 August, 12 August, 19 August 1886; 20 January, 17 March, 14 April, 1 September, 8 September, 15 September 1887; "Alpha," in *Citizen* for 14 April 1887; "Index," in *Citizen* for 7 April 1887; "J. W. O.," in *Citizen* for 20 January, 27 January 1881; Mack," in *Citizen* for 13 October 1881; "Uala," in *Citizen* for 12 January 1882; 24 March, 31 March, 25 August 1887; *The St. Paris Dispatch* for 10 August 1883; *St. Paris Era-Dispatch* for 23 April 1886.

7. *The Mechanicsburg News* for 23 January 1896.

8. *Citizen* for 22 September 1887; 26 January, 2 February, 16 May, 21 June, 12 July, 9 August, 16 August, 8 November, 15 November, 22 November 1888; "Ajax," and reprinted *Era-Dispatch* editorial, in *Citizen* for 7 September 1888.

9. *Urbana Daily Citizen* for 16 February 1889; *Citizen* for 21 February, 28 February, 7 March 1889; *The West Liberty Banner* for 15 August, 29 August 1889; *AR* for 1889: 271.

Bibliography

Aaron, Daniel. *Cincinnati, Queen City of the West: 1819–1838*. Columbus, OH: Ohio State University Press, 1992.

Abbott, Richard H. "The Agricultural Press Views the Yeoman: 1819–1859." *Agricultural History* 42 (1): 35–48. January 1968.

Aldrich, Mark. "A Note on Railroad Rates and the Populist Uprising." *Agricultural History* 54 (3): 424–32. July 1980.

Aley, Ginette. "Bringing about the Dawn: Agriculture, Internal Improvements, Indian Policy, and Euro-American Hegemony in the Old Northwest, 1800–1846." In *The Boundaries Between Us: Natives and Newcomers Along the Frontiers of the Old Northwest Territory, 1750–1850*, edited by Daniel P. Barr, 196–218. Kent, OH: The Kent State University Press, 2006.

———. "Grist, Grit, and Rural Society in the Early Nineteenth Century Midwest: Insight Gleaned from Grain." *Ohio Valley History* 5 (2): 3–20. Summer 2005.

Allen, Lewis Falley. *American Cattle: Their History, Breeding and Management*. New York: Taintor Brothers & Co., 1868.

Anderson, Oscar Edward. *Refrigeration in America: A History of a New Technology and Its Impact*. Princeton, NJ: Princeton University Press, 1953.

Ankli, Robert E. "The Coming of the Reaper." *Business and Economic History*. Second series, volume five, edited by Paul Uselding, 1–24. Urbana, IL: Bureau of Economic and Business Research, 1976.

Annual Report of the Ohio State Board of Agriculture,...for the Year.... [Full volume title varied slightly, always beginning with appropriate ordinal (*First, Second*, etc.) and naming the relevant year (*1846* through *1913*)]. *First Annual Report* printed in Columbus by C. Scott's Steam Press in 1847; most subsequent volumes also printed in Columbus by State Printer, usually a named contractor.

Antrim, Joshua. *The History of Champaign and Logan Counties, from Their First Settlement*. Bellefontaine, OH: Press Printing Co., 1872.

Appleby, Joyce. "Commercial Farming and the 'Agrarian Myth' in the early Republic." *The Journal of American History* 68 (4): 833–49. March 1982.

Ardrey, Robert L. *American Agricultural Implements: A Review of Invention and Development in the Agricultural Implement Industry of the United States*. Chicago: Printed by the author, 1894.

Argersinger, Peter H. and Jo Ann E. Argersinger. "The Machine Breakers: Farmworkers and Social Change in the Rural Midwest of the 1870s." *Agricultural History* 58 (3): 393–410. July 1984.

Atack, Jeremy. "The Agricultural Ladder Revisited: A New Look at an Old Question with Some Data for 1860." *Agricultural History* 63 (1): 1–25. Winter 1989.

———. "Tenants and Yeoman in the Nineteenth Century." *Agricultural History* 62 (3): 6–32. Summer 1988.

Atack, Jeremy and Fred Bateman. "The 'Egalitarian Ideal' and the Distribution of Wealth in the Northern Agricultural Community: A Backward Look." *The Review of Economics and Statistics* 63: 124–29. February 1981.

———. "Land and the Development of Mid-Nineteenth Century American Agriculture in the Northern States." In *Agrarian Organization in the Century of Industrialization: Europe, Russia, and North America*, edited by George Grantham and Carol S. Leonard, 279–312. *Research in Economic History* Supplement 5. 1989 (Part B). Greenwich, CT: JAI Press, 1989.

———. "Marketable Farm Surpluses." *Social Science History* 8 (4): 371–93. Fall 1984.

———. *To Their Own Soil: Agriculture in the Antebellum North*. The Henry A. Wallace Series on Agricultural History and Rural Studies. Ames: Iowa State University Press, 1987.

Atack, Jeremy, Fred Bateman, and William N. Parker. "The Farm, the Farmer, and the Market." In *The Cambridge Economic History of the United States, Volume II: The Long Nineteenth Century*, edited by Stanley L. Engerman and Robert Gillman, 245–84. Cambridge: Cambridge University Press, 2000.

———. "Northern Agriculture and the Westward Movement." In *The Cambridge Economic History of the United States, Volume II: The Long Nineteenth Century*, edited by Stanley L. Engerman and Robert Gillman, 285–328. Cambridge, England: Cambridge University Press, 2000.

Atack, Jeremy, Peter Coclanis, and George Grantham. "Creating Abundance: Biological Innovation and American Agricultural Development—An

Appreciation and Research Agenda." *Explorations in Economic History* 46 (1): 160–67. January 2009.

Atwater, Caleb. *A History of the State of Ohio, Natural and Civil.* Second edition. Cincinnati, OH: Stereotyped by Glezen and Shepard, 1838.

Bailey, Robert C. *Farm Tools & Implements before 1850.* Spring City, TN: Hillcrest Books, 1973.

Baker, Raymond. "Indian Corn and Its Culture." *Agricultural History* 48 (1): 94–97. January 1974.

Ball, Carleton R. "The History of American Wheat Improvement." *Agricultural History* 4 (2): 48–71. April 1930.

Banham, Reyner. *A Concrete Atlantis: US Industrial Building and European Modern Architecture 1900–1925.* Cambridge, MA: The MIT Press, 1986.

Barnhart, John D. *Valley of Democracy: The Frontier Versus the Plantation in the Ohio Valley, 1775–1818.* Bloomington: Indiana University Press, 1953.

Barron, Hal S. *Those Who Stayed Behind: Rural Society in Nineteenth-Century New England.* Cambridge: Cambridge University Press, 1984.

Basch, Norma. "Equity vs. Equality: Emerging Concepts of Women's Political Status in the Age of Jackson." *Journal of the Early Republic* 3 (3): 297–318. Autumn 1983.

———. *Framing American Divorce: From the Revolutionary Generation to the Victorians.* Berkeley: University of California Press, 1999.

———. "Marriage and Domestic Relations." In *The Cambridge History of Law in America, Volume II: The Long Nineteenth Century (1789–1920),* edited by Michael Grossberg and Christopher Tomlins, 245–79, 750–57. Cambridge: Cambridge University Press, 2008.

Bateman, Fred and Jeremy Atack. "The Profitability of Northern Agriculture in 1860." *Research in Economic History* 4: 87–125. 1979.

Beaver, R. Pierce. "Joseph Hough, an Early Miami Merchant." *The Ohio State Archaeological and Historical Society* 45 (1): 37–45. January 1936.

Becher, Bernd, and Hilla Becher. *Grain Elevators.* Cambridge, MA: The MIT Press, 2006.

Becker, Carl M. "Entrepreneurial Invention and Innovation in the Miami Valley During the Civil War." *Bulletin of the Cincinnati Historical Society* 22 (1): 5–28. January 1964.

[Beers]. *The History of Champaign County, Ohio.* Chicago: W. H. Beers & Co., 1881.

Bernstein, Peter L. *Wedding of the Waters: The Erie Canal and the Making of a Great Nation.* New York: W. W. Norton & Company, 2005.

Berry, Ellen T. and David A. Berry. *Early Ohio Settlers: Purchasers of Land in Southwestern Ohio, 1800–1840*. Baltimore, MD: Genealogical Publishing Company, 1986.

Berry, Thomas Senior. *Western Prices before 1861: A Study of the Cincinnati Market*. Cambridge, MA: Harvard University Press, 1943.

Betts, John Rickards. "Agricultural Fairs and the Rise of Harness Racing." *Agricultural History* 27 (2): 71–75. April 1953.

Bidwell, Percy Wells and John I. Falconer. *History of Agriculture in the Northern United States 1620–1860*. Washington, DC: Carnegie Institution of Washington Publication No. 358, 1925.

Black, Robert L. *The Little Miami Railroad*. Cincinnati, OH, 1940.

Blandford, Percy W. *Old Farm Tools and Machinery. An Illustrated History*. Fort Lauderdale, FL: Gale Research Company, 1976.

Bourcier, Paul G. "'In Excellent Order': The Gentleman Farmer Views his Fences, 1790–1860." *Agricultural History* 58 (4): 546–64. October 1984.

A Brief History of the State Board of Agriculture: The State Fair District and Agricultural Societies and Farmers' Institutes in Ohio. Columbus, OH: Fred. J. Heer, State Printer, 1899.

Briggs, Hilton M. *Modern Breeds of Livestock*. New York: The Macmillan Company, 1949.

Brown, William J. *American Colossus: The Grain Elevator, 1843 to 1943*. Cincinnati, OH: Colossal Books, 2009.

Brown, William L. and Edgar Anderson. "The Northern Flint Corns." *Annals of the Missouri Botanical Garden* 34 (1): 1–29. February 1947.

Bruchey, Stuart. "The Business Economy of Marketing Change, 1790–1840: A Study of Sources of Efficiency." *Agricultural History* 46 (1): 211–26. January 1972.

Bruegel, Martin. *Farm, Shop, Landing: The Rise of a Market Society in the Hudson Valley, 1780–1860*. Durham, NC: Duke University Press, 2002.

Buck, Norman. "Improved Minnesota flour." In *Report of the Commissioner of Agriculture for the Year 1875*, 388–90. Washington, DC: Government Printing Office, 1876.

Burke, Thomas Aquinas. *Ohio Lands—A Short History*. Columbus, OH: Ohio Auditor of State, 1987.

Burkett, Charles William. *History of Ohio Agriculture: A Treatise on the Development of the Various Lines and Phases of Farm Life in Ohio*. Concord, NH: The Rumford Press, 1900.

Burnet, Jacob. *Notes on the Early Settlement of the North-Western Territory*. New York: D. Appleton & Co., Publishers; Cincinnati: Derby, Bradley & Co., 1847.

Burns, Sarah. *Pastoral Inventions: Rural Life in Nineteenth-Century American Art and Culture*. Philadelphia: Temple University Press, 1989.

Bushman, Richard Lyman. "Family Security in the Transition from Farm to City, 1750–1850." *Journal of Family History* 6: 238–56. Fall 1981.

Calomiris, Charles W. and Gary Gorton. "The Origin of Banking Panics: Models, Facts, and Bank Regulation." In *Financial Markets and Financial Crises*, edited by R. Glenn Hubbard, 109–73. Chicago: The University of Chicago Press, 1991.

Carson, W. Wallace. "Transportation and Traffic on the Ohio and Mississippi before the Steamboat." *Mississippi Valley Historical Review* 7 (1): 26–38. June 1920.

Casson, Herbert N. *Cyrus Hall McCormick: His Life and Work*. Chicago: A. C. McClurg & Co., 1909.

———. *The Romance of the Reaper*. New York: Doubleday, Page & Company, 1908.

Cayton, Andrew R. L. *The Frontier Republic: Ideology and Politics in the Ohio Country, 1780–1825*. Kent, OH: Kent State University Press, 1986.

———. "The Middle West." In *A Companion to 19th-Century America*, edited by William L. Barney, 272–85. Malden, MA: Blackwell Publishers, 2001.

Cayton, Andrew R. L. and Peter S. Onuf. *The Midwest and the Nation: Rethinking the History of an American Region*. Bloomington: Indiana University Press, 1990.

Chaddock, Robert E. "Ohio before 1850. A Study of the Early Influence of Pennsylvania and Southern Populations in Ohio." In *Studies in History, Economics and Public Law*, edited by the Faculty of Political Science of Columbia University. 31 (2): 187–341. New York: Columbia University: 1908.

Chambers, J. D., and G. E. Mingay. *The Agricultural Revolution, 1750–1880*. London: B T Batsford Ltd, 1966.

Cheetham, Jean Dick, ed. *The Farmers' Centennial History of Ohio, 1803–1903*. Issued by the Department of Agriculture. Springfield, OH: The Springfield Publishing Company, State Printers, 1904.

Chused, Richard H. "Late Nineteenth-Century Married Women's Property Law: Reception of the Early Married Women's Property Acts by Courts and Legislatures." *The American Journal of Legal History* 29 (1): 3–35. January 1985.

———. "Married Women's Property Law, 1800–1850." *Georgetown Law Journal* 71: 1359–425. June 1983.

Clanin, Douglas E. "Internal Improvements in National Politics, 1816–1830." In *Transportation and the Early Nation: Papers Presented at an Indiana American Revolution Bicentennial Symposium*, 30–60. Indianapolis: Indiana Historical Society, 1982.

Clark, Christopher. *The Roots of Rural Capitalism: Western Massachusetts, 1780–1860*. Ithaca, NY: Cornell University Press, 1990.

———. *Social Change in America: From the Revolution through the Civil War*. Chicago: Ivan R. Dee, 2006.

Clark, John E., Jr. *Railroads in the Civil War: The Impact of Management on Victory and Defeat*. Baton Rouge: Louisiana State University Press, 2001.

Clark, John G. *The Grain Trade in the Old Northwest*. Urbana: University of Illinois Press, 1966.

Clark, Victor S. *History of Manufactures in the United States*. Volume I 1607–1860. 1929 edition. New York: McGraw-Hill Book Company, 1929.

Clemen, Rudolf Alexander. *The American Livestock and Meat Industry*. New York: The Ronald Press Company, 1923.

Clemens, Paul G. E. *The Atlantic Economy and Colonial Maryland's Eastern Shore: From Tobacco to Grain*. Ithaca, NY: Cornell University Press, 1980.

Cole, Arthur Harrison. "Agricultural Crazes: A Neglected Chapter in American Economic History." *The American Economic Review* 16 (4): 622–39. December 1926.

———. *The American Wool Manufacture*. Volume I. Cambridge, MA: Harvard University Press, 1926.

Connor, L. G. "A Brief History of the Sheep Industry in the United States." In *Annual Report of the American Historical Association*, 89–197. 1918.

Cousins, Peter H. *Hog Plow and Sith: Cultural Aspects of Early Agricultural Technology*. Dearborn, MI: The Edison Institute, 1973.

Cox, Gregory V. *A Van Meter Chapter in The American Story*. Published privately in October 2001.

Craig, Lee A. "Farm Output, Productivity, and Fertility Decline in the Antebellum Northern United States." *The Journal of Economic History* 50 (2): 432–34. June 1990.

———. *To Sow One Acre More: Childbearing and Farm Productivity in the Antebellum North*. Baltimore, MD: The Johns Hopkins University Press, 1993.

————. "The Value of Household Labor in Antebellum Northern Agriculture." *The Journal of Economic History.* 51 (1): 67–81. March 1991.

Craig, Lee A. and Thomas Weiss. "Agricultural Productivity Growth During the Decade of the Civil War." *The Journal of Economic History* 53 (3): 527–48. September 1993.

Craven, Avery Odelle. *Soil Exhaustion as a Factor in the Agricultural History of Virginia and Maryland, 1606–1860.* University of Illinois Studies in the Social Sciences. 13 (1): 1–179. March, 1925. Urbana: The University of Illinois, 1926.

Crockett, Norman L. *The Woolen Industry of the Midwest.* Lexington: The University Press of Kentucky, 1970.

Cronon, William. *Nature's Metropolis: Chicago and the Great West.* New York: W. W. Norton & Company, 1991.

Cutler, Jervis. *A Topographical Description of the State of Ohio, Indiana Territory, and Louisiana.* Boston: Charles Williams, 1812.

Danhof, Clarence H. "Agricultural Technology to 1880." In *The Growth of the American Economy: An Introduction to the Economic History of the United States,* edited by Harold F. Williamson, 113–40. New York: Prentice-Hall, 1944.

————. *Change in Agriculture: The Northern United States, 1820–1870.* Cambridge, MA: Harvard University Press, 1969.

————. "The Farm Enterprise: The Northern United States, 1820–1860s." *Research in Economic History* 4: 127–91. 1979.

————. "Farm-Making Costs and the 'Safety Valve': 1850–60." *The Journal of Political Economy* 49 (3): 317–59. June 1941.

————. "The Fencing Problem in the Eighteen-Fifties." *Agricultural History* 18 (4): 168–86. October 1944.

————. "The Tools and Implements of Agriculture." *Agricultural History* 46 (1): 81–90. January 1972.

Dart, Joseph. "The Grain Elevators of Buffalo." *Publications of the Buffalo Historical Society* 1: 391–404. 1879.

David, Paul A. "The Mechanization of Reaping in the Antebellum Midwest." In *Industrialization in Two Systems: Essays in Honor of Alexander Gerschenkron,* edited by Henry Rosovsky, 3–39. New York: John Wiley & Sons, 1966.

————. "Path Dependence and Varieties of Learning in the Evolution of Technological Practice." In *Technological Innovation as an Evolutionary Process,* edited by John Ziman, 118–33. Cambridge: Cambridge University Press, 2000.

Davis, Joseph Ray and Harvey S. Duncan. *History of the Poland China Breed of Swine*. Volume I. Poland China History Association, 1921.

Dee, Christine, ed. *Ohio's War: The Civil War in Documents*. Athens: Ohio University Press, 2006.

[Deering] *Official Retrospective Exhibition of the Development of Harvesting Machinery for the Paris Exposition of 1900*. Chicago/Paris: Deering Harvester Company, 1900.

Denison, Merrill. *Harvest Triumphant: The story of Massey-Harris*. Toronto: McClelland and Stewart Limited, 1948.

Derry, Margaret E. *Bred for Perfection: Shorthorn Cattle, Collies, and Arabian Horses Since 1800*. Baltimore, MD: The Johns Hopkins University Press, 2003.

Dodge, J. R. "Short Horn Cattle." In *Report of the Commissioner of Agriculture for the Year 1863*, 190–93. Washington, DC: Government Printing Office, 1863.

———. "Report of the Statistician." In *Report of the Commissioner of Agriculture for the Year 1865*, 54–87. Washington, DC: Government Printing Office, 1866.

Downes, Randolph Chandler. "Evolution of Ohio County Boundaries." *Ohio Archaeological and Historical Quarterly* 36 (3): 340–477. July 1927.

———. *Frontier Ohio, 1788–1803*. Ohio Historical Collections. Volume III. Columbus, Ohio: The Ohio State Archaeological and Historical Society, 1935.

———. "Trade in frontier Ohio." *The Mississippi Valley Historical Review* 16: 467–94. March 1930.

Drake, B. and E. D. Mansfield. *Cincinnati in 1826*. Cincinnati, OH: Printed by Morgan, Lodge, and Fisher, 1827.

Drake, Daniel. *Natural and Statistical View, or Picture of Cincinnati and the Miami Country, Illustrated by Maps*. Cincinnati, OH: Printed by Looker and Wallace, 1815.

Dudden, Faye E. *Serving Women: Household Service in Nineteenth-Century America*. Middletown, CT: Wesleyan University Press, 1983.

Duncan, Colin A. M. "Legal Protection for the Soil of England: The Spurious Context of Nineteenth-Century 'Progress.'" *Agricultural History* 66 (2): 75–94. Spring 1992.

Dupre, Daniel S. "The Panic of 1819 and the Political Economy of Sectionalism." Chapter 9 in *The Economy of Early America*, edited by Cathy Matson, 263–93. Philadelphia: The Pennsylvania University Press, 2006.

Duran, Xavier. "The First US Transcontinental Railroad: Expected Profits and Government Intervention." *The Journal of Economic History* 73 (1): 177–200. March 2013.

Durand, Loyal, Jr. "The Migration of Cheese Manufacture in the United States." *Annals of the Association of American Geographers* 42 (4): 263–82. December 1952.

Earle, Carville. "Regional Economic Development West of the Appalachians, 1815–1860." In *North America: The Historical Geography of a Changing Continent*, edited by Robert D. Mitchell and Paul A. Groves, 172–97. Lanham, MD: Rowman and Littlefield, 1987.

Earle, Carville and Ronald Hoffman. "The Foundation of the Modern Economy: Agriculture and the Costs of Labor in the United States and England, 1800–60." *The American Historical Review* 85 (5): 1055–94. December 1980.

Easterlin, Richard A. "Factors in the Decline of Farm Family Fertility in the United States: Some Preliminary Research Results." *The Journal of American History* 63: 600–614. 1976.

———. "Farm Production and Income in Old and New Areas at Mid-Century." In *Essays in Nineteenth Century Economic History: The Old Northwest*, edited by David C. Klingaman and Richard K. Vedder, 77–117. Athens: Ohio University Press, 1975.

Easterlin, Richard A., George Alter, and Gretchen A. Condran. "Farms and Farm Families in Old and New Areas: The Northern States in 1860." In *Family and Population in Nineteenth-Century America*, edited by Tamara K. Hareven and Maris A. Vinovskis, 22–84. Princeton, NJ: Princeton University Press, 1978.

Edwards, Everett E. "American Agriculture—the First 300 years." In *Farmers in a Changing World: Yearbook of Agriculture 1940*. United States Government Printing Office, 171–276.

Effland, Anne B. W., Denise M. Rogers, and Valerie Grim. "Women as Agricultural Landowners: What Do We Know About Them?" *Agricultural History* 67 (2): 235–61. Spring 1993.

Ellis, L. W. "A Study of Farm Equipment." *Bulletin of the Ohio Agricultural Experiment Station* Number 227. February 1911.

Engerman, Stanley L. and J. Matthew Gallman. "The Civil War Economy: A Modern View." In *On the Road to Total War: The American Civil War and the German Wars of Unification, 1861–1871*, edited by Stig Förster and Jörg Nagler, 217–47. Cambridge: Cambridge University Press, 1997.

Enoch, Cecil Roscoe. "A History of Champaign County, Ohio, to 1860." MA thesis, The Ohio State University, 1930.

Etcheson, Nicole. *The Emerging Midwest: Upland Southerners and the Political Culture of the Old Northwest, 1787–1861.* Bloomington: Indiana University Press, 1996.

Evans, Walter Brigham, Jr. "Cedar Bog: A Plea for Conservation." Edited by Mary A. Skardon. Springfield, OH: Clark County Historical Society, 1974. [reprint of 1944 edition]

Fabian, Ann. *Card Sharps and Bucket Shops: Gambling in Nineteenth-Century America.* New York: Routledge, 1999.

Faragher, John Mack. *Women and Men on the Overland Trail.* New Haven, CT: Yale University Press, 1979.

Farrell, Richard T. "Cincinnati, 1800–1830: Economic Development through Trade and Industry." *Ohio History* 77 (1–3): 111–29, 171–74. Winter, Spring, Summer 1968.

———. "Internal-Improvement Projects in Southwestern Ohio, 1815–1834." *Ohio History* 80 (1): 4–23. Winter 1971.

Ferleger, Lou, ed. *Agriculture and National Development: Views on the Nineteenth Century.* The Henry A. Wallace Series on Agricultural History and Rural Studies. Ames: Iowa State University Press, 1990.

Finn, Chester E. "The Ohio Canals: Public Enterprise on the Frontier." *The Ohio State Archaeological and Historical Quarterly* 51 (1): 1–40. January–March 1942.

Fisher, Franklin M. and Peter Temin. "Regional Specialization and the Supply of Wheat in the United States, 1867–1914." *The Review of Economics and Statistics* 52 (2): 134–49). May 1970.

Fishlow, Albert. *American Railroads and the Transformation of the Antebellum Economy.* Cambridge, MA: Harvard University Press, 1965.

———. "Antebellum Interregional Trade Reconsidered." *The American Economic Review* 54 (3): 352–64. May 1964.

Fite, Gilbert C. *The Farmers' Frontier 1865–1900.* New York: Holt, Rinehart, and Winston, 1966.

Flagg, Gershom. *Pioneer Letters of Gershom Flagg,* edited by Solon J. Buck. Reprinted from the Transactions of the Illinois State Historical Society for 1910. Springfield: Illinois State Journal Co., State Printers, 1912.

Fletcher, Calvin. *The Diary of Calvin Fletcher. Volume I. 1817–1838,* edited by Gayle Thornbrough. Indianapolis: Indiana Historical Society, 1972.

Flint, Charles L. "Agriculture in the United States." In *One Hundred Years' Progress of the United States,* 19–102. Hartford, CT: L. Stebbins, 1872.

Florey, Francesca A. and Avery M. Guest. "Coming of Age Among US Farm Boys in the Late 1800s: Occupational and Residential Choices." *Journal of Family History* 13 (2): 233–49. 1988.

Flynn, Benjamin H. and Margaret S. Flynn. "The Natural Features and Economic Development of the Sandusky, Maumee, Muskingum, and Miami Drainage Areas in Ohio." Department of the Interior United States Geological Survey Water-Supply and Irrigation Paper No. 91. Washington, DC: Government Printing Office, 1904.

Foner, Eric. *Free Soil, Free Labor, Free Men: The Ideology of the Republican Party before the Civil War.* Oxford: Oxford University Press, 1970.

Fornari, Harry D. "Recent Developments in the American Grain Storage Industry." *Agricultural History* 56 (1): 264–71. January 1982.

Freund, Rudolf. "Military Bounty Lands and the Origins of the Public Domain." *Agricultural History* 20 (1): 8–18. 1946.

Friedenberg, Daniel M. *Life, Liberty, and the Pursuit of Land: The Plunder of Early America.* Buffalo, NY: Prometheus Books, 1992.

Fuller, Wayne E. "Changing Concepts of the Country School as a Community Center in the Midwest." *Agricultural History* 58 (3): 423–41. July 1984.

———. *The Old Country School: The Story of Rural Education in the Middle West.* Chicago: The University of Chicago Press, 1982.

Furstenberg, Francois. "The Significance of the Trans-Appalachian Frontier in Atlantic History." *The American Historical Review* 113 (3): 647–77. June 2008.

Gallman, Robert E. "The Agricultural Sector and the Pace of Economic Growth: US Experience in the Nineteenth Century." In *Essays in Nineteenth Century Economic History: The Old Northwest*, edited by David C. Klingaman and Richard K. Vedder, 35–76. Athens: Ohio University Press, 1975.

———. "Changes in Total US Agricultural Factor Productivity in the Nineteenth Century." *Agricultural History* 46 (1): 191–210. January 1972.

———. "Commodity Output, 1839–1899: Trends in the American Economy in the Nineteenth Century." In *Studies in Income and Wealth*. Vol. 24. The Conference on Research in Income and Wealth. Princeton, NJ: Princeton University Press, 1960, 13–71.

———. "Gross National Product in the United States, 1834–1909: Output, Employment, and Productivity in the United States after 1800." In *Studies in Income and Wealth*. Vol. 30. The Conference on Research in Income and Wealth, 3–90. New York: National Bureau of Economic Research, 1966.

Gallman, Robert E. and Edward S. Howle. "Trends in the Structure of the American Economy since 1840." In *The Reinterpretation of American Economic History*, edited by Robert William Fogel and Stanley L. Engerman, 25–37. New York: Harper & Row, Publishers, 1971.

Garber, D. W. *Waterwheels and Millstones: A History of Ohio Gristmills and Milling*. Historic Ohio Buildings Series 2. The Ohio Historical Society, 1970.

Gates, Paul W. *Agriculture and the Civil War*. New York: Alfred A. Knopf, 1965.

———. *The Farmer's Age: Agriculture 1815–1860*. The Economic History of the United States. Volume III. New York: Holt, Rinehart and Winston, 1960.

———. "The Promotion of Agriculture by the Illinois Central Railroad, 1855–1870." *Agricultural History* 5 (2): 57–76. April 1931.

———. "Research in the History of American Land Tenure: A Review Article." *Agricultural History* 28 (3): 121–26. 1954.

Gates, Warren J. "Modernization as a Function of an Agricultural Fair: The Great Grangers' Picnic Exhibition at Williams Gove, Pennsylvania, 1873–1916." *Agricultural History* 58 (3): 262–79. July 1984.

George, John J., Jr. "The Miami Canal." *Ohio Archaeological and Historical Quarterly* 36 (1): 92–115. January 1927.

Gephart, William F. "Transportation and Industrial Development in the Middle West." *Studies in History, Economics and Public Law* 34 (1): 1–273. 1909.

Gilchrist, David T., and W. David Lewis. *Economic Change in the Civil War Era: Proceedings of a Conference on American Economic Institutional Change, 1850–1873, and the Impact of the Civil War*. Greenville, DE: Eleutherian Mills-Hagley Foundation, 1965.

Gilford, Edwin J. "The Agricultural Labor Shortage in the Northwest During the Civil War and How It Was Met 1860–1865." M.A. thesis, Miami University, 1956.

Glymph, Thavolia. "The Civil War Era." In *A Companion to American Women's History*, edited by Nancy A. Hewitt, 167–92. Hoboken, NJ: Blackwell Publishers Ltd, 2002.

Goldstein, Benjamin F. *Marketing: A Farmer's Problem*. New York: The Macmillan Company, 1928.

Goodrich, Carter. "American Development Policy: The Case of Internal Improvements." *The Journal of Economic History* 16 (4): 449–60. December 1956.

———. "Internal Improvements Reconsidered." *The Journal of Economic History* 30 (2): 289–311. June 1970.

Goodwin, Barry K., Thomas J. Grennes, and Lee A. Craig. "Mechanical Refrigeration and the Integration of Perishable Commodity Markets." *Explorations in Economic History* 39 (2): 154–82. April 2002.

Goodwin, Frank P. "Building a Commercial System." *Ohio Archaeological and Historical Quarterly* 16 (3): 316–39. July 1907.

———. "The Development of the Miami Country." *Ohio Archaeological and Historical Quarterly* 18 (4): 484–503. October 1909.

———. "The Rise of Manufactures in the Miami Country." *The American Historical Review* 12: 761–75. 1906–1907.

Gordon, Robert B. "The Natural Vegetation of Ohio in Pioneer Days." *Bulletin of the Ohio Biological Survey*. New Series. 3 (2): xi, 113. Columbus, OH: Published by the Ohio State University, 1969.

Gould, John Stanton, and others. Report of the Trial of Plows, held at Utica, by the N.Y. State Agricultural Society, commencing September 8th, 1867. Albany, 1868.

Greenberg, Dolores. "Reassessing the Power Patterns of the Industrial Revolution: An Anglo-American Comparison." *The American Historical Review* 87: 1237–61. 1982.

Greene, Ann Norton. *Horses at Work: Harnessing Power in Industrial America.* Cambridge, MA: Harvard University Press, 2008.

Greeno, Follett L., ed. *Obed Hussey, Who, of All Inventors, Made Bread Cheap.* Rochester, NY: printed by the author, 1912.

Grossberg, Michael. *Governing the Hearth: Law and the Family in Nineteenth-Century America.* Chapel Hill: The University of North Carolina Press, 1985.

Gruenwald, Kim M. *River of Enterprise: The Commercial Origins of Regional Identity in the Ohio valley, 1790–1850.* Bloomington: Indiana University Press, 2002.

Haines, Donald E. "The Political Career of Joseph Vance, with Especial Emphasis on his Congressional Service." MA thesis, The Ohio State University, 1947.

Haites, Erik F. and James Mak. "Ohio and Mississippi River Transportation 1810–1860." *Explorations in Economic History* 8 (2): 153–80. Winter 1970.

———. "Steamboating on the Mississippi, 1810–1860: A Purely Competitive Industry." *The Business History Review* 45 (1): 52–78. Spring 1971.

Haites, Erik F., James Mak, and Gary M. Walton. *Western River Transportation: The Era of Early Internal Development, 1810–1860.* Baltimore, MD: The Johns Hopkins University Press, 1975.

Hardeman, Nicholas P. *Shucks, Shocks, and Hominy Blocks: Corn As a Way of Life in Pioneer America*. Baton Rouge: Louisiana State University Press, 1981.

Harley, C. Knick. "Steers Afloat: The North Atlantic Meat Trade, Liner Predominance, and Freight Rates, 1870–1913." *The Journal of Economic History* 68 (4): 1028–58. December 2008.

———. "Transportation, the World Wheat Trade, and the Kuznets Cycle, 1850–1913." *Explorations in Economic History* 17: 218–50. 1980.

Hart, John Fraser. *The Look of the Land*. Upper Saddle River, NJ: Prentice-Hall, 1975.

Henlein, Paul C. "Cattle Driving from the Ohio Country, 1800–1850." *Agricultural History* 28 (2): 83–95. April 1954.

———. "Early Cattle Ranges of the Ohio Valley." *Agricultural History* 35 (3): 150–54. July 1961.

———. "Shifting Range-feeder Patterns in the Ohio Valley before 1860." *Agricultural History* 31 (1): 1–12. January 1957.

Higgs, Robert. *The Transformation of the American Economy, 1865–1914: An Essay in Interpretation*. New York: John Wiley & Sons, 1971.

Hinderaker, Eric. *Elusive Empires: Constructing Colonialism in the Ohio Valley, 1673–1800*. Cambridge: Cambridge University Press, 1997.

Hinderaker, Eric and Peter C. Mancall. *At the Edge of Empire. The Backcountry in British North America*. Baltimore, MD: The Johns Hopkins University Press, 2003.

Hitz, Elizabeth. *A Technical and Business Revolution: American Woolens to 1832*. New York: Garland Publishing, 1986.

Hoffman, G. Wright. *Future Trading upon Organized Commodity Markets in the United States*. Philadelphia: University of Pennsylvania Press, 1932.

Hoganson, Kristin. "Meat in the Middle: Converging Borderlands in the US Midwest, 1865–1900." *The Journal of American History* 98 (4): 1025–51. March 2012.

Horowitz, Roger. *Putting Meat on the American Table: Taste, Technology, Transformation*. Baltimore, MD: The Johns Hopkins University Press, 2006.

Horwitz, Morton J. *The Transformation of American Law, 1780–1860*. Cambridge, MA: Harvard University Press, 1977.

Howard, Robert West. *The Horse in America*. Chicago: Follett Publishing Company, 1965.

Howe, Daniel Walker. *What Hath God Wrought: The Transformation of America, 1815–1848*. Oxford: Oxford University Press, 2007.

Howe, Henry. *Historical Collections of Ohio: Containing a Collection of the Most Interesting Facts, Traditions, Biographical Sketches, Anecdotes, etc. Relating to Its General and Local History: with Descriptions of Its Counties, Principal Towns and Villages.* Cincinnati, OH: Published by Henry Howe, at E. Morgan & Co's, 1854.

Hudson, John C. *Making the Corn Belt: A Geographical History of Middle-Western Agriculture.* Bloomington: Indiana University Press, 1994.

Hughes, Jonathan. "The Great Land Ordinances: Colonial America's Thumbprint on History." In *Essays on the Economy of the Old Northwest,* edited by David C. Klingaman and Richard K. Vedder, 1–18. Athens: Ohio University Press, 1987.

Hulbert, Archer Butler. *The Cumberland Road.* Historic Highways of America Volume 10. Cleveland, OH: The Arthur H. Clark Company, 1904.

———. "The Indian Thoroughfares of Ohio." *Ohio Archaeological and Historical Quarterly* 8 (3): 264–95. January 1900.

———. "The Old National Road—the Historic Highway of America." *Ohio Archaeological and Historical Quarterly* 9 (4): 405–519. April 1901.

Hunter, Louis C. *A History of Industrial Power in the United States, 1780–1930. Volume One: Waterpower in the Century of the Steam Engine.* Charlottesville: Published for the Eleutherian Mills-Hagley Foundation by the University Press of Virginia, 1979.

———. *A History of Industrial Power in the United States, 1780–1930. Volume Two: Steam Power.* Charlottesville: Published for the Hagley Museum and Library by the University Press of Virginia, 1985.

———. *Steamboats on the Western Rivers: An Economic and Technological History.* Cambridge, MA: Harvard University Press, 1949.

———. "Studies in the Economic History of the Ohio Valley. Seasonal Aspects of Industry and Commerce before the Age of Big Business." *Smith College Studies in History* 19 (1): 5–49. October 1933.

Hurt, R. Douglas. "The Agricultural Power of the Midwest During the Civil War." In *Union Heartland: The Midwestern Home Front during the Civil War,* edited by Ginette Aley and J. L. Anderson, 68–96. Carbondale: Southern Illinois University Press, 2013.

———. *American Agriculture: A Brief History.* Ames: Iowa State University Press, 1994.

———. *American Farm Tools from Hand-Power to Steam-Power.* Manhattan, KS: Sunflower University Press, 1982.

———. *The Ohio Frontier: Crucible of the Old Northwest, 1720–1830.* Bloomington: Indiana University Press, 1996.

———. "Out of the Cradle: The Reaper Revolution." *Timeline* 3 (5): 38–51. October/November 1886.

———. "The Sheep Industry in Ohio, 1807–1900." *The Old Northwest.* 7: 237–54. 1981.

Hutchinson, William Thomas. "The Bounty Lands of the American Revolution in Ohio." PhD diss., University of Chicago, 1927.

———. Cyrus Hall McCormick. *Seed-time, 1809–1856.* New York: The Century Co., 1930.

———. *Cyrus Hall McCormick. Harvest, 1856–1884.* New York: D. Appleton-Century Company, 1935.

———. "The Reaper Industry and Midwestern Agriculture, 1855–1875." In *Essays in Honor of William E. Dodd by his Former Students at the University of Chicago,* edited by Avery Craven, 115–30. Chicago: The University of Chicago Press, 1935.

Hutslar, Donald A. *Log Construction in the Ohio Country, 1750–1850.* Athens: Ohio University Press, 1992.

———. "Ohio Waterpowered Sawmills." *Ohio History* 84 (1–2): 5–56. Winter–Spring 1975.

Ierley, Merritt. *Traveling the National Road: Across the Centuries on America's First Highway.* Woodstock, New York: The Overlook Press, 1990.

Jacks, David S. "Populists Versus Theorists: Futures Markets and the Volatility of Prices." *Explorations in Economic History* 44 (2): 342–62. April 2007.

Jeremy, David J. "The Diffusion of New Woolen Manufacturing Technology, 1790–1830." In *Transatlantic Industrial Revolution: The Diffusion of Textile Technologies Between Britain and America, 1790–1830s,* 118–40. Oxford: Basil Blackwood Publisher, 1981.

Johnston, John D., Jr. "Sex and Property: The Common Law Tradition, the Law School Curriculum, and Developments Toward Equality." *New York University Law Review* 47 (6): 1033–92. December 1972.

Johnstone, Paul H. "Old Ideals Versus New Ideas in Farm Life: Farmers in a Changing World." In *Yearbook of Agriculture 1940,* 111–70. United States Government Printing Office.

Jones, Robert Leslie. "The Beef Cattle Industry in Ohio Prior to the Civil War." *The Ohio Historical Quarterly* Part I 64 (2): 168–94. April 1955. Part II. 64 (3): 287–319. July 1955.

———. *History of Agriculture in Ohio to 1880.* Kent, OH: Kent State University Press, 1983.

———. "The Horse and Mule Industry in Ohio to 1865." *The Mississippi Valley Historical Review* 33: 61–88. June 1946–March 1947.

———. "The Introduction of Farm Machinery into Ohio Prior to 1865." *The Ohio State Archaeological and Historical Quarterly* 58 (1): 1–20. January 1949.

———. *Ohio Agriculture During the Civil War*. Ohio Civil War Centennial Commission Publication No. 7. Ohio State University Press for The Ohio Historical Society, 1962.

———. "Ohio Agriculture in History." *The Ohio Historical Quarterly* 65 (3): 229–58. July 1956.

Jordan, Philip D. *Ohio Comes of Age: 1873–1900. The History of the State of Ohio*. Volume V, edited by Carl Wittke. Columbus: Ohio State Archaeological and Historical Society, 1943.

Jordan, Terry G. *North American Cattle-Ranching Frontiers: Origins, Diffusion, and Differentiation*. Albuquerque: University of New Mexico Press, 1993.

Jordan, Terry G. and Matti Kaups. *The American Backwoods Frontier: An Ethnic and Ecological Interpretation*. Baltimore, MD: The Johns Hopkins University Press, 1989.

Kaatz, Martin R. "The Black Swamp: A Study in Historical Geography." *Annals of the Association of American Geographers* 45 (1): 1–35. March 1955.

———. "The Settlement of the Black Swamp of Northwestern Ohio: Pioneer Days." *Northwest Ohio Quarterly*. 25: 134–56. Summer 1953.

Kane, Lucile M. *The Falls of St. Anthony: The Waterfall That Built Minneapolis*. St. Paul: Minnesota Historical Society Press, 1987.

Kerridge, Eric. *The Agricultural Revolution*. London: George Allen & Unwin, 1967.

Kindahl, James K. "Economic Factors in Specie Resumption the United States, 1865–79." *The Journal of Political Economy* 69: 30–48. 1961.

King, Isaac F. "The Coming and Going of Ohio Droving." *Ohio Archaeological and Historical Quarterly* 17 (3): 247–53. July 1908.

———. "Flat Boating on the Ohio River." *Ohio Archaeological and Historical Quarterly* 26 (1): 78–81. January 1917.

Kinnison, William A. *Springfield and Clark County: An Illustrated History*. Northridge, CA: Windsor Publications, 1985.

Kirby, Jack Temple. "Rural Culture in the American Middle West: Jefferson to Jane Smiley." *Agricultural History* 70 (4): 581–97. Autumn 1996.

Klein, Maury. *Unfinished Business: The Railroad in American Life*. Hanover, NH: University Press of New England, 1994.

Klingaman, David. "The Significance of Grain in the Development of the Tobacco Colonies." *The Journal of Economic History* 29 (2): 268–78. June 1969.

Kniffen, Fred. "The American Agricultural Fair: The Pattern." *Annals of the Association of American Geographers* 39 (4): 264–82. December 1949.

Knight, W. J. "A History of Pretty Prairie." Manuscript prepared for the Champaign County Historical Society, 1946.

Knodell, Jane. "The Demise of Central Banking and the Domestic Exchanges: Evidence from Antebellum Ohio." *The Journal of Economic History* 58 (3): 714–30. September 1998.

———. "Interregional Financial Integration and the Banknote Market: The Old Northwest, 1815–1845." *The Journal of Economic History* 48 (2): 287–98. June 1988.

———. "Rethinking the Jacksonian Economy: The Impact of the 1832 Bank Veto on Commercial Banking." *The Journal of Economic History* 66 (3): 541–74. September 2006.

Kohlmeier, A. L. *The Old Northwest as the Keystone of the Arch of the American Federal Union: A Study in Commerce and Politics.* Bloomington, IN: The Principia Press, 1938.

Konig, David Thomas, "Jurisprudence and Social Policy in the New Republic." In *Devising Liberty: Preserving and Creating Freedom in the New American Republic,* edited by David Thomas Konig, 178–216. Palo Alto, CA: Stanford University Press, 1995.

Kuhlmann, Charles Byron. *The Development of the Flour-Milling Industry in the United States with Special Reference to the Industry in Minneapolis.* Boston: Houghton Mifflin, 1929.

Kujovich, Mary Yeager. "The Refrigerator Car and the Growth of the American Dressed Beef Industry." *Business History Review* 44 (4): 460–82. Winter 1970.

Kulikoff, Allan. *The Agrarian Origins of American Capitalism.* Charlottesville: University Press of Virginia, 1992.

———. "The Transition to Capitalism in Rural America." *The William and Mary Quarterly* 46 (1): 120–44. January 1989.

Lang, Elfrieda. "Ohioans in Northern Indiana before 1850." *Indiana Magazine of History* 49: 391–404. 1953.

Laning, J. F. "The Evolution of Ohio Counties." *Ohio Archaeological and Historical Quarterly* 5: 326–50. August 1897.

Laning, Paul F. "Sandusky and Cleveland—Railroad Rivals in the 1850s." *Inland Seas* 28 (3): 189–95. Fall 1972.

Larson, John Lauritz. *Internal Improvement: National Public Works and the Promise of Popular Government in the Early United States.* Chapel Hill: The University of North Carolina Press, 2001.

—————. *The Market Revolution in America: Liberty, Ambition, and the Eclipse of the Common Good.* Cambridge: Cambridge University Press, 2010.

Laurent, Jerome K. "Trade, Transport and Technology: The American Great Lakes, 1866–1910." *The Journal of Transport History* 4 (1): 1–24. 1983.

Leavitt, Charles T. "Attempts to Improve Cattle Breeds in the United States, 1790–1860." *Agricultural History* 7 (2): 51–67. April 1933.

—————. "Transportation and the Livestock Industry of the Middle West to 1860." *Agricultural History* 8 (1): 20–33. January 1934.

Lebergott, Stanley. *The Americans: An Economic Record.* New York: W. W. Norton & Company, 1984.

—————. "Labor Force and Employment, 1800–1960." In *Output, Employment, and Productivity in the United States after 1800: Studies in Income and Wealth.* Volume Thirty by the Conference on Research in Income and Wealth, 117–204. New York: National Bureau of Economic Research, 1966.

—————. "United States Transport Advance and Externalities." *The Journal of Economic History* 26: 437–61. December 1966.

LeDuc, Thomas. "Public Policy, Private Investment, and Land Use in American Agriculture, 1825–1875." *Agricultural History* 37 (1): 1–9). January 1963.

—————. "State Disposal of the Agricultural College Land Scrip." *Agricultural History* 28 (3): 99–107). July 1954.

Lee, Guy A. "The Historical Significance of the Chicago Grain Elevator System." *Agricultural History* 11 (1): 16–32. January 1937.

Leet, Donald. "The Determinants of the Fertility Transition in Antebellum Ohio." *The Journal of Economic History* 36 (2): 359–78. June 1976.

Lemon, James T. *The Best Poor Man's Country: A Geographical Study of Early Southeastern Pennsylvania.* Baltimore, MD: The Johns Hopkins Press, 1972.

Levy, Jonathan Ira. "Contemplating Delivery: Futures Trading and the Problem of Commodity Exchange in the United States, 1875–1905." *The American Historical Review* 111 (2): 307–35. April 2006.

Lindert, Peter H. "Long-run Trends in American Farmland Values." *Agricultural History* 62 (3): 45–85. Summer 1988.

Lippincott, Isaac. *A History of Manufactures in the Ohio Valley to the Year 1860.* New York: Knickerbocker Press, 1914.

Lloyd, W. A., J. I. Falconer, and C. E. Thorne. *The Agriculture of Ohio.* Bulletin 326 of the Ohio Agricultural Experiment Station. Wooster, Ohio, 1918.

Loehr, Rodney C. "The Influence of English Agriculture on American Agriculture, 1775–1825." *Agricultural History* 11 (1): 3–15. January 1937.

Lurie, Jonathan. *The Chicago Board of Trade 1859–1905: The Dynamics of Self-regulation.* Urbana: University of Illinois Press, 1979.

———. "Speculation, Risk, And Profits: The Ambivalent Agrarian in the Late Nineteenth Century." *Agricultural History* 46 (2): 269–78. 1972.

Lush, Jay L. and A. L. Anderson. "A Genetic History of Poland-China Swine." *The Journal of Heredity* 30 (4 & 5): 149–56, 219–24. April & May 1939.

Lyon-Jenness, Cheryl. "Bergamot Balm and Verbenas: The Public and Private Meaning of Ornamental Plants in the Mid-Nineteenth-Century Midwest." *Agricultural History* 73 (2): 201–21. Spring 1999.

Macdonald, James. *Food from the Far West or, American Agriculture with Special Reference to the Beef Production and Importation of Dead Meat from America to Great Britain.* London: William P. Nimmo, 1878.

Macmaster, Richard K. "The Cattle Trade in Western Virginia, 1760–1830." In *Appalachian Frontiers: Settlement, Society, and Development in the Preindustrial Era,* edited by Robert D. Mitchell, 127–49, 314–17. Knoxville: The University Press of Kentucky, 1991.

Mahar-Keplinger, Lisa. *Grain Elevators.* New York: Princeton Architectural Press, 1993.

Mahoney, Timothy R. *River Towns in the Great West: The Structure of Provincial Urbanization in the American Midwest, 1820–1870.* Cambridge: Cambridge University Press, 1990.

Mak, James. "Intraregional Trade in the Antebellum West: Ohio, a Case Study." *Agricultural History* 46: 489–97. October 1972.

Mak, James and Gary M. Walton. "Steamboats and the Great Productivity Surge in River Transportation." *The Journal of Economic History* 32 (3): 619–40. September 1972.

Malin, Donald F. *The Evolution of Breeds: An Analytical Study of Breed Building as Illustrated in Shorthorn, Hereford and Aberdeen Angus Cattle Poland China and Duroc Jersey Swine.* Des Moines, IA: Wallace Publishing Company, 1923.

Marti, Donald B. "Agricultural Journalism and the Diffusion of Knowledge: The First Half-Century in America." *Agricultural History* 54 (1): 28–37. January 1980.

———. "Sisters of the Grange: Rural Feminism in the Late Nineteenth Century." *Agricultural History* 58 (3): 247–61. July 1984.

Martin, Albro. *Railroads Triumphant: The Growth, Rejection, and Rebirth of a Vital American Force.* New York: Oxford University Press, 1992.

Marvin, Walter Rumsey. "The Steubenville and Indiana Railroad: The Pennsylvania's Middle Route to the Middle West." *The Ohio Historical Quarterly* 66 (1): 11–21. January 1957.

Mayhew, Anne. "A Reappraisal of the Causes of Farm Protest in the United States, 1870–1900." *The Journal of Economic History* 32 (2): 464–75. June 1972.

McCalla, Alex F. "Protectionism in International Agricultural Trade, 1850–1968." *Agricultural History* 43 (3): 329–43. July 1969.

McClelland, Peter D. *Sowing Modernity: America's First Agricultural Revolution.* Ithaca, NY: Cornell University Press, 1997.

McClelland, Peter D. and Richard J. Zeckhauser. *Demographic Dimensions of the New Republic: American Interregional Migration, Vital Statistics, and Manumissions, 1800–1860.* Cambridge: Cambridge University Press, 1982.

McConnell, Michael N. *A Country Between: The Upper Ohio Valley and Its Peoples, 1724–1774.* Lincoln: University of Nebraska Press, 1992.

McCormick, Virginia E. "Butter and Egg Business: Implications from the Records of a Nineteenth-Century Farm Wife." *Ohio History* 100 (1–2): 57–67. Winter–Spring 1991.

———, ed. *Farm Wife: A Self Portrait, 1886–1896.* Ames: Iowa State University Press, 1990.

McGuire, Robert A. "Economic Causes of Late-Nineteenth Century Agrarian Unrest: New Evidence." *The Journal of Economic History* 41 (4): 835–52. December 1981.

McMurry, Sally. *Families and Farmhouses in Nineteenth-Century America: Vernacular Design and Social Change.* Oxford: Oxford University Press, 1988.

———. *Transforming Rural Life: Dairying Families and Agricultural Change, 1820–1885.* Baltimore, MD: The Johns Hopkins University Press, 1995.

McPherson, James M. *Battle Cry of Freedom: The Civil War Era.* New York: Oxford University Press, 1988.

———. "From Limited War to Total War in America." In *On the Road to Total War: The American Civil War and the German Wars of Unification, 1861–1871,* edited by Stig Förster and Jörg Nagler, 295–309. Cambridge: Cambridge University Press, 1997.

Meinig, D. W. *The Shaping of America: A Geographical Perspective on 500 Years of History. Volume 2: Continental America, 1800–1867.* New Haven, CT: Yale University Press, 1993.

Merrill, Michael. "Putting 'Capitalism' in Its Place: A Review of Recent Literature." *The William and Mary Quarterly* 52 (2): 315–26. April 1995.

Meyer, David R. "Midwestern Industrialization and the American Manufacturing Belt in the Nineteenth Century." *The Journal of Economic History* 49 (4): 921–37. December 1989.

———. *The Roots of American Industrialization.* Baltimore, MD: The Johns Hopkins University Press, 2003.

Middleton, Evan P., ed. *History of Champaign County Ohio: Its People, Industries and Institutions*. Indianapolis, IN: B. F. Bowen & Company, 1917.

Miller, Aaron. "Diary of Aaron Miller." *Ohio Archaeological and Historical Quarterly* 33 (1): 67–79. January 1924.

Miller, Tamara Gaskell. "'My Whole Enjoyment & Almost My Existence Depends Upon My Friends': Family and Kinship in Early Ohio." In *The Center of a Great Empire: The Ohio Country in the Early Republic*, edited by Andrew R. L. Cayton and Stuart D. Hobbs, 122–45. Athens: Ohio University Press, 2005.

Miner, Craig. *A Most Magnificent Machine: America Adopts the Railroad, 1825–1862*. Lawrence: University Press of Kansas, 2010.

Morgan, Dan. *Merchants of Grain*. New York: The Viking Press, 1979.

Moss, Jeffrey W. and Cynthia B. Lass. "A History of Farmers' Institutes." *Agricultural History* 62 (2): 150–63. Spring 1988.

Mould, David H. *Dividing Lines: Canals, Railroads and Urban Rivalry in Ohio's Hocking Valley, 1825–1875*. Dayton, OH: Wright State University Press, 1994.

Muller, Edward K. "Selective Urban Growth in the Middle Ohio Valley, 1800–1860." *The Geographical Review* 66: 178–99. April 1976.

Murray, John E., and Metin M. Coşgel. "Market, Religion, and Culture in Shaker Swine Production, 1788–1880." *Agricultural History* 72 (3): 552–73. Summer 1998.

Nader, John. "The Rise of an Inventive Profession: Learning Effects in the Midwestern Harvester Industry, 1850–1890." *The Journal of Economic History* 54 (2): 397–408. June 1994.

Neely, Mark E., Jr. "Was the Civil War a Total War?" *Civil War History* 37 (1): 5–28. 1991.

Newcomer, Lee. "Construction of the Wabash and Erie Canal." *The Ohio State Archaeological and Historical Quarterly* 46 (2): 199–207. April 1937.

Nordin, D. Sven. *Rich Harvest: A History of the Grange, 1867–1900*. Jackson: University Press of Mississippi, 1974.

North, Douglass, C. "The United States in the International Economy, 1790–1950." In *American Economic History*, edited by Seymour E. Harris, 181–206. New York: McGraw-Hill Book Company, 1961.

Odle, Thomas D. "The American Grain Trade of the Great Lakes, 1825–1873." *Inland Seas* 7: 237–45. Winter 1951; 8: 23–28. Spring 1952; 8: 99–104. Summer 1952; 8: 177–92. Fall 1852; 8: 248–54. Winter 1952.

———. "Entrepreneurial Cooperation on the Great Lakes: The Origin of the Methods of American Grain Marketing." *Business History Review* 38: 439–55. 1964.

Olmstead, Alan L. "The Mechanization of Reaping and Mowing in American Agriculture, 1833–1870." *The Journal of Economic History* 35: 327–52. June 1975.

Olmstead, Alan L. and Paul W. Rhode. "The Red Queen and the Hard Reds: Productivity Growth in American Wheat, 1800–1940." *The Journal of Economic History* 62 (4): 929–66. December 2002.

Opie, John. *The Law of the Land: Two Hundred Years of American Farmland Policy.* Lincoln: University of Nebraska Press, 1987.

Overton, Mark. *Agricultural Revolution in England: The Transformation of the Agrarian Economy 1500–1850.* Cambridge: Cambridge University Press, 1996.

Owsley, Frank Lawrence. *Plain Folk of the Old South.* Baton Rouge: Louisiana State University Press, 1949.

Page, Brian and Richard Walker. "From Settlement to Fordism: The Agro-Industrial Revolution in the American Midwest." *Economic Geography* 67 (4): 281–315. October 1991.

Parker, William N. "From Northwest to Midwest: Social Bases of a Regional History." In *Essays in Nineteenth Century Economic History: The Old Northwest*, edited by David C. Klingaman and Richard K. Vedder, 3–34. Athens: Ohio University Press, 1975.

———. "The Magic of Property." *Agricultural History* 54 (4): 477–89. October 1980.

———. "Sources of Agricultural Productivity in the Nineteenth Century." *Journal of Farm Economics* 49 (5): 1455–68. December 1967.

Parker, William N. and Stephen J. Decanio. "Two Hidden Sources of Productivity Growth in American Agriculture, 1860–1930." *Agricultural History* 56 (4): 648–62. October 1982.

Parker, William N. and Judith L. V. Klein. "Productivity Growth in Grain Production in the United States, 1840–60 and 1900–10." In *Output, Employment, and Productivity in the United States after 1800: Studies in Income and Wealth, Volume Thirty* by the Conference on Research in Income and Wealth, 523–82. New York: National Bureau of Economic Research, 1966.

Paul, Allen B. "The Past and Future of the Commodities Exchanges." *Agricultural History* 56 (1): 287–305. January 1982.

Pauly, Philip J. *Fruits and Plains: The Horticultural Transformation of America.* Cambridge, MA: Harvard University Press, 2007.

Paxson, Frederic L. "The Railroads of the 'Old Northwest' before the Civil War." *Transactions of the Wisconsin Academy of Sciences, Arts, and Letters* Volume 17, Part 1 (4): 243–74. 1911.

Percy, David O. "Ax or Plow?: Significant Colonial Landscape Alteration
    Rates in the Maryland and Virginia Tidewater." *Agricultural History* 66
    (2): 66–74. Spring 1992.

Perkins, Elizabeth A. *Border Life: Experience and Memory in the Revolutionary
    Ohio Valley*. Chapel Hill: The University of North Carolina Press, 1998.

Perry, P. J. "The Shorthorn Comes of Age (1822–1843): Agricultural History
    from the Herdbook." *Agricultural History* 56 (3): 560–66. July 1982.

Peters, William E. *Ohio Lands and Their Subdivisions*. Athens, OH: William E.
    Peters, 1917.

Petty, Gerald M., ed. *Ohio 1810 Tax Duplicate: Arranged in a State-Wide
    Alphabetical List of Names of Taxpayers with an Index of Names of Original
    Entries*. Gerald M. Petty, Compiler & Publisher, Columbus, Ohio, 1976.

Phillips, Kevin. *The Cousins' Wars: Religion, Politics, and the Triumph of Anglo-
    America*. New York: Basic Books, 1999.

Phillips, Sarah T. "Antebellum Agricultural Reform, Republican Ideology, and
    Sectional tension." *Agricultural History* 74 (4): 799–822. Fall 2000.

Plumb, Charles Sumner. "Felix Renick, Pioneer." *Ohio Archaeological and
    Historical Quarterly* 33 (1): 3–66. January 1924.

———. *Types and Breeds of Farm Animals*. Boston: Ginn & Company, 1906.

Porter, Eugene O. "Financing Ohio's pre-Civil War Railroads." *The Ohio State
    Archaeological and Historical Quarterly* 57 (3): 215–26. July 1948.

Porter, Glenn and Harold C. Livesay. *Merchants and Manufacturers. Studies in
    the Changing Structure of Nineteenth-Century Marketing*. Baltimore, MD:
    The Johns Hopkins Press, 1971.

Post, Charles. "Agrarian Class Structure and Economic Development in
    Colonial British North America: The Place of the American Revolution
    in the Origins of US Capitalism." *Journal of Agrarian Change* 9 (4): 453–83.
    October 2009.

Price, H. Bruce. "Grain Standardization." *The American Economic Review* 11
    (2): 227–30. June 1921.

Primack, Martin L. "Land Clearing under Nineteenth-Century Techniques:
    Some Preliminary Calculations." *The Journal of Economic History* 22 (4):
    484–97. December 1962.

Quick, Graeme R. and Wesley F. Buchele. *The Grain Harvesters*. St. Joseph,
    MI: American Society of Agricultural Engineers, 1978.

Quinn, Michael J. "The Late Glacial History of the Cedar Bog Area." In
    Cedar Bog Symposium, edited by Charles C. King and Clara May Freder-
    ick. Ohio Biological Survey Informative Circular No. 4: 7–12. The Ohio
    State University, 1974.

Quinn, Michael J. and Richard P. Goldthwait. "Glacial Geology of Champaign County, Ohio." State of Ohio. Department of Natural Resources. Division of Geological Survey. Report of Investigations No. 111. Columbus, 1979.

Quisenberry, K. S., and L. P. Reitz. "Turkey Wheat: The Cornerstone of an Empire." *Agricultural History* 48 (1): 98–110. January 1974.

Raitz, Karl, ed. *The National Road*. Baltimore, MD: The Johns Hopkins University Press, 1996.

Ransom, Roger L. "Public Canal Investment and the Opening of the Old Northwest." In *Essays in Nineteenth Century Economic History. The Old Northwest*, edited by David C. Klingaman and Richard K. Vedder, 246–68. Athens: Ohio University Press, 1975.

Rasmussen, Wayne D. "The Civil War: A Catalyst of Agricultural Revolution." *Agricultural History* 39 (4): 187–95. October 1965.

———. "The Impact of Technological Change on American Agriculture, 1862–1962." *The Journal of Economic History* 22: 578–91. December 1962.

Rastatter, Edward H. "Nineteenth Century Public Land Policy: The Case for the Speculator." In *Essays in Nineteenth Century Economic History: The Old Northwest*, edited by David C. Klingaman and Richard K. Vedder, 118–37. Athens: Ohio University Press, 1975.

Ratcliffe, Donald J. *Party Spirit in a Frontier Republic: Democratic Politics in Ohio, 1793–1821*. Columbus: Ohio State University Press, 1998.

Rees, Jonathan. *Refrigeration Nation: A History of Ice, Appliances, and Enterprise in America*. Baltimore, MD: The Johns Hopkins University Press, 2013.

Rezneck, Samuel. "The Depression of 1819–1822." *The American Historical Review* 39 (1): 28–47. 1933–1934.

Ridder, Edgar A. *An Atlas of Champaign County Landmarks*. Urbana, OH: Champaign County Genealogical Society, 1987.

Rikoon, J. Sanford. *Threshing in the Midwest, 1820–1940: A Study of Traditional Culture and Technological Change*. Bloomington: Indiana University Press, 1988.

Robbins, Roy Marvin. *Our Landed Heritage: The Public Domain, 1776–1936*. Princeton, NJ: Princeton University Press, 1942.

Rogin, Leo. *The Introduction of Farm Machinery in Its Relation to the Productivity of Labor in the Agriculture of the United States during the Nineteenth Century*. University of California Publications in Economics. Volume 9. Issued July 9, 1931. Berkeley: University of California Press, 1931.

Rohrbough, Malcolm J. "Diversity and Unity in the Old Northwest, 1790–1850: Several Peoples Fashion a Single Region." In *Pathways to the Old*

Northwest: An Observance of the Bicentennial of the Northwest Ordinance, 71–87. Indianapolis: Indiana Historical Society, 1988.

———. *The Trans-Appalachian Frontier: People, Societies, and Institutions 1775–1850*. New York: Oxford University Press, 1978.

Rosenberg, Charles E. *The Cholera Years: The United States in 1832, 1849, and 1866*. Chicago: The University of Chicago Press, 1962.

Ross, Earle D. "The Evolution of the Agricultural Fair in the Northwest." *The Iowa Journal of History and Politics* 24 (3): 445–80. July 1926.

Rothbard, Murray N. *The Panic of 1819: Reactions and Policies*. New York: Columbia University Press, 1962.

Rothenberg, Winifred B. "The Market and Massachusetts Farmers, 1750–1855." *The Journal of Economic History* 41 (2): 283–314. June 1981.

———. *From Market-Places to a Market Economy: The Transformation of Rural Massachusetts, 1750–1850*. Chicago: The University of Chicago Press, 1992.

———. "Markets, Values and Capitalism: A Discourse on Method." *The Journal of Economic History* 44 (1): 174–78. March 1984.

Rothstein, Morton. "America in the International Rivalry for The British Wheat Market, 1860–1914." *The Mississippi Valley Historical Review* 47 (3): 381–406. December 1960.

———. "The American West and Foreign Markets, 1850–1900." In *The Frontier in American Development: Essays in Honor of Paul Wallace Gates*, edited by David M. Ellis, 381–406. Ithaca, NY: Cornell University Press, 1969.

———. "Antebellum Wheat and Cotton Exports: A Contrast in Marketing Organization and Economic Development." *Agricultural History* 40 (2): 91–100. April 1966.

———. "Farmer Movements and Organizations: Numbers, Gains, Losses." *Agricultural History* 62 (3): 161–81. Summer 1988.

Rubin, Julius. "Canal or Railroad? Imitation and Innovation in the Response to the Erie Canal in Philadelphia, Baltimore, and Boston." *Transactions of the American Philosophical Society*. New Series—Volume 51, Part 7. November 1961.

Rugh, Susan Sessions. *Our Common Country: Family Farming, Culture, and Community in the Nineteenth-Century Midwest*. Bloomington: Indiana University Press, 2001.

Salmon, Marylynn. *Women and the Law of Property in Early America*. Chapel Hill: The University of North Carolina Press, 1986.

Salmon, S. C., O. R. Mathews, and R. W. Leukel. "A Half Century of Wheat Improvement in the United States." *Advances in Agronomy* 5: 1–151. 1953.

Sanders, Alvin Howard. *Short-Horn Cattle: A Series of Historical Sketches, Memoirs and Records of the Breed and its Development in the United States and Canada*. Chicago: Sanders Publishing, 1900.

Sanders, Alvin Howard and Wayne Dinsmore. *A History of the Percheron Horse*. Chicago: Breeder's Gazette Print, 1917.

Schafer, Joseph. *The Social History of American Agriculture*. New York: The Macmillan Company, 1936.

Scheerer, Hanno. "'For Ten Years Past I Have Constantly Wished to Turn My Western Lands into Money': Speculator Frustration and Settlers' Bargaining Power in Ohio's Virginia Military District, 1795–1810." *Ohio Valley History* 14 (10): 3–27. Spring 2014.

Scheiber, Harry N. *Ohio Canal Era: A Case Study of Government and the Economy, 1820–1861*. Athens: Ohio University Press, 1968.

———. "The Ohio-Mississippi Flatboat Trade: Some Reconsiderations." *The Frontier in American Development: Essays in Honor of Paul Wallace Gates*, edited by David M. Ellis, 277–98. Ithaca, NY: Cornell University Press, 1969.

———. "The Transportation Revolution and American Law: Constitutionalism and Public Policy." In *Transportation and the Early Nation: Papers Presented at an Indiana American Revolution Bicentennial Symposium*, 1–29. Indianapolis: Indiana Historical Society, 1982.

———. "Urban Rivalry and Internal Improvements in the Old Northwest 1820–1860." *Ohio History* 71 (3): 227–39, 290–92. October 1962.

Schlebecker, John T. *Whereby We Thrive: A History of American Farming, 1607–1972*. Ames: The Iowa State University Press, 1975.

Schmidt, Louis Bernard. "Internal Commerce and the Development of National Economy before 1860." *The Journal of Political Economy* 47: 798–822. December 1939.

———. "The Internal Grain Trade of the United States 1850–1860." *The Iowa Journal of History and Politics* 18: 94–124. January 1920.

———. "The Internal Grain Trade of the United States 1860–1890." *The Iowa Journal of History and Politics* 19: 196–245, 414–55; 20: 70–131. April, July 1921; January 1922.

———. "The Westward Movement of the Wheat Growing Industry in the United States." *The Iowa Journal of History and Politics* 18: 396–412. 1920.

Schneider, Norris F. "The National Road: Main Street of America." *Ohio History* 83 (2): 114–46. Spring 1974.

Schob, David E. *Hired Hands and Plowboys: Farm Labor in the Midwest, 1815–60*. Urbana: University of Illinois Press, 1975.

Schotter, H. W. *The Growth and Development of The Pennsylvania Railroad Company: A Review of the Charter and Annual Reports of The Pennsylvania Railroad Company 1846 to 1926, Inclusive.* Philadelphia: Press of Allen, Lane and Scott, 1927.

Schumacher, Max George. *The Northern Farmer and His Markets during the Late Colonial Period.* Ph.D. Dissertation, University of California, 1948.

Sellers, Charles. *The Market Revolution: Jacksonian America, 1815–1846.* New York: Oxford University Press, 1991.

Shannon, Fred A. *The Farmer's Last Frontier: Agriculture 1860–1897.* Volume V. The Economic History of the United States. New York: Farrar & Rinehart, 1945.

———. "The Homestead Act and the Labor Surplus." *The American Historical Review* 41 (4): 637–51. July 1936.

Shannon, Timothy J. "'This Unpleasant Business': The Transformation of Land Speculation in the Ohio Country, 1787–1820." In *The Pursuit of Public Power: Political Culture in Ohio, 1787–1861,* edited by Jeffrey P. Brown and Andrew R. L. Cayton, 15–30, 191–96. Kent, OH: Kent State University Press, 1994.

Sharp, Paul and Jacob Weisdorf. "Globalization Revisited: Market Integration and the Wheat Trade between North America and Britain from the Eighteenth Century." *Explorations in Economic History* 50 (1): 88–98. January 2013.

Sharrer, G. Terry. "The Merchant-Millers: Baltimore's Flour Milling Industry, 1783–1860." *Agricultural History* 56 (1): 138–50. January 1982.

Shepherd, Rebecca A. "Restless Americans: The Geographic Mobility of Farm Laborers in the Old Midwest, 1850–1870." *Ohio History* 89 (1): 25–45. 1980.

Sherman, C. E. *Original Ohio Land Subdivisions: Final Report Ohio Cooperative Topographic Survey: Volume III.* Press of the Ohio State Reformatory, 1925.

Skaggs, Jimmy M. *Prime Cut: Livestock Raising and Meatpacking in the United States 1607–1983.* College Station: Texas A&M University Press, 1986.

Smith, C. Wayne. *Crop Production: Evolution, History, and Technology.* John Wiley & Sons, 1995.

Smith, Thomas H. *The Mapping of Ohio.* Kent, OH: Kent State University Press, 1977.

Smith, William E. and Ophia D. Smith. *A Buckeye Titan.* Cincinnati: Historical and Philosophical Society of Ohio, 1953.

Sokoloff, Kenneth L. and B. Zorina Khan. "The Democratization of Invention during Early Industrialization: Evidence from the United States, 1790–1846." *The Journal of Economic History* 50 (2): 363–78. June 1990.

Soltow, Lee C. "Inequity Amidst Abundance: Land Ownership in Early Nineteenth Century Ohio." *Ohio History* 88 (2): 133–51. Spring 1979.

———. "Land Fragmentation as an Index of History in the Virginia Military District of Ohio." *Explorations in Economic History* 20 (3): 263–73. July 1983.

———. *Men and Wealth in the United States 1850–1870.* New Haven, CT: Yale University Press, 1975.

Sowers, Edgar. *The Laws of Ohio Relating to Women.* Published by the Cleveland Branch of the Association of Collegiate Alumnae, [1895?] Booklet, 84 pages.

Speth, Linda E. "The Married Women's Property Acts, 1839–1865: Reform, Reaction, or Revolution?" In *Women and the Law: A social historical perspective. Volume II. Property, Family and the Legal Profession,* edited by D. Kelly Weisberg, 69–91. Cambridge, MA: Schenkman Publishing, 1982.

Sprague, G. "Agricultural Associations of Ohio." In *Transactions of the Illinois State Agricultural Society: 1853–1854,* 34–37. 1855.

Stanley, Amy Dru. "Marriage, Property, and Class." In *A Companion to American Women's History,* edited by Nancy A. Hewitt, 193–205. Hoboken, NJ: Blackwell Publishers Ltd, 2002.

Steckel, Richard H. "The Economic Foundations of East-West Migration during the 19th Century." *Explorations in Economic History* 20 (1): 14–36. January 1983.

Steinfeld, Robert J. "Property and Suffrage in the Early American Republic." *Stanford Law Review* 41 (2): 335–76. January 1989.

Steward, John F. *The Reaper: A History of the Efforts of Those Who Justly May Be Said to Have Made Bread Cheap.* New York: Greenberg, 1931.

Stewart, Leola M. "Sandusky, Pioneer Link between Sail and Rail." In *The Ohio State Archaeological and Historical Quarterly* 57 (3): 227–36. July 1948.

Stickley, Pat and Denise Kay Moore. *Champaign County, Ohio Patent Deeds Located in the Land Deed Indices.* Urbana, OH: The Champaign County Genealogical Society, 2003.

Stokes, Melvyn and Stephen Conway, eds. *The Market Revolution in America: Social, Political, and Religious Expressions, 1800–1880.* Charlottesville: University Press of Virginia, 1996.

Stoll, Steven. *Larding the Lean Earth: Soil and Society in Nineteenth-Century America.* New York: Hill and Wang, 2002.

Storck, John and Walter Dorwin Teague. *Flour for Man's Bread: A History of Milling.* Minneapolis: University of Minnesota Press, 1952.

Stover, John F. *History of the Baltimore and Ohio Railroad*. West Lafayette, IN: Purdue University Press, 1987.

———. *Iron Road to the West: American Railroads in the 1850s*. New York: Columbia University Press, 1978.

———. "Iron Roads in the Old Northwest: The Railroads and the Growing Nation." In *Transportation and the Early Nation. Papers presented at an Indiana American Revolution Bicentennial Symposium*, 135–56. Indianapolis: Indiana Historical Society, 1982.

Stover, Stephen L. "Early Sheep Husbandry in Ohio." *Agricultural History* 36 (2): 101–7. April 1962.

———. "Ohio's Sheep Year: 1868." *Agricultural History* 38 (2): 102–7. April 1964.

Swan, John R. *Statutes of the State of Ohio, of a General Nature, in Force August 1854*. Cincinnati, OH: H. W. Derby & Co., 1854.

Swierenga, Robert P. "The Settlement of the Old Northwest: Ethnic Pluralism in a Featureless Plain." *Journal of the Early Republic* 9: 73–105. Spring 1989.

Sylla, Richard, John B. Legler, and John J. Wallis. "Banks and State Public Finance in the New Republic: The United States, 1790–1860." *The Journal of Economic History* 47 (2): 391–403. June 1987.

Taylor, Alan. *The Civil War of 1812: American Citizens, British Subjects, Irish Rebels, and Indian Allies*. New York: Alfred A. Knopf, 2010.

———. "Land and Liberty on the Post-Revolutionary Frontier." In *Devising Liberty: Preserving and Creating Freedom in the New American Republic*, edited by David Thomas Konig, 81–108. Stanford University Press, 1995.

Taylor, George Rogers. "American Economic Growth before 1840: An Exploratory Essay." *The Journal of Economic History* 24 (4): 427–44. December 1964.

———. *The Transportation Revolution, 1815–1860*. New York: Holt, Rinehart & Winston, 1951.

Taylor, George Rogers and Irene D. Neu. *The American Railroad Network 1861–1890*. Cambridge, MA: Harvard University Press, 1956.

Temin, Peter. *The Jacksonian Economy*. New York: W. W. Norton & Company, 1969.

Thackery, David T. *A Light and Uncertain Hold: A History of the Sixty-Sixth Ohio Volunteer Infantry*. Kent, OH: Kent State University Press, 1999.

Thomas, John J. *Farm Implements, and the Principles of Their Construction and Use; an Elementary and Familiar Treatise on Mechanics, and on Natural Philosophy Generally, As Applied to the Ordinary Practices of Agriculture*. New York: Harper & Brothers, Publishers, 1854.

Thompson, James Westfall. *A History of Livestock Raising in the United States, 1607–1860.* Agricultural History Series No. 5. United States Department of Agriculture, November 1942.

Thrower, Norman J. W. *Original Survey and Land Subdivision: A Comparative Study of the Form and Effect of Contrasting Cadastral Surveys.* Fourth in the Monograph Series Published for The Association of American Geographers. Chicago: Rand McNally & Company, 1966.

Towne, Marvin W. and Wayne D. Rasmussen. "Farm Gross Product and Gross Investment in the Nineteenth Century." In *Trends in the American Economy in the Nineteenth Century: Studies in Income and Wealth Volume Twenty-Four by the Conference on Research in Income and Wealth,* 255–315. Princeton, NJ: Princeton University Press, 1960.

Townshend, N. S. "History of Agriculture in Ohio." In *Forty-Second Annual Report of the Ohio State Board of Agriculture ... for the Year 1887,* 359–71. Columbus: Myers Brothers, State Printers, 1888.

Treat, Payson Jackson. *The National Land System 1785–1820.* New York: E. B. Treat & Company Publishers, 1910.

———. "Origin of the National Land System under the Confederation." *Annual Report of the American Historical Association* 1: 233–39. 1905.

Trigger, Bruce G., ed. *Handbook of North American Indians.* Volume 15. *Northeast.* Washington, DC: Smithsonian Institution, 1979.

Trimble, William. "Historical Aspects of the Surplus Food Production of the United States, 1862–1902." In *Annual Report of the American Historical Association,* 223–39. 1918.

True, Rodney H. "The Early Development of Agricultural Societies in the United States." In *Annual Report of the American Historical Association for the Year 1920.,* 295–306. Washington, DC: Government Printing Office, 1925.

Turner, Frederick Jackson. "The Place of the Ohio Valley in American History." *Ohio Archaeological and Historical Quarterly* 20 (1): 32–47. January 1911.

Ulen, Thomas S. "The Regulation of Grain Warehousing and its Economic Effects: The Competitive Position of Chicago in the 1870s and 1880s." *Agricultural History* 56 (1): 194–210. January 1982.

Ulrich, Laurel Thatcher. *The Age of Homespun: Objects and Stories in the Creation of an American Myth.* New York: Alfred A. Knopf, 2001.

US Bureau of the Census. *Census for 1820.* Washington, DC, 1821.

———. *Abstract of the Returns of the Fifth Census ...* Washington, DC, 1832.

———. *Compendium of the Enumeration of the Inhabitants and Statistics of the United States*....Washington, DC, 1841.

———. *The Seventh Census of the United States: 1850*. Washington, DC, 1853.

———. *The Seventh Census. Report of the Superintendent*....Washington, DC, 1853.

———. *Agriculture of the United State in 1860*....Washington, DC, 1864.

———. *Population of the United States in 1860*....Washington, DC, 1864.

———. *Manufactures of the United States in 1860*....Washington, DC, 1865.

Van Metre, T. W. "Internal Commerce of the United States." In Part Two of *History of Domestic and Foreign Commerce of the United States*. Volume I, edited by Emory R. Johnson, 191–323. New York: Burt Franklin, 1915.

Vance, James E., Jr. *The North American Railroad: Its Origin, Evolution, and Geography*. Baltimore, MD: The Johns Hopkins University Press, 1995.

von Ende, Eleanor and Thomas Weiss. "Consumption of Farm Output and Economic Growth in the Old Northwest, 1800–1860." *The Journal of Economic History* 53 (2): 308–18. June 1993.

Wade, Richard C. *The Urban Frontier: The Rise of Western Cities, 1790–1830*. Cambridge, MA: Harvard University Press, 1959.

Walsh, Margaret, *The Rise of the Midwestern Meat Packing Industry*. Lexington: The University Press of Kentucky, 1982.

Walton, Gary M. "River Transportation and the Old Northwest Territory." In *Essays on the Economy of the Old Northwest*, edited by David C. Klingaman and Richard K. Vedder, 225–42. Athens: Ohio University Press, 1987.

Warbasse, Elizabeth Bowles. *The Changing Legal Rights of Married Women, 1800–1861*. New York: Garland Publishing, 1987.

Ward, James A. *Railroads and the Character of America 1820–1887*. Knoxville: The University of Tennessee Press, 1986.

Ware, Joseph. *History of Mechanicsburg, Ohio*. Columbus, OH: The F. J. Heer Printing Co., 1917.

Watson, Harry L. *Liberty and Power: The politics of Jacksonian America*. New York: Hill and Wang, 1990. Revised edition, 2006.

Weber, Thomas. *The Northern Railroads in the Civil War, 1861–1865*. New York: King's Crown Press, 1952.

Weeks, William Earl. *Building the Continental Empire: American Expansion from the Revolution to the Civil War*. Chicago: Ivan R. Dee, 1996.

Weiner, Marli F. "Rural Women." In *A Companion to American Women's History*, edited by Nancy A. Hewitt, 150–66. Hoboken, NJ: Blackwell Publishers Ltd, 2002.

Weld, Mason Cogswell. *The Percheron Horse in America*. New York: O. Judd Co., 1886.

Welke, Barbara Young. *Law and the Borders of Belonging in the Long Nineteenth Century United States*. Cambridge: Cambridge University Press, 2010.

Wentworth, Edward Norris. *America's Sheep Trails*. Ames: The Iowa State College Press, 1948.

Wheeler, David L. "The Beef Cattle Industry in the Old Northwest, 1803–1860." *Panhandle-Plains Historical Review* 47: 28–45. 1974.

White, John H., Jr. *The American Railroad Freight Car: From the Wood-car Era to the Coming of Steel*. Baltimore, MD: The Johns Hopkins University Press, 1993.

———. *The Great Yellow Fleet: A History of American Railroad Refrigerator Cars*. San Marino, CA: Golden West Books, 1986.

White, Richard. *The Middle Ground: Indians, Empires, and Republics in the Great Lakes region, 1650–1815*. Cambridge: Cambridge University Press, 1991.

Wik, Reynold M. *Steam Power on the American Farm*. Philadelphia: University of Pennsylvania Press, 1953.

Wilhelm, Hubert G. H. *The Origin and Distribution of Settlement Groups: Ohio: 1850*. Printed by the author, 1982.

Winberry, John J. "The Sorghum Syrup Industry 1854–1975." *Agricultural History* 54 (2): 343–52. April 1980.

Winkle, Kenneth J. *The Politics of Community: Migration and politics in antebellum Ohio*. Cambridge: Cambridge University Press, 1988.

Winters, Donald L. "Agricultural Tenancy in the Nineteenth-Century Middle West: The Historiographical Debate." *Indiana Magazine of History* 78: 128–53. June 1982.

Wood, Gordon S. *Empire of Liberty: A History of the Early Republic, 1789–1815*. Oxford: Oxford University Press, 2009.

Woods, Terry K. *Ohio's Grand Canal: A Brief History of the Ohio & Erie Canal*. Kent, OH: Kent State University Press, 2008.

Woodworth, Steven E. *Manifest Destinies: America's Westward Expansion and the Road to the Civil War*. New York: Alfred A. Knopf, 2010.

Yang, Donghyu. "Farm Tenancy in the Antebellum North." In *Strategic Factors in Nineteenth Century American Economic History*, edited by Claudia Goldin and High Rockoff, 135–56. Chicago: The University of Chicago Press, 1992.

———. "Notes on the Wealth Distribution of Farm Households in the United States, 1860: A New Look at Two Manuscript Census Samples." *Explorations in Economic History* 21: 88–102. January 1984.

Zakim, Michael and Gary J. Kornblith, eds. *Capitalism Takes Command: The Social Transformation of Nineteenth-Century America*. Chicago: The University of Chicago Press, 2012.

Zerbe, Richard O., Jr. "The Origin and Effect of Grain Trade Regulations in the Late Nineteenth Century." *Agricultural History* 56 (1): 172–93. January 1982.

Index

A

Adams Township, 19, 36, 46, 66, 112, 153, 163–64, 181
agricultural identity, 1, 48, 49, 55, 59, 152, 181, 183
agricultural revolution, 13, 13n1, 104n4
Agricultural Society, Champaign County: during Civil War, 154, 156, 163–65; finances, 148–49, 163–64, 189–91; formation, 103–9; leadership, 110–13, 120, 136, 149, 163–64; purposes, 103, 106, 108, 109, 184, 185, 188, 191
Alderney cattle, 173
Allen, Gideon, 80, 82–83, 88
Allison, Samuel, 126
Armstrong, J. B., 173
Atlantic & Great Western Railroad, 67, 71
Atwater, Caleb, 30, 31, 33, 39
Ayrshire cattle, 173

B

Baltimore, 11, 33, 47, 68, 79, 81, 154
barley, 11, 37, 38n7, 134, 139, 167, 168
Barnett, David, 98, 158
Barnett, Samuel, 166, 175
beef, dressed, 175
Bennett, Alonzo, 89, 100
Bennett, E. M., 166, 175
Berry, E. C., 35

Brand, Joseph C., 72, 97, 106, 106n9, 107, 138, 140, 143
broad-gauge railroad, 67
Buck Creek, 2, 4, 9, 16, 18, 52, 54, 97
buckwheat, 9, 28, 84, 134, 167
Burnet, Jacob, 30, 31, 32
butter, 137, 173–74

C

Canal Commission, Ohio, 43, 45, 45n9, 47, 49
canal, Mad River feeder, 49, 56
canals and railroads, 49, 50, 56–58, 69–70
carding, wool, 35, 141, 145
Cartmel, Nathaniel, 121
Cartmel, Thomas, 121
cattle raising, 9, 11, 39, 62, 76, 104, 104n5, 108, 136–37, 139, 166, 173, 173n6, 175, 176
Cawood, John, 28
census: 1820, 19, 20, 21, 38, 52; 1830, 52, 180; 1840, 20; 1850, 20, 28n10, 53, 54, 64, 98, 113, 115n2, 118, 120, 128, 129, 180; 1860, 53, 54, 64, 101, 111, 112, 113, 115, 118n5, 120, 122, 125, 129, 141, 180; 1870, 180, 182; 1880, 20, 180, 182
Champaign County: creation, 2, 14, 19n14; division, 19, 19n14
Champaign County Fair: beginnings, 103, 104–5, 105n6, 106, 108, 109; during Civil War, 156, 163–65; locations, 105, 107, 110,

Champaign County Fair: locations (*continued*) 148, 190–91; purposes, 102, 105n6, 110, 137, 148, 150, 151, 163, 172–73, 188–89, 191

Chance, William, 117

Chase, Salmon P., 89, 153

cheese, 137

Cheney, Benjamin, 120–21

Cheney, Jonathan, 120–21

Cheney, Samuel, 120–21

Chicago, 63, 71n18, 80, 86, 86n23, 87, 92, 172, 176, 186

cholera, 108, 108n14

Christiansburg (renamed Addison), 18, 45

Cincinnati: flour milling, 38; pork processing, 43, 138, 138n15; as regional trade center, 19, 37, 46, 50, 62, 63–64, 72, 138; as river port, 38, 41–42, 47, 54

Civil War: crop adjustments, 162–63, 167; disruptions, 126, 168; labor, 155, 157, 159; labor-saving farm machines, 157, 159–60; sheep craze, 139, 165–66; as time marker, 27, 64, 75, 87, 100, 114, 134

Clark County, 3, 15, 18, 19, 19n14, 52, 101n13, 106, 108, 115, 128, 137, 187

Clark, George Rogers, 4

Clark, Lewis H., 131

Clarke, William, 158

clover, 77, 101

Coffenberger, Elizabeth, 123–24

Columbus as trade center, 36, 46, 62, 65–66, 68

Columbus, Piqua, & Indiana Railroad, 65, 68, 156, 156n8

Concord Township, 16, 17, 25, 28, 155, 159, 172, 174n9, 180, 181, 182, 190

Congress Lands, 8, 9n6, 14, 15, 16, 18

Cooke, Eleutheros, 56, 56n1

corn: extent, 28, 29, 30, 49, 93, 133n5, 134, 135, 136, 139, 167, 177, 182; markets, 38n9, 50, 71–72, 136, 163; mechanization, 135–36, 151; milling, 10, 36; planting cycle, 27, 75, 76, 176; uses, 9, 10, 10n11, 23, 38, 89, 135, 138, 175, 176; varieties, 10n11, 133

Corwin, Moses, 7, 7n2, 53n4

cradle scythe, 27, 27n8, 29, 78, 84, 91, 179, 179n18

Crain, Clarisa, 118–19, 120n8

Crain, James, 119

Crain, Lewis F., 119

Crain, Louisa, 119

Crain, Lucinda, 119

crop, cash, 10–11, 11n12, 35, 37, 51, 135

crop rotation, 104n4, 132, 177

cultivation customs, 9, 24, 25, 29, 75, 84, 100, 135, 146, 175

Cutler, Jervis, 3, 52

D

dairy, 11, 28, 46, 104, 117, 136, 137, 158, 173

Dallas, James, 57, 110, 111, 133, 187

Dallas, Wilson, 133

Darby Creek, 3, 10, 15, 16

Dayton: canal connection, 46, 47–48; manufacturing center, 83, 85, 86, 145, 161; market center, 21, 22, 36, 39, 62, 72; river access, 37

Democrat, 154, 154n1, 181, 184

Detwiler, Joseph, 181

Diltz, Rachael, 123

Diltz, Samuel, 123

Diltz, Wesley, 123

distilleries, 38, 72, 136

ditching, 99–100, 177, 182

diversified farming, 20, 28, 29, 73, 108, 133, 136, 137, 139, 143, 147, 167, 172

Dorsey, Charles, 6

Downs, William, 25, 90

drain tiles, 100, 177, 182

Drake, Daniel, 7, 31, 33, 39

drill, grain, 82–84, 88, 135, 160, 179

droving, 34, 39, 73, 137, 139, 175

Durham cattle, 104, 104n5, 107

E

Earsom, John, 111, 151n18

Eichelberger, Wes, 181

elevator, grain, 70, 71n18, 178

emigration, 53, 181

Enoch, John, 104, 106n9

Enoch, William, 71

Erie & Kalamazoo Railroad, 58, 58n5

Erie Canal, 32, 33, 43, 46, 47, 67

Evans, John, 140
Evans, Walter Brigham, Jr., 101n13
Everett, Wilson, 48, 48n14, 49, 55
extensive agriculture, 21, 96, 177

F

family farm, 27, 28n9, 29, 93, 128–29, 147
farm hand, 117, 118, 124, 125–26
Farmers' Institutes, 184, 188
fences, 9, 96, 97, 98, 142
fertility, land, 7, 8n4, 48, 100, 181
field trial, 84, 86, 87, 88, 90, 93
Fithian, George, 7, 53n4
Flagg, Gershom, 7, 31
flailing, 76–77
flatboat, 34, 34n7, 37, 38, 42
Fletcher, Calvin, 28, 31
flour: as commercial product, 11, 23, 38,
    38n8, 38n9, 49, 50, 163; as export, 38, 46;
    milling, 36, 37, 38, 132, 177; transport, 36,
    39, 67
Forbes Road, 34
Fox, Henry, 174
fulling, wool, 35, 141
Funk, Joel, 92, 106, 106n9, 109n16, 110, 112,
    138
futures markets, 178
Fyffe, Edward, 154, 155

G

Gatling wheat drill, 82–83, 84, 88
gender, 11, 28n9, 29, 107, 115, 117, 123–24, 150,
    164
General Assembly, Ohio, 43, 44, 49, 57, 60,
    99, 103, 122
Genesee Road, 33
glacier, 2
Glenn's Mills, 38
Gordon, John, 147
Goshen Township, 21, 25, 53, 65, 66, 110, 137,
    140, 143, 149, 153
Grange, 183–85, 184n28, 190
Great Miami River, 1, 2, 14, 23
Greeneville, Treaty of, 6, 13, 31, 33
Greeno, Follett L., 85
gristmill, 10, 17, 36, 38, 177, 178

Guthridge, Mary, 10
Gutridge, Aaron, 25

H

Hamilton County, 15, 79, 81, 103
Harr, Abraham, 90
Harr, Newton H., 85, 151, 164
Harrison Land Act, 14, 15, 18
Harrison Township, 19, 110
Harshman, Jonathan, 37
harvesting process, 27, 28, 75, 81, 84, 91, 92,
    93, 147, 179, 180
hay, 75, 76, 134, 139, 147, 160, 162, 176, 179
Hereford cattle, 136
Heylin, Isaiah B., 47
Hitt, Elizabeth, 107
Hitt, John W., 106n9, 140
hogs: breeds, 42; droving, 34, 39, 42;
    feeding, 23, 136, 140; importance, 49,
    138, 139n17, 148, 174, 188; marketing, 62,
    139, 176; packing, 71, 72, 138, 138n15;
    shipping, 62, 137, 138
Horr, Julia A., 131
Horr, Willis, 131
horse-drawn implements, 78, 82, 83, 84, 93,
    132, 135, 143–44, 160, 162, 179
horse power, 77, 80, 141, 144–45
Howard, Pearl, 146
Howe, Henry, 5
Howells, Joshua, 18
Hughes, Wesley, 24
Hussey, Obed, 78, 79, 80, 81, 85, 87, 103
Hussey's Reaping Machine, 79, 80, 81, 82,
    85, 86, 87, 87n25, 88, 90, 91

I

immigration, 13, 20, 115
improved land, 96, 98, 99, 100, 132, 182
intensive agriculture, 95, 100, 101, 132n4, 177
internal improvement, 43
Irish, 53, 53n5

J

Jackson Township, 6, 19, 20, 77, 110, 153,
    154n1

James, John Henry, 155
James, John Hough, 44, 53, 58, 59, 62, 82,
    103, 104, 104n5, 105, 106, 106n9, 107, 154,
    155
Jennings, A. C., 173
Jersey cattle, 173
Johnson, Jess, 17
Johnson Township, 6, 19, 110, 112, 115n2, 137,
    153, 155
Johnson, Mary Polly, 128
Johnson, Silas, 6
Jones, Daniel, 54
Jones, Hannah, 54
Jones, Justus, 81n13

K

Kansas, "Kansas fever", 131, 181
Kauffman, Jacob, 82, 88, 88n26, 89, 90
Keener, Samuel, 59, 70n17, 81, 82, 91, 92, 93,
    96, 100, 101, 104, 105, 112, 113, 136, 139, 167
Kenaga, Benjamin, 105, 131
Kennard, 72, 181, 183
Kiger, Thomas, 181
King's Creek, 9, 10, 16, 17, 28, 36, 151
Kist, John, 131
Kist, Marshall, 131
Klippart, John H., 30, 32, 112, 127n16, 132,
    138, 159, 187n1
Knight, W. J., 27, 180

L

labor, farm, 9, 21, 26, 27, 28, 28n9, 28n10, 29,
    75, 76, 77, 78, 85, 90–92, 93, 94, 101, 104,
    118, 125, 127, 135, 147, 155, 157, 157n11, 159,
    179, 180
land ownership, 16, 28n9, 115, 117, 118, 126,
    127, 127n17, 157, 158
land policy, federal, 14, 18
Lewis, Martin L., 48
Lincoln, Abraham, 152, 153, 154, 154n1, 169
Little Miami Railroad, 60, 63, 64
Little Miami River, 14, 23
Logan, Benjamin, 4
Logan County, 4, 15, 16, 19, 19n14, 25
Ludlow Line, 8, 15

M

Mad River, 2, 3, 4, 5, 9, 10, 14, 15, 16, 21, 38,
    43, 44, 48, 49, 52, 56, 108, 171
Mad River & Lake Erie Railroad, 49, 57,
    58, 58n5, 60, 61, 63, 64, 65, 66, 67, 69, 72,
    106, 137
Mad River Township, 6, 16, 19–21, 20n15,
    44, 53, 66, 108, 110, 153
manure, 101
market economy, 26, 29, 35n1, 39, 96n1, 101,
    139, 162, 168, 176
market revolution, 32
married women's property rights, 119, 122,
    122n11
Martin, Erastus, 146, 147
McAdams, Samuel, 126
McArthur, Duncan, 7, 16
McCormick, Cyrus, 78, 78n6, 79, 80, 87
McFarland, T. S., 25, 179, 181, 182, 186
Mechanicsburg, 10, 63, 65, 66, 131, 140, 145,
    147, 149, 150, 153, 172, 174, 175, 181, 188, 189,
    190
merchants, 18n12, 35, 37, 37n6, 38n8, 39, 46,
    47, 59, 66, 69, 69n16, 82n15, 134, 137, 160
Merino sheep, 140, 141, 146
Miami & Erie Canal, 37, 38n8, 47, 48, 49,
    50, 52, 56, 132
Middleton, 3
Middleton, Evan, 61, 105n6, 178
migration, pass through, 20, 53, 181
military bounty, 9n6, 17n10, 128
Minturn & Allen, 82, 85
Minturn, Allen & Co, 82, 83, 85, 86, 87, 88
Minturn & Co., 88, 90, 161
Minturn, Barton [father of Jacob, Edward,
    and Smith], 54, 81n13, 112
Minturn, Edward, 54
Minturn, Elizabeth, 54
Minturn, Esther, 54
Minturn, Jacob (1753–1817) [father of
    Barton], 54, 81n13
Minturn, Jacob (1802–1880) [son of
    Barton], 54, 77, 80, 82, 83, 85, 86, 87, 88,
    89, 92, 94
Minturn, Smith, 54, 103, 104, 106n9, 108, 137
moraine, 2, 3, 4
Morgan, E. M., 174, 174n8

Morgan, Simon E., 36, 101, 174, 177
Morgan horses, 146, 150
Morris, F. W., 141
Mosgrove & Wiley, 85, 89, 138, 162
mowers, 78, 82, 84, 85, 86, 87, 88, 90, 92, 93, 151, 155, 160, 161, 179
mowing, 75, 77, 78, 93
mules, 26, 36, 143, 146, 162, 165
mutton, 11, 140, 165, 166
Muzzy, Horace, 105

N

National Road, 31, 32, 33, 43, 52, 108
Native American, x, 3, 4, 4n4, 5n7, 10n9, 17n10, 98
native-born, 53, 55
Nelson, James A., 82, 88, 88n26, 89, 90
New Orleans, 34, 38, 41, 42, 138
New York & Erie Railroad (Erie), 67, 68
New York Central Railroad, 68
newspapers, Champaign County, 35, 43, 45, 53, 53n4, 54n6, 56, 58, 59, 66, 69, 89, 96, 131, 153, 154, 171, 176, 184, 186
Northwest Ordinance, 1, 153
Northwest Territory, 1, 6, 14, 51

O

oats, 11, 28, 50, 84, 134, 139, 147, 162, 167, 168, 186
Ogden, John W., 4n4, 10n11, 11n12, 16, 27, 28n10, 61n11, 88n26, 103, 104, 104n4, 105, 186, 186n1
Ohio & Erie Canal, 45
Owens, William, 6, 6n1
oxen, 9, 11, 24, 26, 136, 137, 145, 146

P

packing, meat, 42, 62, 71, 138, 138n15, 176
panic, financial, 18, 35, 58, 148, 151
Parry, David, 25, 38
pasture, 28, 76, 93, 97, 98, 142, 175
Patrick, William, 31
pioneer conditions, 4n4, 5, 9, 9n7, 20, 24, 26, 35, 76, 96, 139, 187
planting customs and seasons, 9, 29, 82, 132, 133, 135, 176, 188

plows and plowing, 3, 9, 11, 23–26, 27, 51, 96, 97, 98, 100, 101, 111, 132, 133, 135, 155, 160, 176, 177, 179, 182, 188
population patterns, 20, 28n10, 45, 51, 52, 53, 53n4, 112, 115n2, 149, 168, 180, 182, 183
Pretty Prairie, 9, 59, 115, 119, 158n12, 184
provisions, pork, 38, 39, 45, 46, 62, 68, 176

R

racing, horse, 150, 151, 152, 189, 190
railroad financing, 57, 58, 59, 60, 68, 128, 168, 172
raking, harvest, 75, 77, 78, 79, 86, 87, 90, 91, 155, 160, 179
Rawlings, James, 9, 39, 112
Rawlings, William Sanford, 17, 18n11, 18n12, 112
reaping: by hand, 27, 75–76, 84; horse-drawn, 78–82, 84–87, 90–94, 160
refrigeration, 173, 174, 175
Republican, 153, 184
Reynolds, John, 25, 47, 52, 52n2, 80, 99, 100, 103, 104, 105, 109, 136
Rianhard, William, 37, 47, 59
roads: improved, 22, 32, 37, 38, 43–44, 45, 72, 177; unimproved, 30, 31, 34, 36, 39, 40, 44, 47, 60
Roberts, Charles, 15
Roberts, Daniel, 122
Roberts, Hugh, 122
Ropp, Mary, 124
Ropp, Simon, 123
Ross, Philander B., 80, 100, 175
Rush Township, 19, 100, 140, 146, 153
Russell, John, 164

S

Salem Township, 6n1, 16, 21, 24, 70, 77, 92, 101, 104, 110, 112, 115n2, 118, 131, 135, 140, 151, 158, 159, 180n20, 181, 182
Sandusky, 32, 33, 46, 56, 57, 58, 60, 61, 62, 63, 64, 66, 69, 71n18, 137, 146
Saxton, Joshua, 58, 60, 62, 63, 82, 88, 95, 101, 106, 107, 108, 109
Sceva, Mary Huntoon, 122, 123, 124
Scioto River, 5, 6, 31, 39, 43

seed choice, 10n11, 132, 133, 188
self-sufficient agriculture, 21, 35, 35n1, 73
Shawnee, 4, 33
sheep raising, 11, 136, 139–41, 142, 165–66, 174
Sheldon, Erastus, 26
Shorthorn cattle, 104n5, 136, 173, 175
Showers, Abram, 104
Sickle, 11, 27, 76
Springfield: agricultural organizations, 39,
    62, 69, 84, 103, 106; as county seat, 52,
    115; as manufacturing center, 22, 52, 83,
    85, 86, 87, 144, 161, 180; location and
    topography, 2, 3, 4, 52; as railroad route,
    57, 60, 61; surface road connections, 30,
    31, 44, 52, 148
Springfield, Mt. Vernon, & Pittsburgh
    Railroad, 65
State Board of Agriculture, Ohio:
    activities, 88, 108, 108n14, 109, 156, 185;
    creation, 105, 107; questionnaires, 95,
    187n1; recommendations, 98, 149, 150;
    reports, 69, 81, 85, 86, 98, 101, 108, 134,
    135n9, 139, 141, 161, 166, 167, 191;
    secretary, 110, 112, 124n14, 159, 185, 187n1
State Fair, 83, 86, 87, 88, 108n14, 109, 135, 136,
    146, 156, 161, 164, 165
steam power, 51, 72, 77, 82, 141, 144, 144n2,
    145, 160, 178, 179, 180, 186
steam railroad, 58, 70
steam watercraft, 32, 34, 41, 42, 43, 46, 48,
    69, 72, 137, 171
stockyard, 175
Stokes, Frederick, 133
Stuart, Ephraim, 174
subsistence agriculture, 35, 35n1
Sullivant, M. L., 132
surplus, 30, 37, 41, 48, 57, 132, 138
Swimley, William M., 159
Symmes, John Cleves, 14

T

Tax Duplicate, Ohio, 8, 15, 16, 118, 128
Taylor, Alexander, 28
Taylor, John, 17
Taylor, Kirk, 181
Taylor, Mary, 81n13
Taylor, William S., 80, 81, 81n13, 82, 92

Tecumseh, 17, 17n10
telegraph, 64, 126, 182, 186
tenancy, 117, 118, 118n5, 120, 124, 126–27,
    127n16, 159
Terre Haute, 20, 22, 180n20, 184
Texas (renamed Mutual), 152, 172
threshing: by flailing and treading, 27, 76;
    by machine, 71, 77, 78, 92, 126, 144–45,
    155, 160, 179, 180, 180n20
timber, 3n3, 9, 52, 96–97, 98, 182
Toledo, 46, 58, 63
transportation revolution, 32, 33
turnpike, 44, 45, 56, 72, 100, 110

U

unimproved land, 9, 96, 98
Union Township, 7n3, 53, 54, 65, 80, 92, 97,
    104, 108, 110, 111, 112, 115, 117–18, 120, 127,
    128–29, 131, 135, 151, 151n18, 174n9, 175, 181
Urbana: as county seat, 22, 52, 53; as trade
    center, 35, 36, 37, 49, 52, 55, 69, 174; as
    transportation hub, 31, 44, 45, 56, 58, 60,
    61, 62, 63, 64, 66, 67, 172, 178
Urbana & Columbus Railroad, 65
Urbana Banking Company, 18, 58, 59, 106
Urbana Township, 16, 17, 39, 53, 98, 104, 112

V

Vance, Joseph (1786–1852) [the Governor],
    17, 37, 43, 57, 58, 59, 103, 104, 104n5, 105,
    106, 136, 143
Vance, Joseph C. [father of Joseph and
    William], 7, 52
Vance, William, 83, 103, 104, 104n5, 108, 118,
    119, 120, 120n8, 143
Vanmeter, Henry, 59, 97, 103, 104, 128, 129
Vanmeter, Isaac, 129
Vanmeter, Jacob (1791–1867) [father of
    Joseph and William], 111, 120, 128, 129
Vanmeter, Jacob (1750–1808) [father of
    Henry and Jacob], 128
Vanmeter, Jacob (1812–1857), 129
Vanmeter, John R., 128, 129
Vanmeter, Joseph R., 120, 128, 129
Vanmeter, Mary Polly Johnson, 128
Vanmeter, Sarah Reynolds, 128

Vanmeter, William, 126, 129
vegetables, 134, 158, 160
Virginia Military District, 8, 15, 97, 128

W

War of 1812, 7, 17, 20, 32, 34, 39, 139
Ward, Abijah, 96
Ward, Samuel C., 106n9
Ward, William, 104, 104n5
Warder, Benjamin H., 85, 87, 161
warehouses, 66, 69, 70, 71
water power, 3, 10, 38, 39, 141, 144n2
Wayne Township, 3, 110, 112, 174n9
Weaver, Christopher, 19
Weaver, Henry, 59
Weaver, William, 19
Weller, John, 137
"West" as migration ideal, 4n4, 7, 17, 20, 51,
    54, 91, 101, 129, 130, 131, 132, 168, 181
Westville, 22, 69, 83, 179
wheat: as cash crop, 10, 11, 11n12, 21, 38n9, 51,
    135; economic significance, 23, 30, 46,
    47, 50, 130, 131, 132, 133, 134, 136, 139, 163,
    167, 168; as exchange medium, 35, 38, 89;
    labor implications, 27, 29, 85, 92, 159;

milling, 36, 37, 177; season, 76, 176; soil
    preparation, 24, 84; varieties, 11n12
Whig, 64
whisky, 23, 28, 37, 38, 39, 50, 176
Whisler, William, 181
Wiley, William, 89, 138, 162
Wilson, Rezin C., 80, 81, 81n13, 82, 92, 111
Wilson, Robert, 47
woodland, 24, 28, 29, 93, 182
Woods, Robert, 120
Woodstock, 8, 100, 146, 147, 155, 169
wool processing, 80, 141, 142, 142n20, 145,
    165–66, 174

Y

yeoman, 28n9, 111, 124, 167
yield, crop, 10n11, 75, 95, 96, 102, 109, 112, 132,
    133, 133n5, 134, 162, 180, 188
Young, John H., 108, 109, 111, 184

Z

Zane, Isaac, 16–17, 17n10
Zombro, John T., 89, 90, 164